Dear Mike Cohen,

I hope this finds you well.

As suggested to me by Helen Frais in Leeds, I am sending a copy of my book for review. I hope you will find it of interest.

Yours sincerely,

Philip Feldman PhD

philipmfeldman @ gmail.com

Against the Odds

Against the Odds: Jewish Achievement in the Modern World

Philip Feldman

KDP

KINDLE DIRECT PUBLISHING

ISBN 9798538662203

for my children and

grandchildren

Table of Contents

Preface   1

Chapter One   3

Exceptional Jewish Achievement in the West: 1800 to 2017

Chapter Two   20

The Jews of Eastern Europe 1800 to 1933

Chapter Three   45

Careers Open to Talent: The Jews of Central and Western

Europe 1800 to 1933

Chapter Four   58

A Golden Land: American Jewry 1800 to 1945

Chapter Five   67

Old-New Land: Palestine

Chapter Six   79

The Jews' Darkest Years: 1933 to 1945

Chapter Seven   110

Hitler's Bounty: A Talented Remnant Escaped to the West

Chapter Eight   126

Post-war Jewry: Eastern Europe

Chapter Nine   139

Post-war Jewry: Western Europe

Chapter Ten   165

Post-war Jewry: The US

Chapter Eleven   189

Palestine and Israel, 'the hinge of fate': May 8th, 1945 to mid-April 1949

Chapter Twelve   214

Israel: The Main Events, Civilian and Military, 1948 to 2020

Chapter Thirteen   240

Israel among the Nations: International Comparisons

Chapter Fourteen   264

Explaining Exceptional Jewish Achievement: The Inheritance of Potential

Chapter Fifteen   278

Explaining Exceptional Jewish Achievement: The Amplification of Potential

Chapter Sixteen   300

The Next Decade: Jewish Potential in the Diaspora and Israel

Notes   327

Preface

The idea of writing *Against the Odds* had its origin in a *Times Literary Supplement* review (2.4.2004) by a distinguished British historian, Andrew Roberts. The book in question was *Human Accomplishment: The Pursuit of Excellence in the Arts and Sciences, 800 BC to 1950,* by Charles Murray. Roberts' review included the following: "The Jews ... despite making up only a fraction of the global population and suffering from legal restrictions in many areas of endeavour for many centuries, have made an astonishing contribution across the entire gamut of human achievement, especially those originally hailing from Central and Eastern Europe... It makes one wonder how many future global-class achievers perished in the Holocaust."

This book builds on Roberts' powerful summary and Murray's review of the factual evidence of Jewish achievement, updated to 2020. In writing it I have been aware that setting out the factual evidence of exceptional Jewish achievement, as compared to the general population, may be seen as "politically incorrect". Such comparisons are currently seen as both odious and divisive. But solid statistical evidence, rather than being ignored, invites an attempt at explanation. Nobel Prizes in Science and Economics are awarded on merit, as are equally prestigious prizes in Mathematics and Computer Science; all show exceptional Jewish achievement.

In seeking to explain the phenomenon, I have drawn on material relating to both "nature" and "nurture", that is, genetic inheritance and social experience. Neither one can, on its own, tell the full story; they interact in complex ways to produce exceptional achievement. The background context of major events, such as the two World Wars and the Holocaust, also plays a part, as does the perennial presence of antisemitism in the Diaspora. After the establishment of Israel in 1948, notable Jewish achievement became a feature of Israel's research universities and its burgeoning hi-tech sector. But the renewal of Jewish sovereignty, after an interregnum of 1900 years, brings with it another problem that must urgently challenge the finest minds: how to be both Jewish and democratic?

The story I tell is an ongoing one. I take it to 2020, concluding with speculation as to what the next decade will bring.

I would like to thank the following authors for their kind permission to quote from their work: Charles Murray, *Human Accomplishment: The Pursuit of Excellence in the Arts and Sciences, 800 BC to 1950*, HarperCollins; Benny Morris, *1948: A History of the First Arab-Israeli War*, Yale University Press; Anita Shapira, *Israel: A History*, Weidenfeld and Nicolson.

In writing this book I have been greatly helped by my Jerusalem family: my wife Jennie, whose editing greatly improved the text; Elisheva, who read every chapter as I completed it and made many helpful suggestions, particularly with regard to the great and growing importance of female achievement; and Daniel, who collated the references and prepared the book according to the publisher's requirements. I am grateful to them all for their unfailing support and encouragement.

Chapter One

Exceptional Jewish Achievement in the West: 1800 to 2020

'And if, in the course of many centuries, the oppressed descendants of warriors and sages have degenerated from the qualities of their fathers; if while excluded from the blessings of law and bowed down under the yoke of slavery, they have contracted some of the vices of outlaws and slaves, shall we consider this as a matter of reproach to them? Shall we not rather consider it as a matter of shame and remorse to ourselves? Let us open to them every career in which ability and energy can be displayed. Till we have done this, let us not presume to say that there is no genius among the countrymen of Isaiah, no heroism among the descendants of the Maccabees' (Lord Macaulay, 1833, found in Gilbert, 1976[1]).

About a century later, according to Winston Churchill, 'The Jews are the most formidable and the most remarkable race the world has ever seen.' Less given to hyperbole, another distinguished Englishman, Arthur Balfour (he of the Declaration), reckoned the Jews 'had contributed more to the world than anyone since the 6th-century Greeks.'

Others took a different view. 'All foreign Jews are criminals, thieves, sweaters, usurers, burglars, forgers, traitors, swindlers, blackmailers and perjurers' - J. Bannister (1901), cited by Lebzelter[2], in support of the agitation leading to the 1905 Aliens Bill, which sharply restricted immigration into Britain by East European Jews. In the U.S., the results of the newly developed intelligence tests seemed to give scientific support to an equally unfavorable view: 83 percent of the Jews pouring into Ellis Island were found, on arrival, to be 'feeble-minded.' (It was later realized that those being assessed were both exhausted from their voyage and ignorant of English, the language of the tests.)

Today, the evidence for high-achieving Jews supports Churchill and Balfour and is all around us. From Einstein to Freud and Saul Bellow to Isaiah Berlin, many have become household names and there are no longer serious obstacles to high intellectual and artistic achievement – or to more modest professional status – in any of the countries of the West, where the great majority of non-Israeli Jews now live. But it was not always thus. For almost the entire period from the Jewish Exile (70 A.D.) to about 1800, Jews were subject to severe restrictions almost everywhere they lived, and their opportunities for achievement were minimal. How did such a situation come about?

The failed Jewish rebellion against Roman rule in 70 A.D. resulted in a massive expulsion from their historic homeland, and dispersal throughout the Roman Empire. The 4th century saw the rapid rise of Christianity, which regarded Judaism as a rival to be crushed. Increasingly severe restrictions on Jews followed, resulting in a gradual and almost total exclusion from the economic and cultural mainstream.

After a brief flowering in parts of medieval Spain, then under Islamic, rather than Christian, rule, European Jewry was to be relegated once more to the margins of life for several hundred years, occasionally tolerated when convenient to the rulers under whom they lived, more usually hounded and persecuted, from the Atlantic to the Urals. But in the middle of the 18th century there appeared a precursor of a remarkable burst of talent that has continued to this day.

In 1743 a frail and sickly 14-year-old boy entered Berlin through the gate in the city wall permitted to Jews and cattle. Moses Mendelssohn, a promising Talmudic student had come to study with his rabbi who was newly resident in the city. The youth knew only Hebrew and Yiddish. Within two decades, almost entirely self-taught, he became a renowned German philosopher, philologist, stylist, literary critic and man of letters. He remained a practicing Jew to his death in 1786. (With each succeeding generation, however, the bonds with tradition would loosen. Only four of his 56 great-grandchildren were observant Jews, the others converting to Christianity, the passport to opportunity and admission to schools, universities and the professions).

Mendelssohn was almost unique in his day. There were very few Jews of distinction in the arts and sciences before 1800. Only in the United States, where the Jewish community was tiny, did Jews enjoy a relatively equal opportunity to achieve.

An inkling of what could happen when the barriers were lowered had already been provided by Moorish (Muslim) Spain in the Middle Ages when Arab culture was the bridge between the

Greek and Roman worlds and the Christian world of the Middle Ages. What is known as the Golden Age of medieval Iberian Jewry was far from unalloyed. Nevertheless, when a science historian, George Sarton, listed the leading medieval scientists across the world (including East and South Asia, the Arab world and Christian Europe) he came up with 626 names, of whom 95 were Jews; in other words, according to Charles Murray, author of the definitive work *Human Accomplishment: The Pursuit of Excellence in the Arts and Sciences*, 15 percent of the total was produced by a group that comprised about half of one percent of the world's potential scientist-producing population[3]. Of course, the vast majority of both the full 626 and the minority of 95 have left little impact on the broad sweep of scientific history. But the finding showed that given an even reasonably benign environment, Jews might achieve well *beyond* their share of the population. The opportunity to do so did not present itself again for several hundred years. Moorish Spain returned to Christian control. The barriers against Jewish participation in cultural and economic life were raised once more. Under the influence of the Church, Iberian Jewry suffered increasingly severe discrimination and by the end of the 15th century had been expelled from both Spain and Portugal, dispersing to much of the rest of Europe, where they were excluded almost completely from the arts and sciences; not merely discouraged from entering universities and the professions, they were often forbidden by law from doing so. Socially, they were despised. A leading historian of the period, David Vital, wrote: 'Underlying everything was the central fact that ... no Jew was, or could be, a member of civil society. No matter how learned or wealthy or contingently influential he might be within or without Jewry itself, a Jew was held to belong to a moral, and of course, theological category inferior to that of the meanest peasant.'[4] Charles Murray added: 'Until the end of the 18C throughout Europe and well into 19C in most parts of Europe, Jews lived under a regime of legally restricted rights and socially sanctioned discrimination as severe as that borne by any population not held in chattel slavery' (p. 6).

This situation began to change when Napoleon's armies swept through Europe and the ghetto walls were breached. Since 1800, despite continuing disabilities, Jews have achieved, across the board, whenever and wherever they were allowed to do so, far in excess of their share of the European and American general populations. The success has continued despite the destruction of two-thirds of European Jewry in the Holocaust.

Significant figures in the arts and sciences: 800 B.C. to 1950

Charles Murray is one of America's boldest policy intellectuals, provoking debate on sometimes controversial subjects, ranging from welfare to IQ.

At the beginning of the 21st century he directed the mammoth task of producing a definitive listing of key figures in philosophy, sciences and the arts, both Eastern (Arab, Indian, Chinese and Japanese) and Western (European and American), between 800 B.C. and 1950. (As the sciences are universal in method and content, the listings of scientists made no distinction between East and West). Murray and his colleagues assembled the major reference books in each field (composers of Western music, for example) and then listed all those in the field that appeared in at least one of them. Next, they rejected all names that appeared in fewer than 50 percent of the books. They then arranged the listings in order, according to the combined number of column inches devoted to each composer. Finally, each received a score of 1 to 100 according to his or her place in the listing. The results formed what mathematicians call a "Lotka curve", meaning that the scores fell at first steeply, then very gradually, with a small number of "giants" obtaining very high scores and a much larger number receiving progressively lower ones. For example, in Western Music, Beethoven and Mozart scored 100, Stravinsky 45 and Mendelssohn (a grandson of Moses M.) 30. Mahler and Offenbach scored 23 and 6, respectively, and Irving Berlin only 1.

Murray and his team restricted themselves to reference books that had appeared before 1950 and to significant figures already dead (the living continue to produce new work, and appraisal by reference book contributors needs mature reflection).

The listing for Physics begins with a number of giants: Newton and Einstein both score 100; Bohr and Dirac receive 52 and 40, respectively. Pasteur is the only Medicine great to score 100; Paul Ehrlich scores 59, Sigmund Freud 37 (for his early work on

Neurology). In Western Literature, Shakespeare, with 100, towers above his fellows, with Goethe and Dante (62) coming next.

Significant Jewish figures in the arts and sciences: 1800 to 1950

Murray chose 1800 as his starting date for calculating Jewish achievement in the arts and sciences, because that was when the barriers against Jewish entry to the universities and the professions began to be lifted throughout most of Europe. Until 1933 progress was fairly steady across Western and Central Europe; in Russia and Eastern Europe it was much more patchy, with advances followed by reversals.

Who is a Jew?

According to Orthodox Jewish religious law, a Jew is a person born to a Jewish mother; it is the maternal side that is crucial. Murray is more liberal; for his analysis of Jewish achievement, two Jewish grandparents qualify someone to be considered Jewish. The paternal side is given equal weight with the maternal (as is done in the Reform denomination of Jewry). Moreover, he regards someone as Jewish even if he converted to Christianity at some time in his life – a not unusual occurrence in the 19th century, when conversion opened doors that otherwise would have remained closed. Karl Marx's father had the six-year-old baptized to ease his future passage into the practice of law. The 12-year-old Benjamin Disraeli was baptized following his father's quarrel with his synagogue; without this, Disraeli's rise to the position of prime minister – one of Britain's most distinguished – would have been greatly delayed, at the very least. Heinrich Heine, one of the leading 19th-century German poets, who underwent baptism as an adult, referred to conversion as "a passport to European civilization." All three were baptized early in the 19th century. As time went on, such a radical step became less necessary to secure access to the universities and the professions.

Jewish self-identity plays no part in Murray's listings. Disraeli, with a score of 5 in the Literature Inventory (he was a significant novelist as well as a statesman), was always proud of his Jewish origins. Heine (with a score of 22, again in Literature) constantly shifted his position. Marx (surprisingly not included in Murray's Philosophy Inventory) was unchangingly and virulently antisemitic.

So, we are left with the single criterion for entry to the inventories of significant figures (and also to the lists of Nobel Prize winners and of other major awards of distinction reviewed later in this chapter) – having two Jewish grandparents.

How many Jews?

To test the assertion that Jews achieve well beyond their share of the population, we need reliable estimates of that share. The proportional figures that follow are generally accepted – but tend to err on the side of *over-estimation*.

In 1800 when Jewish achievements became possible beyond the occasional Moses Mendelssohn, the population of Europe was approaching 200 million; the Jewish share was around 1.5 percent. The total population of the United States was about 5 million, with a minuscule Jewish presence of approximately 8,000. By 1900, the general European population and the Jewish proportion had both grown considerably; the former to about 425 million, the latter to 8.7 million – a little over 2 percent. In 1900 the population of the United States was 76 million; the Jewish share was one million – less than 1.5 percent. Finally, by 1939 the total European population had reached over 500 million and the Jewish share had fallen to below 2 percent, due to continuing emigration to the United States (particularly in the first quarter of the century) and, to a much lesser extent, to Palestine. A dramatic increase had occurred in U.S. Jewry: out of a total American population of about 130 million in 1939 the Jewish share had risen to almost 5 million – nearly 4 percent.

By 1948 the dust had settled after the massive depredations of World War II. Many millions of Europeans, both combatants and civilians, had been killed or displaced. The losses suffered by European Jewry were disproportionately severe. Jews, their numbers depleted by some 6 million, now represented less than 1 percent of the total. In the U.S., by contrast, Jewish numbers had fallen only slightly, to about 3.5 percent.

Overall, from 1800 to 1950 there was a continuous rise in the European and American populations that had produced most of the significant individuals listed in Murray's inventories of Western arts and sciences. Until the Holocaust, the Jewish share of those populations remained consistent, at nearly 2.5 percent. For the 150-year period as a whole we should expect no more than one in forty of the significant individuals to be Jewish. However, by 1950 the Holocaust had reduced the Jewish share of the population of "the West" to about 1.25 percent. Some potentially major figures probably perished before their work had reached a sufficiently high level for Murray's review to pick them out as actually significant. Moreover, about 1.5 million Jewish children died in the Holocaust; we can never know how many would have appeared in a 2050 review of significant figures for the period 1950 to 2000; some, almost certainly, would have been awarded Nobel or other prizes in the latter years of the 20th century and the early years of the 21st.

Significant Jewish Figures: An Overview

During the years 1800-1870, Jews were gradually allowed to enter the universities and the professions throughout Europe. (In that period America imposed only minor restraints on its very small Jewish community.) In response, they burst forth into all the fields of European endeavour: 'The long pent-up Jewish talent, hitherto dammed up behind the wall of Talmudic learning spilled over into all fields of Gentile cultural activity.'[5]

Many of those who entered this hitherto unknown world had to pay a price – "voluntary" conversion to Christianity. And we should note Patai's reference to Talmudic learning. For many such students, religious studies consumed their daily lives. Moving forward two hundred years we find a similar situation today in the ultra-Orthodox Jewish communities of Israel, the US and the UK, where many thousands of young men pursue Talmudic studies to the exclusion of "Gentile cultural activity." (Their wives both raise large families and often earn the family income, typically in relatively low-level jobs). For this group the "wall" is self-imposed (or at least rabbinically imposed and maintained). Can we expect their situation to change in the rest of the 21st century?

The following were Murray's findings for the four decades from 1830 to 1870:

'When the first Jews to live under emancipation reach their forties [which allows enough time to achieve distinction], 16 significant Jewish figures appear [in the Sciences, Art, Literature and Music]. In the next four decades, from 1870 to 1910, when all non-Russian Jews are living in societies that offer equal legal protections if not social equality, that number jumps to 40. During the next four decades until 1950 – including the years of the Third Reich and the Holocaust – the number of Jewish significant figures almost triples, to 114' (2003, p.277).

Table 1
The sudden emergence of Jewish significant figures (as percentages of total significant figures), 1800-1950

Period			
Area	1800 - 1850	1850 – 1900	1900 – 1950
Total Sciences	3	13	28
Art	0	4	18
Literature	3	8	19
Music	19	9	22

(Source: Murray, 2003 p.277)

Table 2 (adapted from Murray, p.279) shows how these figures work out as percentages of all significant figures for the three half-centuries from 1800 to 1950. In Philosophy, not shown in Table 1, Jews contributed 6 out of the 18 significant figures from 1900-1950). From a standing start at the beginning of emancipation (except for Music, where achievement was already high), Jewish accomplishments in the arts and sciences accelerated for the next 150 years. A glance at Table 1 makes clear that these achievements are well beyond the Jewish share of Western populations. But exactly how far beyond are they? To work this out, Murray took 2.2 percent as his figure for the Jewish proportion of the populations of Europe and the U.S. (where all the Jewish significant figures lived or worked). He then calculated the expected as against the actual Jewish share of significant figures in the arts and sciences. For example, if literature has 100 significant figures you would expect approximately 2 of them to be Jews. If the actual number is, say, 20 the Jews are disproportionately represented by 10 times their share of the population. Murray's findings are set out in Table 2.

Table 2
Disproportionate Representation of Jewish Significant Figures: 1870-1950

Area	Expected significant figures	Actual significant figures	Ratio of actual to expected significant figures
All sciences	14.5	94	6:1
Astronomy	1.0	1	1:1
Biology	2.3	18	8:1
Chemistry	2.4	13	6:1
Earth Sciences	0.8	2	3:1
Physics	3.0	26	9:1
Mathematics	1.1	13	12:1
Medicine	1.8	14	8:1
Technology	2.1	7	3:1
Visual Arts	3.1	16	5:1
Literature	6.8	26	4:1
Music	3.1	14	5:1
Philosophy	0.6	8	14:1

(Source: Murray, 2003, p.279)

In every case but Astronomy, the disparity is at least 3 to 1, at the extreme reaching 14 to 1 (Philosophy); Mathematics (12:1) and Physics (9:1) are also striking. Such disparities are well beyond being statistical accidents and need to be explained. Overall, for the period 1870-1950, 1,277 significant figures were added to the Western inventories. Of these, it would be expected that 28 would have been Jews if they had performed according to their population share; instead, the actual number was 158. (And, Murray adds: 'Data on ethnicity were not available for many of the less prominent significant figures and some Jews have undoubtedly been missed', 2003, p.279).

Country-by-country Comparisons

The majority of the nearly 1,300 significant figures for the period 1870-1950 lived and worked for most of their lives in just six countries. Murray worked out the Jewish share of significant figures for each of the six, together with the Jewish to Gentile ratios after taking population sizes into account (Table 3).

Table 3
Disproportionate Representation of Significant Jews by Country, 1870-1950

Country	Total Jewish significant figures	Total Gentile significant figures	Ratio of Jewish to Gentile significant figures after controlling for population
Austria	21	50	7:1
Britain	8	170	8:1
France	18	185	19:1
Germany	40	155	22:1
Russia	9	63	4:1
USA	48	261	5:1

(Source: Murray, 2003, p.280)

It is clear that for each of the six, the ratios far exceed 1:1 – quite startlingly so in the cases of Germany and France, where there were growing Jewish opportunities despite much antisemitism. In addition, they were the countries at the very forefront of Western culture: France in the arts, Germany in the sciences. The opportunities were there for all citizens (although being formally Christian helped); Jews seized them particularly well. Why the lower ratios for Britain and the U.S., despite both being relatively free of officially approved antisemitism? For most of the period from 1880, when mass emigration from the Czarist Empire began, to 1950, the Jewish populations of both countries consisted largely of poverty-stricken recent immigrants with imperfect English, struggling to earn a living in sweatshops, small workshops or as salesmen, all on low wages for long hours. It was their children, and more notably their grandchildren, who would enjoy the opportunity to achieve in the years after 1950.

The case of Russia is also intriguing. As Murray puts it: 'Russia drove out a large part of its Jewish population. It persecuted the ones who remained, through legal restrictions and virulent antisemitism. After the Revolution, Stalin killed substantial numbers of the most able elements of the remaining Jewish population. Socially, antisemitism remained a fact of Soviet life as it had been of Czarist life. And despite all that, the Jews are disproportionately represented among Russian significant figures from 1870 to 1950 by a ratio of 4:1(2003, p.281).

In his *A History of Russia,*[6] Riasanovsky names eight outstanding Soviet scientists, of whom three are or were Jewish – a small sample, but an interesting illustration of Murray's general point.

Nobel Prizes
The first Nobel prizes were awarded in 1901. Instituted through the will of Alfred Nobel, the Swedish chemist who invented dynamite, they are thus far the most prestigious international prizes in their fields. The prizes for Physics, Chemistry, Physiology/Medicine and Literature are awarded annually by academic committees based in Sweden. A prize for Economics, financed by the Swedish National Bank, was first awarded in 1969. An annual prize for the greatest contribution to world peace, again funded by Nobel's legacy, is awarded by a committee of the Norwegian parliament. Murray analyzed the results for all the prizes except the Peace Prize, for total sciences as well as separately for each science and for literature, first for the period 1901-1950 and then for 1951-2000 (Tables 4 and 5).

Table 4

Percentages of Jewish Nobel Prize Winners in Literature and the Sciences During the Two Halves of 20C

Prize	1901-1950	1951-2000
Total Sciences	17%	29%
Chemistry	12%	22%
Medicine	22%	32%
Physics	15%	32%
Literature	4%	15%
Total	**14%**	**29%**

Source: Murray, 2003, p.282

Table 5

Ratios of Actual to Expected Jewish Nobel Prize Winners in Literature and the Sciences During the Two Halves of 20C

Prize	1901-1950	1951-2000
Total Sciences	8:1	13:1
Chemistry	5:1	10:1
Medicine	10:1	14:1
Physics	7:1	14:1
Literature	2:1	7:1
Total	**6:1**	**12:1**

Source: Murray, 2003, p.283

In the first half of the 20th century Jews won 29 of the prizes in the sciences and literature – that is, 14 percent of the total awarded, about six times what might have been expected from their share of the population. In the second half of the century, they won 96 prizes, 29 percent of the total awarded, despite the losses of the Holocaust, suggesting that any previous obstacles had become unimportant. The ratio of actual as opposed to expected prizes improved in every area; but literature still trails the sciences in the size of the disparity (7:1 for literature as against 13:1 for the sciences). It is worth noting that until well into the 20th century many Jewish writers, particularly those who remained in Russia and Eastern Europe, wrote in Yiddish, from which translations were relatively limited, reducing their accessibility for Nobel prize literature committees; subsequent generations, born or raised in the West, were much more likely to write in English.

The figures given above reflect Murray's assumptions: (a) that the Jewish share of the "Nobel Prize population" was still 2.2 percent even after the Holocaust and (b) that Nobel laureates were still drawn only from Europe and the U.S. In fact, in the second half of the 20th century the Nobel Committee explicitly sought to expand its remit to include the entire world and award science and literature prizes to people in Asia, Africa and Latin America.

As a proportion of today's developed world, Jewry numbers no more than 1.25 percent. By including the entire world, the proportion falls to 0.25 percent. If we average the Jewish share of the "Nobel population" to one percent, the Jewish:Gentile ratios for 1951-2000 now range from 15:1 (Literature) to 35:1 (Medicine and Physics). The inescapable conclusion is that the estimates in Tables 4 and 5 are *radically understated.* Yet even as they stand, they are a clear demonstration of Jewish achievement; their explanation poses a challenge.

The same disparity can be seen among recipients of the most recently (1969) established prize, for Economics. In the years 1969-2000 Jews won 18 (39 percent) of the 46 prizes awarded (in some years the prizes are shared). On the basis of a 2.2 percent population share this means a ratio of 17:1; my more accurate reckoning, taking Jews to constitute 1.25 percent of the entire developed world, yields a ratio of 32:1.

The Nobel Prize for Peace was awarded to 14 organizations and 83 individuals between 1901 and 2000 (43 and 40 in the first and second half centuries, respectively). Individual Jews won 2 and 7 of those prizes. Though these numbers are rather small for drawing reliable conclusions, it can at least be said that Jews have not lagged behind the general population in this sixth prize (albeit they have not won any in the 21st century thus far).

Nobel prizes awarded between 2001 and 2019 for the sciences, economics and literature, and the ratio of Jewish laureates, are shown in Table 6.

Table 6
Percentage representation of Jews among Nobel Prize winners, 2001 – 2020

	Number	Jewish	Percentage Jewish
Total Sciences	149	38	25.5
Chemistry	50	12	24.0
Physics	51	14	27.4
Physiology/Medicine	45	11	25.0
Literature	19	6	31.6
Economics	29	14	48.2

For total sciences, the Jewish share – just over one quarter – is a little lower than in earlier years; for economics (nearly half) the share is much the same. In literature the share doubled between 1950-2000 and 2001-2020. (No literature prize was awarded for 2017.)

The Fields Medal
Awarded every four years by the International Mathematical Union, at the International Congress of Mathematicians, to individuals who are aged up to 40, the Fields Medal, known informally as the Nobel Prize in Mathematics, is generally considered to be the single most prestigious award in the field. To date (2020) 27 percent of recipients have been or are Jewish or part Jewish.

The ACM (Association for Computing Machinery) A.M. Turing Award
The Turing award is the most prestigious in the field of computer science. By 2020, 30 percent of recipients were or are Jewish (or of partial Jewish descent).

Women

Between 1901 and 1950 only 11 women won Nobel prizes for the sciences, about 3 percent of the total, 367. In the first half of the 20th century there were no Jewish women among the female winners. In the second half there were 3 out of 7 (5.7 percent of the overall total, 123). There were 2 Jewish women Nobel Science winners from 2001 to 2020 out of a total of 18 women (11.2 percent of the total, 162). Economics remains even more a male preserve: only 2 women winners from 1969 to 2020. The results for the Literature Prize (not awarded in 2017) are more positive for women: 9 out of 97 from 1901 to 2000 (less than 10 percent) but 7 out of 20 for 2001 to 2020 (35 percent).

Table 7

Representation of Jewish women among female Nobel Prize winners in Literature and the Sciences during the two halves of 20C

Prize	1901 - 1950		1951 - 2000	
	All women	Jewish women	All women	Jewish women
Total Sciences	4	0	7	3
Literature	5	0	4	2
Total	**9**	**0**	**20**	**5**

For the years 2001 to 2020, there were five Jewish Nobel winners out of a total of 21 women laureates. Women are catching up across the board (12 Science winners out of a total of 149, most notably the two joint Chemistry winners for 2020). There were 7 women Literature Prize winners out of 19, again a proportional advance.

It should be no surprise that women have trailed far behind men, both in the inventories of significant figures and in the winners of Nobel prizes. The obstacles to female success may have diminished very recently but it will be some time before women can compete on equal terms. It will not be fair to compare outstanding male and female achievements until at least another generation has passed. Meanwhile, some notable advances can be registered. Half a century ago only 10 percent of British medical students were women; today the proportion is at least a half. The same is true for law students. The situation is much the same throughout the developed world. Females have already outstripped males in school performance up to the age of 18, and they are now also doing so at university level.

It is clear that women have in the past been seriously disadvantaged at all stages, from secondary school to university to competing for the senior academic positions from which the winners of the Nobel Science and Economics prizes are drawn. A succession of official reports indicates that the situation is changing but the timescale is very long. The playing field has not been level even for those women who have managed to obtain relatively senior positions in the sciences. There is repeated anecdotal evidence that they have been pushed aside in the Nobel race. A case in point is Rosalind Franklin, a member of a distinguished Anglo-Jewish family. Her contributions, in the field of x-ray crystallography, to the Nobel won by James Watson and Francis Crick (1952) and later by Aaron Klug (1982) are now – many years after her death at the age of 38 – recognized as having been vital for the others. It is a reasonable conclusion that had she been a man she would have been either a one-third winner with Watson and Crick, or, had she lived, a shared winner with Klug (Nobel prizes are not awarded posthumously).

A recent American example is that of Vera Rubin, who died on Christmas Day, 2016. According to very laudatory obituaries in *The Economist* and *The New York Times,* she established the existence of dark matter, as well as making other notable contributions to astronomy and physics, but never won the Nobel Prize for Physics which, it was widely thought, she deserved. It is likely that there are many other examples throughout the (still) male-dominated world of science. Perhaps ushering in a new era, the 2020 Nobel Prize for Chemistry was shared by two women.

Even in literature there are numerous examples of women having to struggle to secure due recognition: in the 19th-century Mary Anne Evans chose to write under the pen name George Eliot.

In general, it seems women continue to be disadvantaged in fields in which male-dominated committees make the awards. Given equal opportunities, at all stages, they can be expected to achieve equally, and this will be true for both Jewish and non-Jewish women. But there is another aspect of the question: it has been argued that women's brains differ from those of males in some fundamental way, so that even given equal opportunities there will still be a disparity in achievement. It is true that at present women are less likely to become, for example, computer scientists; can this and other disparities between the sexes be explained by different training and expectations rather than by innate biological differences? The argument seems to favour the former: the gender gap in maths and physics has narrowed over the years; it is a reasonable expectation that it will continue to do so in the future. The gap between Jewish and non-Jewish female achievement may or may not continue to parallel the disparity among males.

Across the Board

Jews have succeeded well beyond their numbers in areas as diverse as the composition of popular music and the performance of classical music, as well as in chess, statecraft, high finance and commerce (quite extraordinarily so in the US – see an exhaustive review by Stephen L. Pease in *The Golden Age of Jewish Achievement*).[7] Only in sport have Jews performed approximately in line with their population share. The exception was boxing between the wars when the number of Jewish world champions went well beyond that share. It has not been a case of "all intellect and no muscle." Jews contributed at least equally to the armies of the main protagonists in both world wars, particularly to the Soviet Army in World War II. And the effective performance of the Israel Defence Forces (IDF) ensured Israel's survival during its first quarter century of often difficult existence.

Chapter Two

The Jews of Eastern Europe 1800 to 1933

Background

At the time of the destruction of the Second Temple, in 70 CE, there were between 4.5 and 7 million Jews in the world. The eclipse of commerce and urban life that followed the dismantling of the Roman Empire, together with the restrictions and persecutions which marked the feudal period, led to a sharp reduction in the Jewish population. By the 15th century there were probably fewer than 300,000 on the European continent; worldwide there were fewer than 1 million, most of whom were concentrated in the Near East. With the revival of commerce, and the relaxation of Jewish disabilities, there was a gradual increase in the population of European Jewry.

Following the failed rebellion against Roman rule in their ancestral homeland, the most fateful period in the history of the Jewish people came centuries later, between the French Revolution and the Nazis' accession to power in Germany in 1933. It was a period that, prior to the Holocaust, gave Jews in most countries, most of the time, unparalleled opportunities for development in most areas.

The early 19th century saw the culmination of a century and more of conflict between Britain and France for the mastery of Europe. Napoleon's domination of continental Europe was brought to an end by the defeat of the French armies at the battle of Waterloo in 1815. The defeat was mainly the due to success of the British army under Wellington, but a substantial part was played by the Prussian army. For the rest of the century, the story of continental Europe is that of the rise of Germany as the dominant power, built around the ascent of Prussia within the German Confederation. The key figure, particularly in the third quarter of the 19th century, was Otto von Bismarck, known as the Iron Chancellor. Prussia defeated first Austria and then France, to establish Germany as unassailable on the landmass of Europe.

Ten years before Waterloo, the British fleet under Nelson had crushed the French fleet at Trafalgar. This removed Napoleon's threat to invade Britain by crossing the English Channel. Even more important, Nelson's victory established Britain as the dominant naval power in Europe and the sea lanes of the world, a domination which lasted until World War I. However, Germany's rapidly growing economic power during the century, built upon excellence in science and industry, led to a naval contest between Britain and Germany that culminated in World War I, with France on the side of Britain.

An overview of the Jews of Europe

At the beginning of the period most of world Jewry lived in Eastern Europe. At the time of the Congress of Vienna (1815), which followed the Napoleonic Wars and saw a great redrawing of the boundaries of European states, the Jews of Europe numbered about 2,450,000. About one and a half million lived under Russian rule. Under Hapsburg rule – that is, the Austro-Hungarian Empire – there were about 400,000 Jews; the German states comprised some 350,000. To the west and south the numbers were far smaller: Italy 30,000, France 40,000, Holland 50,000 (half in Amsterdam), England 25,000. Nowhere did these totals reach more than 2 percent of the general population. By the middle of the 19th century, the Jewish population of the world had climbed to about 4,750,000, of whom 72 percent lived in Eastern Europe, 14.5 percent in Western Europe, about 1.5 percent in America, and 12 percent in the Ottoman Empire (North Africa and the Middle East). By the beginning of the 20th century, with their distribution radically changed, the number of Jews in the world had risen to about 10.5 million.

The Jews of Europe followed a range of occupations but, almost without exception, their places of residence and sources of livelihood were limited. They were subject to a multitude of restrictive measures. In Alsace, a Jew who wished to spend a day in Strasbourg had to pay a special tax; in Rome, he was obliged to attend a number of conversionist sermons each year; in Saxony, only with the king's permission could a tailor take a Jewish apprentice; in Frankfort, the annual number of Jewish marriages was limited to 12. At the beginning of the period most Jews in

Eastern Europe lived in small towns, called shtetls, in the majority of which Jews formed the larger part of the local population.

A common factor shared by the overwhelming majority of Jews everywhere was membership in the local Jewish community. This was, as it were 'a state within a state'. Throughout Europe, both in large cities and in innumerable small towns and rural centres, in places as far apart as London and the Ukraine, the local Jewish community enabled the Jew to lead a life in accordance with the precepts of his religion (subject always to the overriding restrictions of the surrounding state). This self-governing community provided a political and religious centre for the Jew, beyond which he had no recognised existence. It was a culture founded on respect for Jewish scholarship and for study, and for peaceful values. It did not see itself in need of reform – least of all from the outside.

The emphasis on learning was noted by a German-Jewish visitor to Riga in 1840[8]:

'A poorly clad couple entered, the man carrying a boy of about six wrapped in a prayer shawl. Both father and mother were weeping with joy, grateful to God who had preserved them that they might witness this beautiful and meaningful moment. The teacher took the hero of the celebration into his arms and stood him upon a table. He then sat down near the youngster, placed a card of the printed alphabet before him and, taking a long pointer, began the first lesson by blessing his newly initiated pupil that he may be raised for the study of the Torah, married, and for good deeds'.

Even earlier, in 1818, a senior official of Russian controlled Poland, wrote of Polish Jews:

'Almost every one of their families hires a tutor to teach its children... We [Gentiles] do not have more than 868 schools in towns and villages and 27, 985 pupils in all. They probably have the same number of pupils because their entire population studies. Girls too can read; even the girls of the poorest families. Every family, be it in the most modest circumstances, buys books, because there will be at least ten books in every household. Most of those inhabiting the huts in [Gentile] villages have only recently heard of an alphabet book.' (Quoted in Vital[9]).

This marked emphasis on education, particularly in verbal skills, prepared the ground for later secular studies, when Jews began to enter the *gymnasia* (grammar schools). In turn, a substantial rate of entry into the gymnasia led on to university level education (frequently subject to quota restrictions).

Linguistic skills were widespread among the Jews of Europe. Typically, they were at home in three languages: Yiddish, the universal language of the Jewish street; the vernacular language of the country in which they lived; and the language of high culture, which – except for in Russia – was German, both in the sciences and in the arts. It was also, at least in Herzl's day and beyond, the language of Zionism.

In most of Europe, Jews were the most literate sector of the population. The discrepancy between Jewish and non-Jewish literacy was particularly marked in Eastern Europe where between a quarter and a third of the general population was still illiterate in the 1930s. In the Soviet Union in 1939, 94 percent of Jews were literate, the highest figure for any Soviet nationality. The high rate was partly a function of urbanisation, but even compared with other city dwellers, there was greater literacy among the Jews. Most Jewish males in Eastern Europe were doubly literate since they could read and write in both Hebrew/Yiddish and at least one other language; the same was true for most Jewish women. Given their high rate of literacy and a disproportionate participation in commerce, it is hardly surprising that Jews played an important part in the publishing of both books and newspapers.

For Jewish children, reading began early. They read the same books as their Christian neighbours, but in addition read texts in Yiddish, including translations of, for example, Grimms' fairy tales and the children's stories of Oscar Wilde. Even poor people often spent significant sums on books, and copies circulated between friends. By the early 20th century, even quite small Jewish communities in Eastern Europe had libraries, some of them associated with particular movements – Orthodox, Zionist, or Socialist.

In the Soviet Union, Hebrew books remained available in some public libraries in the early 1920s, but thereafter they were withdrawn, even from specialist collections. By the late 1930s, private ownership of Hebrew books, particularly any deemed anti-Soviet, had become hazardous.

The French Revolution and the Napoleonic Wars

The French Revolution ushered in the idea of emancipation of the Jews, but it was qualified. In a debate in the French National Assembly in December 1789, a speaker, Clermont Tonnerre, stated:

"As a nation the Jews must be denied everything: as individuals they must be granted everything; their judges can no longer be recognised; the only recourse must be to our own exclusively; legal protection for the doubtful laws by which Jewish corporate existence is maintained must end; and they cannot be allowed to create a political body or a separate order within the state; it is necessary that they be citizens individually".

The French Revolution had literally demolished the walls of the Frankfurt ghetto and enabled the Rothschilds to begin their phenomenal, unprecedented economic ascent. Before 1789, Mayer Amschel Rothschild and his families' lives had been circumscribed by discriminatory legislation. No matter how hard Mayer Amschel worked, first as a rare coin dealer, then as a bullion broker and merchant banker, there were strict upper limits to what he could achieve. But when the French exported their revolution to South Germany, the legal restrictions on Frankfurt Jews were also largely removed. The Rothschilds were presented with major business opportunities by the Revolutionary Wars. As the scale and cost of the conflict between France and the rest of Europe rose, so too did the borrowing needs of the combatants. The disruption of established patterns of trade and banking created room for ambitious risk takers.[10]

Likewise, revolution and war made possible the rapid ascent of Mayer Amschel's son, Nathan, who progressed from exporting British textiles from Manchester, to financing the British war effort against Napoleon in the City of London. In 1810, Mayer Amschel designed the partnership structure that was to endure, modified but essentially the same, for very nearly a century, binding together the male line over four generations. The Rothschild sons established themselves, one per city, in London,

Paris, Berlin, Vienna, and Naples. By the middle of the 19th century – according to Ferguson, the chronicler of the Rothschild dynasty – the Rothschilds were the richest people in the world; indeed, the richest family in all history. Their success inspired competition, and a hundred years later the London and Paris banks were simply two among a number of private banks.

The Jews of Russia

Jews were encouraged to enter occupations and trades that had previously been closed, and throughout much of Europe were subject to obligatory military service. This was particularly the case in Western Europe but later also, increasingly, in Eastern Europe, where the establishment of the Pale of Settlement, from the 1790s on, confined the vast bulk of Russian Jewry to the western provinces of the Tsarist Empire. This inevitably slowed any inroads that assimilation might otherwise have made. Differences between Jews and the rest of the population were accentuated by the expansion of tsarist legislation on taxes, residence, occupation, etc. that applied to Jews alone. The accession of Tsar Nicholas I saw the conscription of Jewish boys from the age of 12 into special schools where they would be prepared for military service of 25 years.

The tyranny of Nicholas 1 was largely ended by the Crimean War (1854-5). It was followed in the 1860s by liberalising and modernising policies for both non-Jews and Jews: emancipation of the serfs, the introduction of elected organs of local self-government, judicial reform, etc. All had their parallel in the Jewish sphere. It became possible for the better educated and wealthier Jews to live outside the Pale. Jews could enter state service (for example as physicians) and live within large cities formerly closed to Jews but still within the Pale. (However, in 1891, thousands of Jews who had been allowed to live in Moscow and St Petersburg, outside the Pale, were forced to return to it).

A Jewish middle and upper class developed and participated in the industrialisation of the Russian Empire: Jews were involved in the Ukrainian sugar industry, the construction of the Russian railway network, water transport, the oil industry in the Caucasus, and private banking. There was an increased entry of young Jews into Russian universities – within legally prescribed limits.

The Pale of Settlement, especially the large urban centres, became a ferment of ideas and publications. There was a struggle between reformers and traditionalists, Hebraizers and Russifiers, Yiddishists and Westernizers: all competed for a hearing. The Jewish Enlightenment movement, known as the Haskalah, was the dominant trend. It preached assimilation into general Russian culture. However, there also came an antisemitic reaction. It was fed by traditional Christian sources but also by more recent phenomena, such as pan-Slav nationalism, a left-wing view of the Jew as capitalist and exploiter, and a right-wing view of him as subversive and a troublemaker. Dostoyevsky stated: "The Jew and his bank now dominate everything, Europe and Enlightenment, the whole civilisation, especially socialism, for with its help the Jew will eradicate Christianity – destroy the Christian civilisation. Then nothing is left but anarchy. The Jew will command everything". Constantine Pobedonostev, the chief theoretician as well as the leading practitioner of reaction in Russia in the last decades of the 19th century, allegedly remarked that the Jewish problem in Russia was to be solved by the conversion to Russian Orthodoxy of one-third of Russian Jews, the emigration of one-third, and the death of the remaining third. (Those who converted to Christianity escaped the disabilities imposed on the others).[11]

Criticism could be heard of the increasing number of Jewish students at secondary schools and universities. A pogrom in Odessa in 1871 seemed an isolated event. But those that took place a decade later were not. The trigger was the assassination of Alexander II (falsely attributed to Jews). Pogroms in the South (which may have been officially instigated) spread rapidly throughout the Pale, involving looting, arson, rape, and physical violence, including murder. A distressing aspect of this wave of violence was the lack of response with which most liberals looked on. Moreover the Jews of Russia were the hardest hit by the May laws of 1882 that accompanied the pogroms. They forbade the acquisition by Jews of property, required the expulsion of Jews from Moscow and imposed a quota for Jewish students in secondary schools and universities.

In 1894 Nicholas II succeeded his father, Alexander III, as Tsar. He was easily persuaded that his greatest enemies were his Jewish subjects. The main instrument in the propagation of this notion was *The Protocols of the Elders of Zion*, a forgery specially prepared for the Tsar and fabricated by the Paris office of the Russian Police between 1901 and 1905. It was only after 1919 that copies were circulated widely, particularly in Western Europe. The Protocols purported to show, from reports of an alleged International Jewish Congress, that there was a widespread international Jewish movement to destroy existing Christian organisations and to replace them by Jewish world domination. (This is essentially the same plot that was "exposed" in France by Drumont, and in England by Belloc, both of them avid antisemites.) The Russian Revolution of 1917 was claimed as evidence that this fantastic Jewish plot had begun to be realised: "After all was not Trotsky Jewish?" The message of the *Protocols* was clear: resistance to liberalism and socialism was vital if the world was to be rescued from a malevolent Jewish conspiracy. A response was rapidly forthcoming in southern Russia, where anti-Bolshevik forces slew thousands of Jews. Translations and annotations of the Russian original of the *Protocols* appeared in most of the languages of Western Europe. In 1921 the *London Times* exposed them as an outright forgery but it was already too late. They were used by antisemites in most lands. In the United States they were circulated by Henry Ford and by Father Coughlin, both influential public figures.

The sharp increase in the Jewish population of the Russian Empire made the situation worse. Between 1820 and 1880 the number of Jews in the Empire grew from 1,600,000 to 4 million, an increase of 150 percent, far greater than the 87 percent increase in the general population. By 1910 the total Jewish population was more than 5,600,000, with a clear link between population growth and poverty, exacerbated by the continued existence within the restricting confines of the Pale of Settlement of an ever-increasing number of artisans and middlemen, forced to compete between themselves for a shrinking market. Jewish workers had little access to capital, tools, credit or raw materials and were frequently driven into the ranks of those who were either unemployed or worked in establishments that were no better than sweat-shops. By the turn of the century one-third of Russian Jews existed on the relief provided by Jewish charitable organisations.

Germany and Central Europe

Here events took a generally different form. In 1812 the citizenship of all Jews living in Prussia was recognised and they were granted the same civic rights, duties and freedoms as those enjoyed by Christians. In the intellectual and social spheres there was a growing relationship between Jews and Germans, exemplified by the literary friendships of Moses Mendelsohn and of later Jewish writers and scholars. Economic liberation was demonstrated by the increasing proportion employed in professions such as medicine and teaching – in Prussia this reached about 4 percent, well ahead of the Jewish population share. Similar advances were found in banking and manufacturing. Overall, there were almost three times as many professional men and major businessmen in the western provinces of Prussia as in Posen, one of the less developed regions. In the latter there were more than twice as many Jewish artisans and less skilled workers as professionals and businessmen. (Throughout the 19th century there was a distinct trend away from handicrafts, as professions, industry and commerce were increasingly favoured.)

Jewish participation in politics was usually in support of European forces seeking change. This was particularly marked in the revolutionary years of 1848-9. Throughout Western Europe Jews tended to look to the higher culture of a country, whether German in Prussia or Magyar in Hungary, inevitably resulting in a racially-tinged hostility to Jews by Poles, Croats and Czechs.

Nevertheless, there was a strong movement towards assimilation, for example in religious reforms that sought to model Jewish synagogue worship on the Christian environment. One prayer book, for example, eliminated the universal reference to hopes for a return to Zion. However, Jews did continue to exist as a distinct entity, irrespective – in part, at least – of their political allegiance as Frenchmen, Germans or Russians.

The German Jew who rose highest in German society during the Imperial years was Gerson Bleichroder, Bismarck's banker. His success dramatizes the power of money. The richest man in Berlin, possibly in Germany, he managed the Chancellor's money and made the Chancellor rich as well. He was the first German Jew to be ennobled without converting to Christianity. Bleichroder hungered for acceptance into Prussian society. He gave lavish balls to which no Jews, not even relatives, were invited lest the other guests take offence. His daughter had to stay at home because no young man would ask her to dance. Bismarck's antisemitism was bland but ingrained. He gave Bleichroder the honorific term *von* but never allowed the banker to forget his origins.

Albert Ballin, who built his Hamburg-America line into the largest steamship company in the world, was a Hamburg Jew. By 1899 his company possessed more tonnage than the combined Merchant Marine of every nation other than Great Britain or Germany. Ballin's first meeting with the Kaiser, Wilhelm II, was in 1891. For the Kaiser, the development of a great merchant marine was vital for the expanding Imperial Navy, as the naval rivalry with Great Britain, hitherto the undisputed master of the seas, intensified. The Kaiser began to dine at Ballin's house. He did not bring his wife, however. The Kaiserin did not approve of her husband's friendship with the Jewish Ballin.

Ballin realised that however many warships Germany built, Britain would always build more and would do whatever was necessary to maintain her naval supremacy; Germany was unlikely to overtake her. Why not, therefore, stop at a point which Britain found unthreatening? However, he failed to persuade Tirpitz, the head of the German Navy.

Antisemitism

Beginning in the 1880s, there was a resurgence of antisemitism throughout the German lands in response to the perceived failure of Jews fully to assimilate. As Jews began to be involved in society, they became the targets of those seeking an explanation for the apparent increase in materialism and decline in Christianity. The term antisemitism was first used in 1879 by Wilhelm Marr; three years later, the first International anti-Jewish Congress was held in Dresden. Lueger was repeatedly elected mayor of Vienna on an explicitly antisemitic programme in the late 19th and early 20th centuries.

What was new in the antisemitism of the 1880s was its claim to have a biological basis: Jews were seen as being biologically inferior, so that marriage with them damaged and weakened the native Christian stock. In a Reichstag debate in 1895, an antisemitic deputy, Hermann Ahlwardt, referred to Jews as cholera bacilli and urged the authorities to exterminate them. In 1899 the antisemitic German Social Reform Party called for "a final solution of the Jewish question, to take the form of complete separation and (if self-defence requires it) ultimately the annihilation of the Jewish people".

Antisemitism, of course, had an economic as well as a biological basis; economic grievances were as important as fears of miscegenation. Those who felt the Rothschilds and their like had made illicit profits, by manipulating the stock exchange, were not particularly interested in racial hygiene. These were often men of the left. Hostility to the Jews was expressed by both the French Socialist Proudhon and the Russian anarchist Mikhail Bakhunin. The figure of the unscrupulous Jewish financier crops up in the literature of most European countries in the 19th century, including works by Balzac and Zola, and Anthony Trollope's *The Way We Live Now*.

Jews were indeed successful. Towards the end of the 19th century, 31 percent of the richest families in Germany were Jewish. Jews were also strikingly better represented among professionals: in the second quarter of the 20th century, one in nine German doctors was Jewish, as was one in six lawyers. Jews were under-represented in only one of Germany's elite occupational groups, the officer corps of the army – from which they were for the most part deliberately excluded.

German Jews were also to be found among the poor – a growing number of them had migrated from Eastern Europe to Germany in the late 19th and early 20th centuries. By 1914 around a quarter of the Jews in Germany were defined as Eastern. Relatively poor, orthodox in their faith, Yiddish in their speech, the so-called *Ostjuden* elicited much the same response among well-established German Jews as among German gentiles: disquiet, bordering on revulsion. Over time these impoverished

Jews would make their way in German society, as they did in Britain and the United States

Jewish responses to antisemitism

The response to antisemitism took three forms at an individual level; at the level of the Jewish collective, there were three further responses.

The first individual response was to **convert to Christianity**. According to Elon[12] Jewish conversions to Christianity in Germany were the highest in Europe since the 15th century, when some 60 percent of the Jews of Spain reportedly converted. (Of course, a good deal of coercion was involved; the Jews of Spain were offered the options of conversion, death, or expulsion.) In 19th-century Germany the pressure to convert came from a desire for social and professional advancement. The distinguished German Jewish historian, Heinrich Graetz, claimed that in Berlin alone, no less than half of the Jewish community converted, including four of Moses Mendelsohn's six children.

Heine called the baptismal certificate an "entrance ticket to European culture". In Germany conversion was mostly a middle-class and upper-middle-class phenomenon. Often, the richest, most talented and cultured men and women were the first to convert. The rich hoped to enter the aristocracy. Intellectuals rationalised their conversion as bringing them a step closer to the ideal of a universal religion.

` The second individual response was to **marry out**, that is, to enter the wider non-Jewish world but without actually converting to Christianity. Legal obstacles to marriage between Jews and non-Jews in Germany were removed in 1875, bringing the Reich into line with Belgium, Britain, Denmark, France, Holland, Switzerland and the United States. In 1876 around 5 percent of Prussian Jews who were married had non-Jewish spouses. By 1900 the proportion had risen to 8.5 percent. For the Reich as a whole, the percentage rose from 7.8 in 1900 to 20.4 in 1914. In Germany intermarriage rates were highest in those places where the Jewish communities were largest, namely in the cities of Berlin, Hamburg and Munich. The figures were markedly lower in Austria-Hungary – even in Vienna, Prague and Budapest. In the United States too, there was much less intermarriage than in

Germany at this time, reflecting the large proportion of Jews in the US who had recently migrated from poorer and less assimilationist Eastern Europe; indeed, it was not until the 1950s that American Jews began to marry out, the way German Jews had done in the 1900s.[13]

Lying low was the third response. In the decades before the Nazi period, many Jews in Europe, particularly of the middle and upper middle classes, tried to de-emphasise what were thought to be Jewish characteristics. The most obvious of these, and the easiest to change, was the family name: for example, in Britain Cohen became Collins or Conway. Often the change was a commercial decision: a German Jewish singer, Paula Levi, adopted the stage name Lindbergh. A new name might be politically expedient: Moshe Faintuch, a leading figure in the French Communist Party's bureau for aid to the Republican cause in Spain, gallicized himself as Jean Jérôme. Perhaps the most important way of lying low was to behave discreetly, speak quietly and dress in a restrained manner.

The three responses to antisemitism at a **collective** level were: to move elsewhere; to try and change the society in which Jews lived; to emigrate specifically to Palestine, an intended Jewish homeland.

Emigration

This came in response to a rapidly worsening economic and political situation. The Jews of the Russian Empire were far from the only people to move to the New World, but in proportion they considerably exceeded any other group. Between 1881 and 1914, 2.75 million left Eastern Europe – about three quarters of them from Russia, and nearly half a million from Austria-Hungary. The world Jewish population was about 10 million at that time, one in four of whom was on the move. About 2 million Jews went to the United States; other destinations were Canada, Argentina, Britain, South Africa, with an initial trickle going to Palestine. This produced an entirely new map of world Jewry, in which there was now a rough numerical equivalence between West and East. Locally, the composition of whole communities was transformed.

Socialism and the Bund

This was the second solution for those who remained in Russia – becoming immersed in socialism and political activism. In Western Europe socialist Jews did not propose anything in the nature of special Jewish rights, or even acknowledge the existence of a distinctly Jewish question; this was seen as a backward step that would preserve the ghetto itself.

In Eastern Europe, however, one version of Socialism took a specifically Jewish form. This was the Bund. Its members sought not only to join the movement demanding democratic and social rights in Russia, but also to defend the specific interests of Jewish workers, to carry on the struggle for their civic rights, and above all to combat discriminatory anti-Jewish laws. Jews were seen as suffering not only as workers but also as Jews. Within a few years the Bund moved in a Jewish-nationalist direction. It demanded for Russian Jewry not only civil and political emancipation but also national and cultural autonomy, though within Russia. The Bund was a way of life; as the Jewish worker lost his place within the traditional Jewish community, the Bund preserved for him some of his ancient links with the past, particularly the continued use of Yiddish.

Zionism

Initially, this was a middle-class movement, drawing on the writings of Leon Pinsker, a Russian physician whose book, *Auto-Emancipation,* argued that antisemitism was inevitable and inescapable: Jews needed their own country. At a meeting in Katowitz, in 1884 the 30 delegates were mainly middle class, but the Zionist appeal was then broadened to include workers, under the name of *Poalei Zion* (workers of Zion). The core belief of this Russian Zionism was that Jews had to move to Palestine (then a part of the Ottoman Empire) to set up agricultural settlements quite separately from the long-established ultra-Orthodox communities (mainly in Jerusalem), which centred around religious observance rather than work and were heavily subsidised by contributions from world Jewry. This farm settlement movement had begun in 1881 and was known as the *Biluim,* an acronym of a biblical Hebrew phrase: "House of Jacob let us arise and go now". Climatic conditions for the settlers were extremely difficult as was the widespread prevalence of malaria. They persevered, financially supported by, amongst others, Baron Rothschild.

Shortly afterwards, a Zionist movement with a rather different emphasis developed in Western Europe, the key figure being a Viennese lawyer, journalist and author, Theodor Herzl. His own experience of antisemitism, much strengthened by the false accusation of spying against a French Jewish officer, Alfred Dreyfus, led him to a view similar to that of Pinsker: Jews had to have their own country. Herzl understood that emancipation had not only failed to bring with it an increased degree of tolerance, but in fact brought intolerance by virtue of its very success. He organised and dominated the first Zionist Congress, held in Basle in 1897. Herzl published what became a key founding document of the Zionist movement, *Altneuland.* Once again, as in Eastern Europe, the Basle delegates were entirely middle class.

Herzl's view was that the support of the major powers, particularly Germany and Great Britain, was essential to achieve the object of Zionism: to establish for the Jewish people a publicly assured home in Palestine. He pursued this top-down political approach, as opposed to the bottom-up settlement aims of the Eastern European Zionists, with immense vigour. Herzl wrote in his diary after the First Zionist Congress: "At Basle I founded the Jewish state. If I said it out loud today, I would be greeted by universal laughter. In five years, perhaps, and certainly in 50 years everyone will perceive it". Just 50 years later the General Assembly of the United Nations decided by the requisite two-thirds majority to partition Palestine between Arabs and Jews, providing the essential legitimacy for a two-state solution. The Jewish state, named Israel, was founded less than a year later.

World War I and its aftermath

This was fought in Europe between the Triple Entente powers – Britain, France and Russia, against the Central Powers – Germany and the Hapsburg Empire. Also involved on the Allied side, from late 1917, was the United States, active on the world stage for the first time. Jewish soldiers fought in large numbers on both sides and suffered heavy losses – a total of 1,500,000 combatants and 175,000 dead – mostly in the Russian army.[14]

On December 1, 1916, the German Minister of War ordered a census of all Jewish soldiers in the German army, following complaints that some were shirking their duties. This thinking had existed in German officialdom across the previous hundred years, as Jews took advantage of unprecedented opportunities to advance. German Jews were accused by German antisemites of not doing their fair share; at the same time, it was made very difficult for well-qualified Jewish soldiers to become officers. Those who did so often cherished their medals and combat records, but these did not help them refute the post-1918 charge that the Jewish 'stab in the back' had been responsible for the German defeat. There were distinguished Jewish scientists on both sides: Fritz Haber's expertise assisted German chemical warfare; Chaim Weizmann was called on by Churchill to supply a key ingredient in heavy artillery shells.

November 11th, 1918, the Great War ends

Most of the hundreds of thousands of Jewish soldiers, chiefly from Eastern Europe, were from traditionally observant homes. The overriding demands of wartime service made keeping the usual practices difficult, if not impossible. Those who returned often found resuming previous religious practices something of a struggle. While Western European Jewish civilians had no great difficulty in keeping kosher homes, this was not the case for the masses of their Eastern counterparts, many of whom fled their homes as the tide of battle swept over them, with Russia's reverses against Germany.

Winston Churchill described the consequences of World War I, then known as the Great War:
"Victors and vanquished were ruined. All the emperors or their successors were slain or deposed... All were stricken; everything they had given was in vain. Nothing was gained by any... Those that survived, the veterans of countless battles, returned, whether with the laurels of victory or tidings of disaster, to homes engulfed already in catastrophe."[15]

This gloomy overview was certainly appropriate as regards the regimes of Central and Eastern Europe. It was not true for those of the victorious Allies whose homelands had not been physically touched by the war – essentially, the United States and Great Britain. And it was only partially true of France: much of the country had been occupied for several years by German armies and administrations, but France was on the winning side and enjoyed some of the spoils of war, at least for a time, due to the reparations agreed at the Treaty of Versailles,. In contrast, Germany, being the loser (although this was attributed by the Prussian military caste to the "stab in the back by the Jews") was driven, in part by the initial Allied rapacity at Versailles, to seek vengeance. For more than a year, well before the Nazi rise to power, Germany collapsed into anarchy and Red Revolution. It was saved by the Army and by the rampaging Freikorps. (There was also the previously unthinkable mutiny of the Imperial Navy.) Running street battles and bloody riots flared in a starved and defeated Berlin. Jews, such as Rosa Luxemburg and Karl Leibknecht, were to the fore on the eventually defeated Communist side. The Weimar Republic, headed by the Social Democratic Party was finally able to take office.

The Bolshevik Revolution of November 1917

The collapse of the multinational tsarist Empire facilitated an antisemitism that derived from a powerful combination of Christianity and nationalism. In these years (1917-1920) in more than 500 communities, over 150,000 Jews fell victim to the attacks of Ukrainians, White Russians, Poles and the Red Army, in the creation and leadership of which Trotsky (born Lev Davidovitch Bronstein) played a major role. Western involvement in attempts to stifle the nascent Revolution added to the suffering of helpless civilians, Jewish and gentile. Thus far, the revolution had brought nothing but suffering and economic catastrophe to the millions of Russian Jews.

When the Revolution did establish itself in power, it brought a decidedly ambiguous message. On the one hand, it made a sincere attempt to suppress overt antisemitism and in this it was, apparently, largely successful. On the other hand, the Jews of Russia suffered in their dual capacity as a religious entity that was reactionary by definition, and as a national political entity that lacked the concentrated territorial nature of other ethnic minorities.

The Bolshevik victory also had positive consequences for Russian Jews, including urbanization (leaving behind the shtetl life) and entering the universities and different professions, in disproportionately large numbers. The pattern of Central and Western Europe reproduced itself in Soviet Russia. In respect of urbanisation, for example, the Jewish population of Moscow grew from 8,100 in 1895 to 131,000 in 1926, and to around 350,000 by 1939; that of Leningrad (St Petersburg) from 17,000 in 1890 to 131,000 in 1926, and to some 250,000 in 1939. Young Russian Jews benefited from increased educational opportunities earlier than their non-Jewish contemporaries, particularly in the less developed constituent republics of the Soviet Union; for example, in White Russia and the Ukraine, in 1926, Jewish medical students formed 46.6 percent and 44.8 percent, respectively, of all medical schools. Other heavily favoured faculties were economics, industry and technology. By 1938, as non-Jewish groups caught up the proportion of Jewish students at universities and colleges declined to 13 percent, although their absolute numbers continued to grow and they were still well ahead of the Jewish population share. On the eve of war, of the 1,400,000 gainfully employed Jews in Russia nearly 18 percent (253,000) earned a livelihood in the liberal professions. There was not all that much difference between the degree of urbanisation and occupational concentration in the totalitarian Soviet Union, and that elsewhere in Europe. (A generation later, Jewish professionals, particularly in the sciences and medicine, would struggle to leave the Soviet Union, some successfully. Some 15 to 20 years further on, nearly all of those who applied to do so were allowed to depart.)

The cost of these advances was the suppression of all aspects of Jewish culture and self-government (Yiddish, religious observance, Zionism and the Bund). Emigration was first allowed then stopped – as the US largely barred entry. There were initial attempts to suppress antisemitism, but Stalin (the victor in 1926 over his great rival Trotsky) turned to it intermittently over the next three decades of his dictatorship, often savagely and with great loss of Jewish life, in a succession of "purges" and "plots". In essence, Jews could advance when convenient to Stalin, but not as Jews. (This echoes the statement of Clermont-Tonnerre, quoted earlier, following the French Revolution.)[16]

The great Jewish writer Isaac Babel (1894-1940) was a product of the Russian Revolution. He fought in the Tsar's army, and when the Revolution came, served in the Cheka (secret police), and also as a Bolshevist operative raiding farms for food. Finally, he got his wish, to fight alongside the Cossacks. From his experiences he produced a masterpiece, *Red Cavalry*,[17] a volume of stories describing in brilliant, sometimes dismaying detail, his efforts to acquire, as he put it, the simplest of proficiencies, 'the ability to kill my fellow men'. The difficulty a Jew finds in escaping his cultural background, especially in dealing with death, is a recurrent, poignant theme. In due course he was arrested and he subsequently disappeared. He was probably shot early in 1940 in one of Stalin's "purges", for the alleged offence of "taking part in a literary conspiracy".

Polish Jewry between the wars

Along with other Central and Eastern European cities, Warsaw was caught between the armies of the Russian Empire and the Central powers, and was occupied by both sides. Warsaw entered the war not as a capital city, but as the third city of the Russian Empire, after St Petersburg and Moscow. It was occupied by the Russians until 1915, and then by the Germans until the war ended in 1918, after which Poland received its independence (at the Congress of Versailles). Russian rule was not very friendly to the Jews of Warsaw during the first year or two of the war. Jews became suspected of spying and were called "enemy aliens", a category they shared with ethnic Germans. There was also a crackdown and complete banning of the Yiddish language press in Warsaw as the Russians prepared their evacuation.

Warsaw and other such cities in Central and Eastern Europe during this period were not yet the 'blood lands' they would become during World War II, but they were certainly 'war lands', where death, starvation and disease afflicted their citizens on a severe scale. During the course of the war an estimated 200,000 Jewish refugees passed through Warsaw, a crisis that caused mass hysteria in the Polish press at the time. There were widespread claims that these Jewish refugees created public health concerns for the city.

There were still three million Jews in Poland and much literary activity, particularly in Yiddish. The cultural level and diversity of Polish Jewry is shown by the following: in 1928, 622 Yiddish works were printed and in 1930, 180 Jewish periodical publications were issued, 135 in Yiddish, 28 in Polish, 17 in Hebrew.

But none of this could disguise the steadily worsening impoverishment of Polish Jews through the state's policy of excluding them (with the enthusiastic support of the Church) from many sectors of the economy, which it controlled. In some communities, as many as half the Jews were wholly or partly dependent on communal funds.

Brief Lives

1. Heinrich Heine (1797-1856)

Heine exemplified the constant conflict between the old certainties and the new opportunities. Born Haim Heine, Germany's greatest 19th-century poet was descended from a family of Court Jews. His was one of a number of Jewish families who were useful suppliers of financial and administrative services to kings, princes and bishops throughout Europe from the 16th century on. Heine himself struggled unsuccessfully to become a businessman, achieving only bankruptcy. Wealthy relatives paid for his studies and subsidised him for many years during his writing career.

Arriving in Berlin in 1821 to study law, Heine created an immediate stir. He was both a gifted poet and of a striking appearance, slight, pale with dreamy blue eyes and long blonde hair. He was lionised by the leading literary hostesses of the day, themselves often Jewish, who introduced him to critics and major writers. In 1823, seeking a public position, he passed his doctoral exams in law, but found the bar associations closed to Jews. He was contemptuous of the many who converted to Christianity, usually for material advancement. Nevertheless, for those same pragmatic reasons, and although disgusted with himself, in 1825 he took the same path. He wrote to a friend, "I am becoming a proper Christian, I sponge off rich Jews". Despite his rapidly rising reputation as a poet, he failed in his bids for a series of university positions in departments of literature (his known political liberalism did not help). Rejected for a legal position he was offered the post of Paris correspondent for a liberal German newspaper. He lived in Paris, in effect exiled from his culture, from 1831 until his death 25 years later, constantly under surveillance by Prussian and Austrian agents. Admired by France's leading writers, he felt 'like a fish in water', wrote his best poetry and voiced some startlingly accurate prophecies regarding German militarism and nationalism.

Heine left a massive literary legacy. As early as 1912 there were over 4,000 musical settings of his poems by great German and Austrian composers. His works influenced Wagner's operas and inspired countless writers including George Eliot, Shaw and Longfellow, and have been translated into most languages. He left an indelible mark on German culture, one that even the Nazis were unable to erase. But while the critics hailed the lyricism of his poetry, they snidely referred to his Jewish origins and resented a Jew having such a perfect ear for German. He was seen as a double outsider – both as a Jew, despite his conversion, and as a radical.

Heine's political prescience was as remarkable as his poetry. In 1817, while still a student, he wrote: 'wherever they burn books they also, in the end, burn human beings'. He was referring to a recent book-burning in Germany, accompanied by fiery antisemitic speeches. In 1834 he warned the French: 'the German thunder ... rises slowly at first, but it will come. And when you hear it roar, as it has never roared before in the history of the world, know that the German thunder has reached its target'. During Heine's lifetime, Communism was an obscure political movement, but his intuitions about its future were remarkable, conveying only fear and foreboding. In 1842, he wrote: ' though Communism is at present little talked about... It is destined to play a great, if transitory, role in the modern tragedy... There will be only *one* shepherd with an iron crook and *one* identically bleating human herd'.

Heine struggled all his life with his ambivalence towards his fellow Jews and Judaism. At an early stage in his career he rejected all religions, asserting that his true fatherland was the German language – "our most sacred possession". But he deeply regretted his conversion, noting that it had brought him nothing but misfortune. Much of the bitterness and self- punishing irony of his later writings stems from this act of opportunism. Both before and after his conversion he was scornful of Germany's new Jewish reform movement, which introduced prayer books in German and organ music. At the same time he denounced the restrictions of Orthodox Judaism. But once he had overcome his initial physical revulsion, he found himself admiring the unkempt, traditionally observant Polish Jew in his shtetl for steadfastly bearing the stamp of freedom. He disliked the enlightened, Europeanizing Jew even more than the Orthodox and Reform types, noting that four out of Moses Mendelssohn's six children had converted, and in 1850 stated: "I make no secret of my Judaism because I have never left it". His change of mind had begun with the Damascus Affair (1840), a trumped-up charge of ritual murder against the Jews of that city. His later poetry drew heavily on Jewish themes. But he died still seeking reconciliation between his conflicting aspirations and experiences. The Jewish-born poet, who was later baptised as a Protestant, and married in a Catholic ceremony to please his French wife, was laid to rest in a general cemetery without religious rites – in accordance with his last wishes. (Extracted and paraphrased from Elon, *The Pity of it All*).[18]

2. Fritz Haber (1868-1934)

A key figure in Germany's rise to industrial dominance early in the 20th century, Haber was born to ordered comfort, but also to the loneliness of his father's widowhood within months of Haber's birth. His father remarried nine years later; in the interim, the young Haber was treated with a Spartan severity that fitted well with the times. Driven by the juggernaut of Bismarck's ambitions, Germany had recently unified and was well on the way to European hegemony. Haber's childhood coincided with Prussia's glorification of German arms and German unity. A photograph of him as a four-year-old presenting arms with a toy gun is prophetic of his later close ties with the army and his lifelong attachment to discipline and rank.

His academic bent was for science, in particular, chemistry, and he received his doctorate in 1891. Along the way he did the requisite one-year army service. When he sought an academic career he found, as had Heine nearly 70 years earlier, that his being a Jew raised huge obstacles. He converted in 1892 – but without any of the agonising and self-disgust that Heine experienced. He was ambitious and pragmatic and his Jewish attachment was not very deep. Yet he retained his pride in the collective suffering and achievements of the Jews, and most of his friends were Jewish, or of Jewish descent. From 1894 to 1911 he worked at the Technical Institute of Karlsruhe, becoming a respected member of the international scientific community.

However, his hopes for a chair at the prestigious University of Vienna were dashed when it became known that he was a 'baptised Jew'. He wrote to a colleague that Jews, even converted Jews, were not wanted in the major positions. (This did not apply to those of even more exceptional eminence: Paul Ehrlich, the inventor of chemotherapy, and an eventual Nobel prize winner, encountered difficulties but did not have to convert; nor did Einstein, recognised early in his career as a genius.)

In 1906 he was finally made a full professor and in 1911, moved to Berlin to head the newly financed Kaiser Wilhelm Institute for Physical Chemistry and Electrochemistry; his distinction as an applied scientist, of special value to Germany's industrial predominance, was now plain to all. His greatest single achievement, together with a British colleague, was the fixation of nitrogen from the air. Accomplished with immense effort over a ten-year period, this breakthrough was a vital step in the commercial production of ammonia that in turn underpinned Germany's preparations for the obviously impending conflict. As the son of a highly patriotic family, Haber enthusiastically supported the war, which broke out in 1914, placing himself at the disposal of the war effort.

One of his discoveries – a process for producing nitric acid – filled a key gap in the manufacture of explosives and fertilisers, which were vital to the war front and to the home front, respectively. Across the English Channel another Jewish chemist, Chaim Weizmann, performed a similar service for the British government: he had developed a new technique for the production of acetone, a vital ingredient in the manufacture of cordite, the propellant explosive used by the British forces. (Weizmann was born in a benighted corner of Eastern Europe; he had acquired a European education and a chemistry lectureship at Manchester University in the north of England. There he pursued his twin passions, for science and for the Zionist movement. His success in the former helped him to pursue the latter, through his contacts with British statesmen. On this occasion, Haber and Weizmann were on parallel tracks. Nearly 20 years later, their paths intersected in very different circumstances.)

Haber became the most important organiser of Germany's wartime science. He supervised a massive increase in the production of saltpeter, without which German military capacity would have been exhausted by the spring of 1915. His work on the production of poison gas became even better known – though it was morally ambiguous, to say the least. In its favour, it was argued that it might break the horrific stalemate of trench warfare. It did not, of course. Fritz Stern, a distinguished American historian of German-Jewish origin, charged that Haber 'had helped to make barbarism scientific'. (In the next world war, similar moral issues surrounded another project in which Jewish scientists were heavily involved – the development of the atomic bomb.) In 1919 Haber's name appeared on the Allied list of war criminals to be extradited for trial. But the appetite for justice rapidly waned as it did after World War II, and Haber, together with many others so named, was able to resume civilian life. He did so to the plaudits of his fellow countrymen for his brilliant successes.

In the post-war world Haber continued to put his scientific talents at the service of his country. He became a roving ambassador for German science, travelling incessantly in an attempt to restore Germany's pre-eminent position. Indeed, he was abroad when Hitler came to power in January 1933. In March of that year, a new law required the removal of non-Aryan professors (with the initial exception of war veterans). Haber could have stayed at his institute, but he balked at dismissing his Jewish colleagues. On 1 October 1933 he resigned, his health and spirit broken. But in helping others to emigrate, he was brought into close contact with Weizmann, who hoped that some of those who were expelled might join him at his newly established research institute in Rehovot, Palestine. Haber himself planned to visit Rehovot. By now he had lost his long-held illusions and wrote to Fritz Stern's father: "Lucky is the person who did not grow up in the German world and is not growing up there now!" In January 1934 he died of a heart attack in Basel, on his way to Palestine. (Extracted and paraphrased from Elon.)[19]

Chapter Three

Careers Open to Talent: The Jews of Central and Western Europe 1800 to 1933

German Jews to 1933

Michael Ignatieff (cited by Wasserstein)[20] has claimed that 'the entire cultural renaissance of Central Europe was made possible by the emancipation and urbanisation of Central European Jewry.'

Ignatieff's sweeping assertion is perhaps a little hyperbolic, but not drastically so. From Nobel laureates in the sciences, to luminaries in the arts across-the-board, German and Austrian Jews did perform extraordinarily well. The extent to which this was so in Germany, before 1933, and in Austria, before 1938, is made clear by Amos Elon in *The Pity of It All.*[21] (Elon also reviews those who left, having lost their positions, were forcibly expelled, were murdered, or committed suicide during or after those crucial years.) German and Austrian Jews also had a great influence on economic life. Both of those years, 1933 and 1938, mark a clear watershed between relative plenty and relative famine in the cultural life of Germany and Austria. The wounds to the scientific, cultural and economic life of those countries were entirely self-inflicted by their Nazi regimes; the two countries have taken many years to recover from them – if indeed they have done so entirely, even more than eighty years on. Other countries, most notably Britain and the U.S. benefited greatly, both immediately and for many years afterwards.

German Jewish Nobel laureates included Haber in chemistry, Ehrlich in medicine and Einstein in physics. Of the last named it was said that he was the most famous scientist in the world. Lazarus and Steinthal created the field of social psychology; Walter Benjamin was a particularly influential social philosopher and critic; Martin Buber was a key figure in philosophy and theology.

The Weimar Republic, which continued until 1933, began in 1919 in an atmosphere of hope. According to Elon,[22] despite turmoil and uncertainty, it was a showpiece of intense creativity until the very end. Arts, sciences and advanced thought flowered as never before and like nowhere else in contemporary modern Europe. In literature, music, film, theatre and design, Weimar evoked a marvellous sense of the new, a vanguard admired to this day. However, from the first the regime was mercilessly under attack, despised and derided by political extremists on both the left and the right.

A key figure in the Republic was an assimilated Jew, Walter Rathenau. In February 1922, against much opposition and his own mother's strong misgivings, he agreed to become foreign minister. He worked hard to reconcile Germany with its former enemies, but his policy of strict compliance with the terms of the unpopular Treaty of Versailles infuriated the nationalist right. On 24 June 1922 he was assassinated. His assailants, who were linked to an extreme right-wing group were sentenced to only four years in prison.[23] At the time few suspected that such thugs might ultimately form a government of criminals under the charismatic leadership of a psychopath preaching a religion of violence and death. The Weimar Republic was identified not only with Rathenau and Rosa Luxemburg, a leading Communist, but with the humiliating terms of the Versailles Treaty. Every unresolved problem and all the worlds' evils from the crucifixion of Christ to capitalism, communism, syphilis, and the last war were projected onto a tiny minority representing 0.9 percent of the German population. In 1923, Hitler led an abortive putsch in Munich which prefigured his ascent to power in 1933.

However, things did improve considerably due to successful currency reforms, Allied concessions on reparations, and sustained economic growth. American loans helped Germany to meet its diminishing reparation payments. Perhaps as a result, the number of Nazi deputies in the Reichstag dropped to only 12; the Nazis seemed destined to remain a tiny fringe party.

The first volume of Hitler's *Mein Kampf* was published in 1925. Few people read it. But the traditional ruling class was exemplified by the officer corps whose arrogance remained unchanged. The Versailles Treaty was being grossly violated and the infrastructure for a vastly larger military force than was laid down in the treaty was maintained clandestinely, as were training programmes, some in collusion with the Soviet Union. Paul von Hindenburg, a former field marshal, became president in 1925. In

1929 a world-wide economic slump gave Hitler his opportunity. His opponents were divided and played into his hands. In the 1930 elections, the Nazi representation in the Reichstag increased nearly tenfold to 207 deputies, making it the second largest after the Social Democrats, with more than 6 million votes. The Communists came in third, increasing their support by 40 percent. But the moderate parties of the centre were vastly reduced. The stage was set for a fight to the end between extremes. Many Jews saw the Nazi upsurge as a temporary blip in what was, 'after all, a civilised country'.

The early 1930s saw the beginning of the end of parliamentary democracy. Nazi and Communist militias clashed in the streets and Jews were attacked by Nazi hoodlums. The Nazi vote continued to grow. The election of July 31, 1932 saw the Nazis emerge as the dominant party in the Reichstag. Hindenburg vainly tried to placate Hitler with the offer of the Vice Chancellorship. Hitler rejected it – only the top spot would do. On January 30, 1933, he was appointed Chancellor of the new Cabinet in which Nazi ministers were initially in a minority of two. This was soon to change, as was the life of the Jews of Germany.

Vienna, to 1933

According to an essay in *The Economist* of December 24, 2016: 'From the late 1880s to the 1920s Vienna was the city of the century. The ideas and art endured. Those Viennese who escaped Nazism went on to sustain the West during the Cold War, and to restore the traditions of empiricism and liberal democracy.'

Vienna was both an imperial city and a national capital. By 1910 Vienna had a population of 2 million, the sixth biggest city in the world, of whom 175,000 were Jews. Fortunes made in the fast-industrialising Empire, many by Jewish or assimilated Jewish families, such as the Wittgensteins and the Efrussis, changed the urban landscape. Sigmund Freud founded and developed psychoanalysis; Arnold Schoenberg changed classical music. The logical positivism of the Vienna Circle, dominated by Moritz Schlick, set the scene for modern analytical philosophy with its strong affinity for the sciences. The most accomplished of the circle was Otto Neurath who also revolutionised the transmission of knowledge with new ways of transmitting complex information.

It was the city where Adolph Hitler lived for five years, from 1908 to 1913, in obscurity and poverty. But some of his antisemitic obsessions developed during that period. He much admired Vienna's antisemitic mayor, Karl Lueger. The rise of Lueger's Christian Social Party made a deep impression on Hitler for its deliberate and successful appeal to the classes whose existence was insecure – the lower-middle-classes and the artisans. What he also took from Lueger was his command of the masses, the moulding of the movement to attain his purposes, his use of propaganda to influence the psychological instincts of his supporters. In Hitler's Vienna there were large numbers of poor Jews, many having recently fled from pogroms. In one district, a third of the down-at-heel population was Jewish, many dressed in traditional garb. In Brigittenau, a depressing district in which Hitler spent his last three years in Vienna, some 17 percent of the inhabitants were Jews.[24]

Kaiser Franz Joseph had occupied the Habsburg throne for more than 50 years. He symbolised apparently unchanging imperial might in a world which was changing around him. Franz Joseph refused to allow Lueger to become mayor, for two successive elections which he had won, but finally had to succumb.

According to Hannah Arendt: "The school of fame that the Jewish youth of Vienna attended was the theatre.[25] As individuals rather than a collectivity, Jews played a vital part in much of Central and Eastern Europe. Max Reinhardt, described as the presiding genius of European theatre in the early 20th-century, born to Orthodox Jewish parents in Vienna, made his name as director of the Deutsches Theater in Berlin. In the 1920s and 1930s he directed plays and operas in Berlin, Vienna, and Salzburg. Reinhardt was one of the hundreds of playwrights, directors, actors, cabaret artists and critics of Jewish origin who transformed the European stage, particularly in the German-speaking lands in those years.

In Central and Eastern Europe a further aspect of theatre that was disproportionately Jewish was the audience. In Poland, it was said that without the Jewish audiences, theatre "could save itself the expense of turning on the lights". Antisemites accused Jews of dominating and perverting the theatre in Central and Eastern Europe for their own purposes. But the only avowedly Jewish theatres were the Yiddish ones. In Warsaw, the centre of European Yiddish theatre between the wars, four major dramatic companies as well as several popular musical companies competed for audiences. The Habimah theatre company left Russia in 1926 and settled in Palestine, later becoming the national theatre of Israel

In film as on the stage, the role of Jews as entrepreneurs, directors and players was enormous. The European – in particular, the German – film industry, was almost as much a Jewish creation as was Hollywood. Fleeing Nazism, directors Ernst Lubitsch and Billy Wilder made their stellar careers in the United States.

Antisemites accused the Jews in all European countries of 'controlling' the press. That was manifestly not true in Britain or France, but in Central Europe matters were apparently different. Before the rise of the Nazis, the German-language press in Vienna, Berlin and Budapest had indeed, to a considerable degree, been owned and produced by Jews – although not by *the Jews*, since the Jewish pressmen did not act in concert. The foremost example of such a newspaper was the *Neue Freie Presse*, the leading newspaper of Vienna from the late 19th century until 1938 and the Nazi takeover of Austria. It developed into the chief organ of the Viennese liberal bourgeoisie and had considerable political influence. In addition, in the heyday of the Viennese cultural flowering between the 1880s and 1914, it was also a major arbiter of taste in literature and the arts. Nearly 80 percent of the editorial staff in the inter-war period was Jewish. But notwithstanding its heavily Jewish ownership, staff and readership, the *Neue Freie Presse* did not see itself as a Jewish publication. Instead, it followed a universalist, liberal outlook, seeking a general audience and striving not to make special claims on behalf of Jewish interests. For example, the editor-in-chief, Benedikt, took extra care to avoid pleas on behalf of Zionism, despite Herzl's involvement with the paper. The liberal, universalist, approach of such papers, made them prime targets of right-wing nationalist forces, whose animosity extended beyond the producers of the newspapers to Jews in general.

Hungary, to 1933

The Jewish population of Hungary grew rapidly during the 19th century, particularly during the latter half. Jews succeeded in establishing a strong position in the country and played a considerable role in the development of its economy. From the 1880s, large numbers entered the liberal professions and also contributed to literary life, particularly in journalism (Theodore Herzl was born in Budapest and spent his early life in Hungary). Before World War I, 55 to 60 percent of merchants were Jews, as were 13 percent of the owners of large and medium-sized estates and 45 percent of the contractors. As compared to Germany and Austria, Jewish professional success was even more conspicuous in Hungary, where Jews accounted for a larger share of the urban population, particularly in the capital Budapest (23 percent of the population). Of those professionally engaged in literature and the arts, 26 percent were Jews (of the journalists, 42 percent), in law 45 percent, and in medicine 49 percent. On the other hand, only a small number of Jews were employed in public administration.

Almost inevitably, antisemitism increased in the 1880s and the rise was particularly sharp early in the 20th century. During World War I, the Jews suffered heavy losses of both life and property. At the same time, anti-Jewish feeling was strong, having increased further because of the presence of numerous Jewish refugees from Galicia, which had been occupied by the Russians.

The communist regime that came into power in Hungary after its defeat in World War I included a considerable number of Jews in its upper ranks, led by Bela Kun. After the communist regime was suppressed, the establishment of the new regime was accompanied by riots and acts of violence against Jews – the White Terror – which led to the deaths of some 3,000. Even when the political situation stabilised and violence against Jews abated, the declared policy of the government remained antisemitic. In 1920 a bill was passed restricting to five percent the number of Jews in institutions of higher learning. Matters improved during the following years but took a sharp anti-Jewish turn during the middle to late 1930s as a result of growing Nazi influence. The Fascist Arrow Cross organisation became increasingly powerful.

In 1938 the "First Jewish Law" was passed, restricting to 20 percent the number of Jews in the liberal professions and in commercial and industrial enterprises. (The term 'Jew' included not only members of the Jewish religion, but also those who had converted to Christianity after 1919, or who had been born of Jewish parents after that date.) In 1939, Parliament passed the "Second Jewish Law" which extended the application of the term Jew on a racial basis, ultimately including some 100,000 Christians (converts and their children), and also reduced the number of Jews in economic activities, fixing the limit at five percent. Under the new law the political rights of Hungarian Jews were restricted, and some 250,000 lost their sources of livelihood.

As in Germany, one reaction on the part of Jews to the anti-Jewish legislation was an increased emphasis on their patriotic attachment to Hungary, voiced by their official representatives. In general, Jews believed that the anti-Jewish current was only a fleeting phenomenon.

France, to 1933

The Jewish community of France was the first in Europe to benefit from Napoleon's meritocratic dictum: all careers are open to the talented. At the time of the Dreyfus Case, the Jews in France numbered no more than 86,000 out of a total population of nearly 40 million. The community was administered through a government-sponsored central consistory, under a ministry which laid down rules for the election of rabbis, and fixed and contributed to their salaries, so that French Judaism had some of the characteristics of a state church – and behaved like one. When J.-H. Dreyfus was installed as Grand Rabbi of Paris in 1891, his theme was the links between the French genius and the fundamental spirit of Judaism, especially the moral affinities between the two races, the French being "the elect people of modern times".[26]

The Jewish laity combined a low profile with great patriotism. They competed energetically for the glittering prizes of the French state – and won them. Many leading Jews argued that antisemitism was a German import that could gain no more than a superficial hearing in France. Unfortunately, this was not so. In

1853 a French diplomat, de Gobineau, published a book that became the handbook of the German antisemites and had an enormous influence on, for example, Richard Wagner. Some years later, Edouard Drumont published a massive two-volume *La France Juive*, which in a short time ran into over 100 editions and enabled him to found the antisemitic League and his vicious daily paper, *La libre Parole.*[27]

Hence, the first layer of French antisemitism was pseudo-scientific. The second was envy. If the Jews were racially inferior, why were they so successful? The answer was obvious: because they cheated and conspired. (Jewish children of the *haute bourgeoisie* tended to carry off the prizes.) And after London, Paris was the centre of European finance; its bankers' roll-call was studded with Jewish names.

There was a third, clerical, layer of French antisemitism. This was a paranoid belief of the official Roman Catholic hierarchy that there was a Jewish plot against Catholicism, linked with Freemasonry and with the Protestants, both a minority in France.[28]

This background of hatred and slander was compounded by the aftermath of Russian pogroms of 1881. As did Britain and the United States, France took in, over a generation, 120,000 Jewish refugees, more than doubling the size of French Jewry. These were poor, and obviously "Jewish", seemingly corresponding to the caricatures that were being peddled.[29]

They were joined by a steady stream from the Alsace Jewish community, which could not abide the German occupation (Germany had seized Alsace after defeating France in the war of 1870), among them the Dreyfus family who were fierce French patriots. Getting a commission in the French army had been a boyhood ambition of Alfred Dreyfus. It was a matter of great pride to him that, after the general staff was reorganised to give it a wider social basis, he had been the first Jew to be selected for staff duties. Fearful of further German assault, in January 1894 France signed a secret military convention with a new ally against Germany, Tsarist Russia. Unfortunately, this made the Jews still more suspect in French eyes, for it was known that they hated the Tsarist regime more than any other group. All the Paris synagogues offered a special prayer on the birthday of Alexander III, the most antisemitic of the Tsars. It made no difference. Every patriotic gesture the Jews made was received by the antisemites with implacable cynicism: "They would, wouldn't they?"[30]

The Dreyfus Affair

In July 1894, a spendthrift gambler, Major Count Esterhazy, offered his services to the German embassy. Next month he gave the embassy a letter listing certain papers he intended to hand over in return for cash. On 26 September, it reached Major Henry of the general staff statistical section (a cover name for counter-espionage). All the internal evidence pointed to Esterhazy. But the head of the section, Colonel Sandherr, was a German-hating, antisemitic, Catholic convert. When Major Henry, another antisemite, produced Dreyfus's name, Sandherr was delighted.

There was no antisemitic army plot against Dreyfus. All concerned acted in good faith. The only exception was Henry, who actually forged evidence against Dreyfus. It was Drumont and his newspaper, *La libre Parole,* who broke the story that a Jewish officer had been secretly arrested for treason. Dreyfus was convicted and sent to Devil's Island; the leaders of the Jewish community accepted his guilt. They simply wanted the whole thing buried. Dreyfus's own family were convinced of his innocence and worked quietly behind the scenes amassing evidence, hoping for a pardon. A celebrated Jewish lawyer, Joseph Reinach, took up the case. Many young Jews joined the cause, including Marcel Proust. Non-Jewish radicals became interested. Among them was Emile Zola, then France's most popular writer. He investigated the case, wrote an enormous article in defence of Dreyfus and gave it to a rising politician, Georges Clemenceau, who ran a liberal newspaper. It was Clemenceau's idea to print it on its front page (13 January 1898) under the headline "J'accuse!" That was the real beginning of the Dreyfus affair. Four days later antisemitic riots broke out in Nantes and spread to many other French towns. Nothing could now stop the polarisation. The army, asked to admit it had made a mistake, refused and closed ranks. When one of its number, Major Picquart, produced evidence pointing to Esterhazy, it was Picquart who was arrested and jailed. Zola was tried for libel and had to flee the country.

The Dreyfus affair convulsed France for an entire decade. It became an important event not just in Jewish history but in

French, indeed in European, history. The Dreyfusards formed a national organisation, the League of the Rights of Man, to get Dreyfus freed. The anti-Dreyfusards replied with the League of the French Fatherland, to defend the honour of the army and France. Over 70 percent of them were highly educated: students, lawyers, doctors, university teachers, artists and men of letters. Behind the passion on each side, tragic issues were taking shape. The Dreyfus affair was a classic example of a fundamentally simple case of injustice being taken over by extremists on both sides.

The real breakthrough for the Dreyfusards was the sudden death of the violently anti-Dreyfus President of France, Felix Faure. After this, the anti-Dreyfus front began to bend. Dreyfus was brought back from Devil's Island, white-haired, malarial, scarcely able to speak. The left won an overwhelming electoral success in 1906. Dreyfus was rehabilitated and returned to the army. Picquart ended up Minister for War. But there was a price to pay, and in the end, it was the Jews of France who paid it. Antisemitism was institutionalised. The League of the French Fatherland went on to become, after the 1914-18 war, a pro-fascist, antisemitic movement which formed the most vicious element of the Vichy regime (1941-44) and helped to send many thousands of French Jews, native and refugee, to their death.

Britain, to 1933

There was no settled Jewish community in Britain until after the Conquest of 1066 by Duke William of Normandy, who invited French Jewish businessmen to relocate to England – they were entitled to lend money on interest, repayment being guaranteed by the King. But in difficult economic times debtors rioted against the Jewish moneylenders. The Jews of York were massacred in 1190. Over time the position of the scattered Jewish community of about 5,000 deteriorated further. Eventually, in 1290, King Edward 1 expelled the remaining Jews to Northern France.

Jews were allowed to return to Britain under the regime of Oliver Cromwell in 1660. Those who did so were the descendants of the Spanish and Portuguese (Sephardi) Jews who had been expelled from those countries in 1492 and had been welcomed in

Holland for their international links. For some 220 years growth was slow. By 1734 the numbers had reached 6,000 and by 1882, 46,000. At that point, the Jewish masses of Eastern Europe, seeking refuge from poverty and pogroms, poured into Britain, as they did to the United States. Between 1882 and 1914 11 ships a week left the major ports of Germany, bringing 300,000 Russian, Galician and Rumanian Jews. (Many went on to the U.S.) The great majority settled in London, but there were also between 10,000 and 20,000 in both Leeds and Manchester. They lived in great poverty working largely, when they had work, in tailoring (40 percent), boot and slipper making (12 percent) and the furniture trade (10 percent). By 1900, there were specifically Jewish trade unions in nearly 20 trades.[31]

The Jewish community which they joined, and in numerical terms overwhelmed, had come mainly from Germany, already established in the middle class, and had gradually prospered further during the 19th century. The disabilities from which this community suffered were relatively minor. Their social emancipation had been complete almost from the beginning. They were subjected to no special regulations of great stringency, and the few disabilities which proved the rule were shared by many among the general population who belonged to dissenting forms of Christianity. The Jew lived where he would, and could enter almost any walk of life, and mix freely with Gentile society. The main enduring disability was the requirement that members of Parliament take an oath on the Christian Bible. In 1858, after many years of striving, Baron Lionel Rothschild took his seat in the House of Commons as MP for the City of London. This section of London Jewry was particularly prominent in banking, as exemplified by the Rothschild dynasty.

The most remarkable Jewish figure in 19th-century Britain was Benjamin Disraeli. He was born Jewish from an originally Italian family, but was baptised by his father, Isaac, when he was 12 both to make his entry into British life easier and because Isaac had fallen out with the synagogue he nominally attended. In addition to serving twice as Prime Minister, three times as Chancellor of the Exchequer and for four decades in the House of Commons, Disraeli published 11 novels, as well as shorter works of fiction, and much partisan journalism. He was sure that he was a genius, and he liked to stress that his forebears had been traders in Venice, the greatest European empire of the Middle Ages, when many of the ancestors of his fellow parliamentarians were simple farmers, scraping out a subsistence on the edge of the known world. Throughout his Parliamentary life he encountered much antisemitism, both from his fellow MPs, and in the form of newspaper cartoons. Much later, the Conservative party, of which he was a member, raised him to the status of the founder of the modern party. He was a great favourite of Queen Victoria, whom he made Empress of India, and he was one of the key figures in the creation of the British Empire. Despite his conversion to Christianity, he always regarded himself as a Jew and was very proud to be regarded as such.

The life of the Jews of the East End of London was very different from that of the long-established Jewish community which they joined in their large numbers in the 1880s. The visible concentration of so many outsiders in such a small space, foreign in appearance, their Yiddish dialect, the smell of their food – particularly fried fish - and their reportedly unsanitary style of living, all served to excite feelings of hostility. They were also perceived as a threat to the livelihoods of native Englishmen, whose jobs the Jews were accused of taking. Agitation to restrict the entry of alien Jews grew over the next two decades. Finally, in 1905 Parliament passed the Aliens Act which sharply restricted Jewish immigration from Eastern Europe. The act gave immigration officers the right to deport any 'undesirable immigrant'. The flow of Jews was reduced by 40 percent.

Over the years, the mass of Eastern European Jews settled into British life; many served in the First World War. There was little or no antisemitism at an official level, but there was a constant strain of literary antisemitism, from popular crime novels featuring Bulldog Drummond, Sexton Blake and the like, to the modernist poetry of T.S. Eliot. Some of the virulent antisemitism of the Nazi regime did seep into British life during the middle and late 1930s when Oswald Mosley, a talented former Labour party politician, founded and led the British Union of Fascists which, at its peak, had several tens of thousands of mainly working- class members. The Anglo-German Fellowship and the more shadowy Right Club included a number of aristocrats and Conservative

MP's, and greatly admired Hitler. Shortly after the outbreak of war in 1939, several hundred British Fascists, including Mosley himself, were interned until 1943, under a special Defence regulation, 18B.

Chapter Four

A Golden Land: American Jewry 1800 to 1945

American Jewry was different from European Jewry from the start. Jews were largely equal and their equality was blessed by George Washington himself: "May the children of the stock of Abraham, who dwell in this land, continue to merit and enjoy the goodwill of the other inhabitants, in which everyone shall sit in safety under his own vine and fig-tree, and there shall be no one to make him afraid" (Washington addressing the Hebrew congregation of Newport, 1790).

Moving forward nearly 200 years, by about 1980, American Jewry was the largest Jewish community in the world and certainly the wealthiest and most successful. Today, it is still the most wealthy and successful, but no longer the largest; that distinction belongs to Israel.

Colonial period, 1654-1820

By the end of the period, there were about 3,000 Jews in the United States; they had come first from Brazil and the West Indies, where there were already small Jewish communities, and from Europe. The general American population was about 3 million, living almost entirely along the coasts of the United States. The Jews' international connections helped them to develop as traders.

The Virginia Bill of Rights of 1776 had proclaimed that all men were 'equally entitled to the free exercise of religion, according to the dictates of conscience', a principle thereafter adopted everywhere in the U.S. The First Amendment to the Federal Constitution, which forbade Congress from 'enacting any law respecting an establishment of religion, or prohibiting the free exercise of religion', carried the Jews to an almost complete equality with their fellow citizens.

Immigration 1820-1880.

This was from Central Europe, mainly from the German-speaking lands, where Jews had found that their hopes of better civil rights in the lands of their birth were not fully met. By 1840 the

American Jewish population had reached 15,000, and by 1880 it had accelerated to 250,000.

Some of those arriving were craftsmen, few were professionals. Many who had been itinerant peddlers graduated to small stores. They went on to open larger stores and then department stores, such as Strauss and Gimbel. The Jews were spread over the country, rather than being concentrated in a few large cities. By and large, they were accepted as one more strand in a great diversity.

During the Civil War Jews sided with where ever they happened to live: 6,000 volunteered for the Northern Army and 1,200 for the Confederate Army.

These American Jews tended to see themselves as a religion and not as any sort of a separate national entity. The first Reform Synagogue was established in Cincinnati in 1854, headed by the charismatic Rabbi Isaac Wise. He was instrumental in establishing, by 1873, a central agency, the Union of American Hebrew Congregations, and within the next decade, the Hebrew Union College in Cincinnati, and a Central Conference of American Rabbis. Finally, at the Pittsburgh Conference of 1881 a statement of principles was laid down that defined the Jews as a religious denomination, rather than as a national entity.

The Reform Movement sought to dispense with portions of the ritual deemed anachronistic, preferred English as the language of prayer, and expected a sermon as part of the service, as was the practice among Protestants. It also judged the Sabbath and the dietary laws to be less binding than was traditional. The leaders argued that Judaism, like other religions, was not static but had developed in accordance with the conditions of time and place. What had been obligatory for the patriarchs had not been obligatory in Spain or Poland, and it certainly did not need to be in the United States. The central belief was that the principles of ethical monotheism, rather than formal ritual worship, were the permanent element of Judaism. To lead a moral life, therefore, was more important than adherence to customs. Religious precepts were taught in Sunday schools. Nearly 100 years on, the considerable participation of Reform Jews in the Civil Rights Movement of the 1960s can be traced back to that initial decision.

During this period a number of Jews became prominent both in political life and in civil law, serving as senators and judges.

Official government discrimination on the European model was absent and systematic antisemitism did not exist. Beginning in the 1870s, however, antisemitism in the form of social discrimination was increasingly evident and was accompanied by the development of ideological antisemitism. The refusal of accommodation to Joseph Seligman, a prominent New York Jewish banker, at the Grand Union hotel in Saratoga Springs in the summer of 1877, drew widespread adverse comment in the public press, but it symbolised a growing tendency towards the exclusion of Jews from areas involving leisure time facilities. Summer resort advertisements such as "we prefer not to entertain Hebrews" were common after the 1880s. From the resorts, social discrimination worked back into the cities. Important social clubs, such as the Union League Club, barred Jewish members, elite private schools were closed to Jewish children and, in general, Jews were often unwelcome at any institution or association that conferred prestige and status.

Bernard Baruch was an adviser to many presidents. Thanks to his wife's Protestant pull he got into the Social Register at a time when it still banned the leading Jewish bankers. But at any moment there was liable to be a twitch on this thread, telling him: thus far, no further. He was mortified when in 1912 his daughter, Belle, was mysteriously refused admission to the Brearley School in Manhattan despite having passed the entrance exam. He himself never got into the University Club or the Metropolitan.[32]

Immigration 1880-1930

By 1880, American Jewry was stable, prosperous and diverse. At that point, masses of poor Jews from Eastern Europe poured in, seeking a 'Golden Land'. Between 1880 and 1914 2 million Russian Jews entered, as did 125,000 Rumanian Jews. They sought economic opportunities at a time while these were diminishing – millions of non-Jewish immigrants, for example, from the Irish famines of the middle 19th-century, had also come to America.

The German Jewish immigrants had found in America freedom of movement, of contacts, of religion, freedom from hatred and discrimination, freedom to roam and vanquish a vast country abounding in innumerable opportunities. The Russian Jew, on the other hand, came to an America that had already entered a more advanced stage of development, where to earn a living in the city one had to labour day after day, night after night, where exploitation was part and parcel of the capitalist system. His task was harder, but even so his life was freer and more secure than it had been in Eastern Europe, and no restrictions were placed on him, at least at the early stages. The immigrant's awareness of this, and of the potential opportunities available to him, had a liberating effect as he was finally freed from the confinement which centuries of discrimination and prejudice had imposed on him.[33]

The Jews crowded into the main cities, particularly New York, which by 1900 had a larger Jewish population than any other city in the world. It has kept this position ever since. Living in cramped tenements, they were heavily involved in the clothing and allied trades. In 1904 one New York area had 64,000 Jewish families living in fewer than 6,000 tenement buildings. It also had 306 synagogues, 307 schools of religious instruction and four theatres.[34] The movement from poverty was slower than the flood of new entrants; even by the 1920s three- quarters of the Jewish population of New York were proletarians – when they had work.

The new immigrants were heavily involved in trade union activity and in left-wing politics. For the most part they continued to observe the Orthodoxy which they brought with them from Europe. Many, however, sought a compromise between Orthodoxy and Reformism, and the Conservative Movement saw strong development.

Some of these immigrant Jews became criminals, engaging in such activities as protection rackets and arson. The established Jewish society responded with crime prevention programmes, including reformatory schools. Such efforts were largely effective with small-time Jewish crime. However, the enactment of Prohibition afforded new opportunities for shrewd operators to rationalise and organise the 'bootlegging' of alcohol. The pioneer of big business crime was Arnold Rothstein, portrayed as 'The Brain' in Damon Runyon's Broadway stories. And then there was Mayer Lansky, who created and lost a gambling empire, and had his application for Israeli citizenship turned down in 1971.

According to Johnson[35] organised Jewish crime never enjoyed the slightest communal sanction, and hence proved to be a temporary phenomenon.

However. Jewish criminals were also prominent in a different area: violence and murder. Louis Buchalter helped to organise and run 'Murder Incorporated'. He was executed in 1944, Other Jews were prominent in the Detroit Purple Gang which ran the city's East Side until the Mafia took over. In the run-up to Israel's War of Independence in 1948, Jewish mobsters were invaluable in both procuring arms and organising their transport to the Jews of Palestine, at a time when a general embargo on official channels of supply was in force. Teddy Kollek, later a long-serving mayor of Jerusalem, was a key liaison with American Jewish criminals.

Hollywood

Jews were pioneers in more salubrious fields, particularly in the film industry and in Broadway musicals. From the start Jews were pre-eminent in Hollywood. In 1912 there were more than 100 small production firms. They were quickly amalgamated into eight major ones. Of these, Universal, 20th Century Fox, Paramount, Warner Brothers, Metro-Goldwyn-Mayer and Columbia were essentially Jewish creations, and Jews played a major role in the other two, United Artists and RKO Radio Pictures.

Nearly all these Jewish movie men conformed to a pattern: they were immigrants or of immediate immigrant stock. They were poor, some desperately poor. Many came from very large families. The Warner brothers were among the nine children of a poor cobbler from Poland. They worked in a variety of jobs from selling ice cream to repairing bicycles. In 1904 they bought a film projector and ran their own show, with their sister Rose playing the piano and the 12-year-old Jack singing treble. In Hollywood they made the breakthrough into sound. They were small in stature. As the film historian Philip French put it: "one could have swung a scythe 5 1/2 feet off the ground at a gathering of movie moguls without endangering many lives: several would scarcely have heard the swish."[36]

Their new cinema culture was not without traditional Jewish characteristics, especially in critical humour. The Marx Brothers provided an underdog view of the conventional world, rather in the way Jews had always seen majority society. From *Animal Crackers*, via *A Night at the Opera*, to *Duck Soup*, they represented a disconcerting intrusion into long-established institutions[37]. More than a generation on, Mel Brooks and Gene Wilder carried on this tradition.

The development of musical theatre on Broadway was largely due to the children of immigrant Jews. The key names include Oscar Hammerstein II, Jerome Kern, and George Gershwin. The tradition they established in the 1920s and 30s continued into the 1940s and 50s, and beyond.

In the 1920s Jews were prominent in the writing of plays and novels, often from a left-wing point of view. And Jews were heavily over-represented among New York's theatregoers, audiences at classical concerts, book purchasers, and art collectors. Jews also emerged as major philanthropic patrons of the arts.

Education and the professions

At university level education and the professions, Jewish success led to a counter movement. Many institutions restricted the admission of members of minority groups, including Jews, but particularly Jews, because they tended to be the most successful. The use of quotas was rarely admitted, but they were a persistent feature of numerous private institutions. In 1922 the Harvard President, Lowell, defended the existence of a ten percent quota for Jews at Harvard, expressing concern about "the large and increasing proportion of Jewish students in Harvard College", and his policy was supported by Harvard undergraduates who claimed that "Jews do not mix... they destroy the unity of the College".

Jews were also discriminated against in the major professional schools, such as medicine and engineering; indeed, in medicine, during the 1920s the proportion of Jewish medical students declined. There was a clear linkage between medical school discrimination and the desire of many non-Jewish senior medics to reduce competition to their professional practices. Law schools did not discriminate against Jewish students, but it was very difficult for Jews to enter the largest and best-established law offices.

In this period, Jews encountered considerable resistance as they attempted to move into white-collar fields. Employers increasingly specified that 'Christians were preferred' for office, sales and executive positions. Banking, insurance and public utilities were in the forefront of anti-Jewish prejudice. Few Jews were employed in the large corporations that dominated heavy industry, such as oil, steel and automobiles.

As economic difficulties grew in the 1920s and 30s, Jews were increasing blamed – both for taking jobs and for conspiring against non-Jews. *The Protocols of the Elders of Zion* made its way into the United States via the automobile mogul, Henry Ford, who had his own antisemitic newspaper, and Father Coughlin, who had an influential radio programme.

Jewish self-help organisations were established over the years, the first being the Hebrew Immigration Aid Society, which dates from 1884 and did important work in meeting and helping the arriving crowds of Eastern European Jewish immigrants. Shortly afterwards, in 1893, the National Council of Jewish Women was established. Perhaps the most important organisation of all, particularly from the point of view of distressed European Jewry, with whom it has done sterling work over the decades, was the American Joint Distribution Committee, established in 1914 and always known as 'The Joint'. The powerful and well-funded Council of Jewish Federations was set up in 1935.[38]

World War II

In 1939, the Jewish population of the United States was about 4,770,000. They were on the way to a reasonable level of prosperity, both through their own efforts and America's economic recovery under President Roosevelt. But the outside world impinged on them: Father Coughlin denounced the Jews on the radio to an audience numbering millions; in the late 1930s German Jewish refugees had begun arriving in the United States. In 1939 the United Jewish Appeal was founded to support Jewish humanitarian programmes in the United States and abroad. This was to be a major source of financial aid for the new State of Israel. During 1942, American Jews became aware of the massacre of Jews in Eastern Europe; this spurred prominent

Jewish individuals such as Henry Morganthau, and representative Jewish organisations, to try to persuade Roosevelt to do something to help. In 1944 he established the War Refugee Board, but the practical effects were rather limited.

During the course of World War II, over half a million Jewish men and women served in the Armed Forces of the United States, amounting to 4.23 percent of all US soldiers, as against a population share of about 3.25 percent. Twenty-two Jews attained the most senior ranks in the armed forces, and about 60 percent of all Jewish physicians in the United States under 45 years of age served in the military. The total number of Jewish war casualties was over 38,000, of whom 11,000 were killed. (Bureau of War Records.)

Nevertheless, antisemitic attitudes persisted and were fairly widespread. Polls taken from the mid-thirties to the late 1940s showed that over half of America's non-Jewish population saw Jews as 'greedy' and 'dishonest'. In 1938, 41 percent thought that Jews 'had too much power in the US', a figure that by 1945 had risen to 58 percent. In 1939, a Roper poll found that while nearly 40 percent thought that 'Jews should be treated like other people', 53 percent believed that Jews should be 'restricted' and 10 percent thought that Jews should be 'deported'. Several surveys, carried out between 1940 and 1946, concluded that Jews were a greater threat to the welfare of the United States than any other national, religious or racial group. Attitudes to immigrants in general tended to be negative in this period, mainly because of fears of competition for jobs and resources – but in the case of Jews antisemitism also played a part.

The Nazi regime drove increasing numbers of its Jewish victims to the United States. Owing to economic conditions and to the hostility of US consuls empowered to grant visas, total Jewish immigration to the United States, most of it from Germany, did not exceed 33,000 from 1933 to 1937. With the extreme worsening of the situation 124,000 arrived from 1938 to 1941, mostly from Germany and the lands it had taken. Refugee immigrants encountered great difficulty in adjusting, owing mainly to economic conditions and most of them had to start, and long remain, at a level beneath that which they enjoyed in Europe.

Several thousand of these refugees were scientists and academic intellectuals, whose symbolic leader was Albert Einstein. A few hundred of them wielded tremendous intellectual influence in research and teaching in the US in such fields as music, art history, psychiatry and psychoanalysis, history, sociology, and, above all, in nuclear physics. This intellectual migration, nearly all Jewish, ensured the transfer of the world's intellectual leadership from Europe to the United States (although Britain also gained very considerably.)

The New Deal of President Franklin D. Roosevelt, attracted enthusiastic Jewish loyalty, vigorous Jewish support for Roosevelt himself and an unprecedented number of high-level Jewish officials (antisemites spoke of the 'Jew deal'), but yielded very little governmental aid for Jews in peril abroad beyond sympathetic presidential statements.

During the public debates between 1939 and December 7, 1941, concerning US foreign policy during World War II, US Jews were generally found on the side favouring maximum aid to Britain and France, and later Russia. Jewish sympathies were less with Britain, seen as imperialist – and the White Paper of 1939 on Palestine was deeply resented – but their fear and loathing focused on Nazi Germany. The America First Committee attracted antisemites. In 1941 it sponsored a speech by Charles Lindbergh (a charismatic, popular hero) charging that Jews were attempting to draw the United States into war. The December 1941, the entry of America into World War II ended the debate over isolation and also proved a blow against antisemitism, which was identified with the Nazi enemy.

While battles raged throughout the world, European Jewry was being systematically murdered by Nazi Germany. Information about this became public during the fall of 1942, and subsequent stages in the Nazi 'final solution' were widely known. US Jewry, fearful of appearing to ask for special treatment, or of encouraging propaganda that it was a 'Jewish war', shied away from demanding direct US intervention to save Jews under Nazi rule. As with Britain, the view taken by the Administration was that early victory was the sole means to rescue European Jewry.

Chapter Five

Old-New Land: Palestine

From tiny beginnings, in the early 1880s, the Zionist movement developed over the next 67 years to the declaration of the State of Israel on May 15th, 1948.

A distinguished English historian, Macaulay, stated that history 'was but the story of great men'. If this is the case, Zionist history is the story of three great men: Herzl, Chaim Weizmann, and David Ben-Gurion. All three were visionaries. But they also had a practical, pragmatic side to their work. Herzl's was focused on the attainment of a Charter from the Ottoman Sultan, Palestine then being a part of the Ottoman Empire. Weizmann's encompassed both practical developments in Palestine and forging vital links with the leading figures in the dominant great powers of the day, particularly Great Britain. Ben-Gurion focused much more on the steady building of a modern Jewish community in Palestine.

From the beginning there was strong opposition to the Zionist idea from within the Jewish world: ultra-Orthodox and assimilationists, revolutionaries and capitalists, dreamers and pragmatists. In the last quarter of the century the bulk of European Jewry lived in Eastern Europe, in the Russian Empire and in Poland. In the latter there was a great flourishing of Hebrew culture at that time, which contributed to the dominant influence of Hebrew as the Zionist enterprise developed in Palestine.

And there was also massive opposition from the Ottoman Empire to the Zionist aim of building a Jewish community in Palestine. In response to this, an element within the Zionist movement considered some geographical alternatives. The most salient of these was the East African country of Uganda, then part of the British Empire. However, the Russian Zionists, although the most in need of a secure physical alternative, rejected this idea (as did both the British Cabinet and the local white settlers). From then on, apart from an occasional excursion, for example, to Argentina, Palestine remained the key focus of the Zionist settlement endeavour.

There were important background factors in favour of the Zionist enterprise: from the middle of the 19th century the major powers, particularly Britain and France, had taken a great interest in the Holy Land. Consulates were opened and churches were built. Thousands of Christian pilgrims made their way to Palestine. This activity was assisted by regular steamship passage to Palestine from various European ports and the opening of the Suez Canal in 1869.

Building up Palestine

The first Jewish farming settlement was established in 1882 and others followed. The settlers saw themselves as the "New Yishuv", in contrast to the much longer established ultra-Orthodox Jews, who lived mainly in Jerusalem and were seen as the "Old Yishuv". Eastern European Jewish immigration continued over the next 20 years, in all around 60,000 people (about half of whom left during that time). Collectively this wave of immigrants was known as the First Aliya, literally "going up". From then on, each wave of immigrants was known as an Aliya.

On the eve of the Second Aliya, in 1904, the Jewish community of Palestine numbered about 55,000. In the following decade some 40,000 more came; once again at least half left. The Second Aliyah included an elite group of about 3,000 – young, single, men and women – who went to Palestine out of idealism. According to David Ben-Gurion, who came from Poland in 1906 when he was 20 and later became Israel's first prime minister, most of them also wound up leaving. But it was the members of this small group who shaped the national ethos, and the leadership.

The 30 agricultural settlements of the First Aliya were dispersed around the country; their positioning helped to determine the future national boundaries. From Russia, the members of the Second Aliya brought the notion of political parties: the most important of these was Poalei Zion, established by the 20-year-old David Ben-Gurion. They sought to become a proletariat and looked initially for work as manual labourers in the farming settlements, known as moshavot. These had become dependent on local Arab labour. The ensuing clash between the idealistic new youngsters and the established Jewish farmers was won by the former, much assisted by the Palestine Office which had been set up in 1908 by Arthur Ruppin, a very practical and highly educated Prussian Jew. This established a new settlement model: instead of a small number of European Jewish plutocrats funding the moshavot, the Palestine Office supplied the funds for Jewish workers on the land being leased to them. This was seen not as philanthropy but as a national enterprise.

Almost from the beginning of Zionist activity there was local Arab resentment of the newcomers, led initially by well-educated Christian Arabs, at a political level. There were also sporadic attacks on the Jewish settlements by local Arab peasants. In reaction, the settlers established a defence organisation, Hashomer (the watchman). Decades later, the newly established Israel Defence Forces could trace their origins to Hashomer.

The new Zionist society

A key development in the New Yishuv was secularisation, which began with the farmers of the First Aliya but was much more pronounced in the young people of the Second Aliyah. This secularisation was intermingled with the retention of Jewish festivals and rites of passage – circumcision, barmitzvah, Jewish marriage and funeral – a pattern that has continued into present-day Israel, with even many who describe themselves as secular maintaining some traditions. An important feature of the Second Aliyah, brought from Eastern Europe, was openness to the great classics of world literature which had been translated into Hebrew in Russia and Poland. In addition, they emphasised Hebrew as an everyday language, in addition to being the language of the Bible, literature, school textbooks and newspapers. There was a lengthy battle for the use of Hebrew, as opposed to Yiddish, which was resolved in favour of the former. In this work of Hebraisation a key role was played by the teachers of the New Yishuv, who made sure that the children of the newcomers spoke Hebrew as an everyday language. By 1910 there were several Hebrew-language newspapers in the country.

On the eve of World War I the Old and New Yishuvs together formed 12 percent of the total population of Palestine (up from 5 percent in 1880). The fact that Turkey was on the side of the Central Powers (Germany and the Austrian-Hungarian Empire) facing the Allied Powers caused great difficulties for the Jews of Palestine, particularly for the farming communities: the Ottoman administration demanded total loyalty whereas many of the settlers saw that their long-term interests lay with the alliance of Britain and France. The military conflict in Palestine between the British and the Turks was resolved in favour of the former. On December 11, 1917, the commander of the British forces, General Sir Edmund Allenby, entered Jerusalem to take possession from the defeated Turks. He did so on foot, as a mark of respect. His entry opened a new period in the history of Palestine, Zionism, and the Jewish people.

"Dr Weizmann: it's a boy!"
In late 1917, Weizmann was waiting outside the British Cabinet Office for the decision on a declaration concerning the future of the newly captured Palestine. It was brought to him by Sir Mark Sykes ("Dr Weizmann, it's a boy!"), a senior official in the British Government and already heavily involved in British Middle East machinations. Weizmann had been born in 1874 in a small town in the Pale of Settlement and managed to have a university education in Germany, before taking up an academic appointment at the University of Manchester in England. At the same time he was extremely active in the Zionist movement in the years after Herzl's death. While in Manchester he combined a scientific career with his Zionist work, which included making repeated contacts with political leaders, notably Churchill, Lloyd George and Balfour. He impressed them all with his eloquent but restrained case for Zionism. Their receptiveness was assisted by their common background in the Old Testament, but also by a very keen understanding of the value to the British Empire of a Jewish national home in Palestine. As early as 1908 Churchill, who was about to become a Cabinet minister (Under Secretary of State for the Colonies) at the age of 33, put it this way:

'I am in full sympathy with the historical, traditional, aspirations of the Jews. The restoration to them of a centre of true racial and political integrity would be a tremendous event in the history of the world.

Jerusalem must be the only ultimate goal. When it will be achieved it is vain to prophesy, but that it will someday be achieved is one of the few certainties of the future. And the establishment of a strong, free, Jewish state, astride of the bridge between Europe and Africa, flanking the land roads to the east, would not only be an immense advantage to the British Empire, but a notable step towards the harmonious disposition of the world among its peoples.'[39]

'The British had identified Palestine as a target ... as a buffer against any threat to the Suez Canal...one of the empire's most vital arteries... under British control since 1888'[40]. In addition, the Port of Haifa was crucial – potentially the Mediterranean terminal of a future pipe-line from the oil fields of Iraq and Persia.

The Balfour Declaration

The Declaration was the seminal event in the history of the Zionist movement, suiting both Jewish aspirations and British imperialist aims. But in 1917, when it was issued, Palestine was very much a part of the Ottoman Empire, strongly opposed to Zionist hopes. And in the war that still raged, Turkey was on the side of the Central Powers. Had Turkey chosen differently – either remaining neutral or opting to join the Entente – it would have ended the war still in control of Palestine. A further complication was that the Bolshevik Revolution of 1917 was followed by Russian withdrawal from the Entente, swinging the balance of forces towards the Central Powers and their possible victory, again leaving Turkey in control of Palestine. However, the entry of the USA into the war, with its limitless resources of men and materiel, swung the balance back again, making an Entente victory eventually inevitable (as in World War II). In late 1917, Britain, solidly in control of Egypt, attacked and defeated the Turkish Army thus gaining control of Palestine– as described earlier. The stage was set for the Balfour Declaration.

The Declaration read:
'His Majesty's government views with favour the establishment in Palestine of a national home for the Jewish people, and will use their best endeavours to facilitate the achievement of this object, it being clearly understood that nothing shall be done which may prejudice the civil and religious rights of existing non-Jewish communities in Palestine, or the rights and political status enjoyed by Jews in any other countries.'

In practice, the implementation of the Declaration took a few years, until the newly established League of Nations assigned the Mandate for Palestine to Britain. The steady work of immigration and building a nation in embryo continued. Not surprisingly, the Arabs of Palestine reacted with intermittent hostility. The riots of 1921 took a number of lives on both sides; Jewish self-defence was organised, amongst others, by Vladimir Jabotinsky. He had been a decorated officer in the British Army in World War I and was a person of considerable intellect, charisma and personal charm. But he had a strong tendency, which became clearer over the subsequent years, to take the more extreme of possible views, and to eschew moderation and pragmatism in pursuit of the common objective of a Jewish state.

This was exemplified in 1923 when Churchill, as colonial secretary, separated Transjordan from Palestine, making it a solely Arab state under King Abdullah. Jabotinsky and his adherents continued to demand a Jewish state 'on both sides of the River Jordan' – a song embodying this aspiration remained central for many years to the canon of what was later called the Revisionist section of the Zionist Movement, and then the Herut party in the Israeli Parliament, headed by Menachem Begin following Jabotinsky's death in 1940.

British rule in Palestine, 1918 to 1948.
The first decade, roughly 1918 to 1929, was characterised by relative quiet and by steady Jewish development. This stability was ended by the Arab riots of 1929 and a series of British decisions that curbed the development of the national home. These were exemplified by the 1930 White Paper, which tended to restrain economic development in the Jewish sector. (This had been also held back by the US stock market crash of 1929, which led to emigration from Palestine rather than immigration.) The Great Crash sent shockwaves throughout Europe and encouraged a tendency to fascist and hence antisemitic regimes. In turn, these led to increased immigration to Palestine, seen as a relatively safe haven. The Jewish population grew from 170,000 in 1929 to 400,000 in 1936. Arab resistance was now openly directed, not only against the Jews of Palestine, but also against the British mandatory authorities. The Arab Revolt (1936 to 1939) was aimed

at forcing Britain to curb Jewish immigration – at a time of greatest Jewish need. The Revolt was suppressed by the British, very forcibly, with much loss of Arab life,

The British government sent to Palestine a high-level commission. It concluded (1938) that a mixed Jewish-Arab population in Palestine was simply not working, and that instead the country should be partitioned, with an exchange of populations between the two resulting sections – on the lines of the population exchange between Greeks and Turks in the 1920s, following the collapse of the Ottoman Empire. While the Zionist Executive, under Weizmann, accepted the concept of partition (albeit with significant modifications) the Arab leadership flatly rejected it, and the British Cabinet, after a period of reflection, also did so. On the eve of the Second World War the British government, conscious of the need to placate the Arab world, issued a further White Paper, which restricted Jewish immigration to 75,000 over the following five years, to be followed by a complete halt.

The development of the Yishuv in the inter-war years
The Third Aliyah began at the end of 1919. It continued until the end of 1923 and included leading intellectuals from the Russian-Jewish intelligentsia as well as many enthusiastic but penniless young people. They were not only drawn by the Zionists of Palestine but also repelled by the terrible loss of life during the Civil War that followed the Bolshevik Revolution and cost some 150,000 Russian Jewish lives in a wave of pogroms. The young people of the Third Aliyah shared the same hopes as the Soviet revolutionaries for a brave new world – but in Palestine, not the Soviet Union.

The Soviet Revolution, together with the enormous damage caused to the old Jewish world by World War I, meant that most of the young people of the Third Aliyah had only a limited Jewish education; their world view combined Jewish nationalism with world reform. Of the 37,000 people in the Third Aliyah, 14,000 were young and single. They had no possessions to speak of, were prepared to do hard physical work and were eager to build a new society in Palestine. The partnership begun in the Second Aliyah between the Palestine Office and the young settlers continued with the Third Aliyah, with whom the Zionist Organisation and its various bodies, headed by Weizmann, developed a strong alliance. But the Zionist Organisation was perennially short of money.

The Fourth Aliyah began in 1924, and in the space of two years about 60,000 Jewish immigrants came to Palestine; as a proportion of the existing Jewish population this was a record that lasted for many years. At the same time, the exit gates of the Soviet Union were beginning to close, and would be shut altogether in 1930. In addition, the United States imposed massive restrictions on immigration. This meant that there was a brief window of opportunity for immigration to Palestine, in the second half of the 1920s. At the same time, the Polish government imposed severe restrictions on the merchant class, which included many Jews. The Fourth Aliyah was largely a middle-class immigration.

There was a further surge after the Nazis came to power in 1933, leading to the Fifth Aliyah. It bought both well-educated, often professionally qualified people and many with financial means. This influx considerably strengthened both the Hebrew University, which had been founded in 1926, Chaim Weizmann being very much to the fore, and the Haifa Technion.

An important way to move to Palestine the assets of German immigrants was the Transfer Agreement, signed in 1933 between the German Government and unofficial Zionist bodies, but with the knowledge and consent of the Zionist Executive. It was an ingenious scheme, whereby money deposited by Jews in Germany, was used to purchase German goods to be imported into Palestine. In Palestine, the money was restored to its owners in local currency. Both sides benefited from this: the Germans by the promotion of their exports, and the departure of their unwelcome Jews, while German Jews seeking to escape the Nazis could save some of their assets. However, the agreement was bitterly criticised by the Revisionist wing of the Zionist Movement, led by Jabotinsky. They proposed instead, and attempted to enforce, a world-wide boycott of German goods. Not surprisingly, the boycott failed; the transfer agreement succeeded in its aim of bringing German Jews and their capital to Palestine. On the basis of this capital inflow, industry expanded considerably, helping both the economic development of the Yishuv and the local Allied war effort in World War II.

The growth of the Jewish population during the 25 years of the Mandate, from 56,000 to 650,000, laid the foundations for the establishment of a productive agricultural and industrial economy, Equally important, the distribution of Jewish settlements throughout the country, particularly on what became its borders, were the foundations on which the future Jewish state were built.

An important contribution to the development of the kibbutz (communal settlement) movement was made over many years, before World War II, by Hechalutz (the Pioneer) organisation which had branches in many European countries, particularly in Eastern Europe, and which prepared young people on training farms for life in Palestine in general, and on the communal settlements in particular. It was a vitally important source of young people for the developing Yishuv. When World War II broke out in 1939, some 100,000 members of Hechalutz were in training throughout Europe, but mainly in Poland, where they were stranded by the speed of the German advance. An unknown number was lost to the Holocaust.

Political and cultural developments up to 1939

A gradual political process culminated in 1930 with the founding of the Mapai party, an acronym from the Hebrew name: the Party of the Workers of the Land of Israel. The year 1920 had already seen the formation of the Histadrut, the General Federation of Jewish Workers in the Land of Israel. This had a constructive arm, concerned with building the country through settlement, cooperatives and contract work, and a professional one, representing the workers in relation to their employers. The former was rather unusual, the latter was a standard trade union, although embracing all sections of the economy. The Mapai party included workers, liberal-minded intellectuals, and well-off people, much like the British Labour Party, or the Democratic Party in the United States. (The Revisionist Party, founded in 1925 and headed by Jabotinsky, was essentially middle-class.)

The Histadrut played a leading part in helping newcomers to settle and gave them access to an employment exchange. Members received medical help from a sick fund, and kitchens served inexpensive meals. At Histadrut cultural centres workers could read books and newspapers, and a Histadrut school system and cultural institutions were set up. The Histadrut also built workers' housing. David Ben-Gurion was to the fore in all these developments, which together constituted a distinctive Yishuv culture. The fierce rivalry between Mapai and the Revisionists foreshadowed future intra-Yishuv civil strife, which flared up during World War II and in the years immediately afterwards.[41]

Brief Lives

3. Martin Buber (1878-1965)

More than most philosophers of religion, Buber looked the part: whether as a youth, or aged 85, he gazes out from photographs with a profoundly benign air, conveying an unchangeable belief in human benevolence. Born in Vienna, he was three when his parents separated and he was raised in Lemberg, Ukraine, by his grandfather, a noted scholar of midrashim – the vast store of Jewish lore that explicates the Talmud, the repository of religious commentary. But he was also drawn to general European culture, and in adulthood his active religious observance ceased. He studied at several universities, mostly philosophy.

Buber joined the Zionist movement in 1898, one year after Theodor Herzl, the founder of its political wing, convened the First Zionist Congress in Basel. He spoke at the Third Congress in 1899, advocating education rather than political propaganda, and in 1901, as editor of the main weekly organ of the Zionist movement, he emphasised the need for a new Jewish cultural creativity. For the next eight years, he devoted himself, to the exclusion of public affairs, to the study of Hasidism, one of the most important Jewish religious movements of the past 500 years: he was to produce many books during the decades that followed. But in 1909, he returned to public affairs, as he was to do repeatedly throughout his long life, while maintaining his devotion to the study of religious philosophy and in writing about it in superb German. That year, he delivered to student audiences three addresses that greatly influenced Jewish youth in Central Europe and marked his move toward a form of utopian socialism, which he saw as rooted in personal relationships, in contrast to the authoritarian nature of Communism, which denied any connection between man and God, a constant theme of Buber's writings.

His public work during World War I included a committee that supported Jewish communities living under German occupation in Europe, and those of the yishuv, the Jewish community in Palestine, during the First World War, until Palestine was conquered by the British. From that point he became the spokesman for what he called Hebrew humanism – which argued that Zionism should be different from other nationalist movements. In an address to the Zionist Congress of 1921, he proposed 'a common homeland with the Arab people', in marked contrast to the central Zionist theme of a *Jewish* homeland. (The idea met with little favour from his fellow Jews and none from the Arabs of Palestine, who wanted the Balfour Declaration abrogated and Zionists to leave Palestine). Essentially, he was advocating a binational state, and he continued to do so for many years.

Buber's public work went hand-in-hand with his academic and educational career. From 1925 he taught Jewish religion and ethics at the University of Frankfurt, and was appointed professor of religion there in 1930. But in 1933 he was forced by the Nazis to leave his position. He was immediately put in charge of the education of Jews who had remained in Germany after being compelled to leave German educational institutions, and in this role fostered something of a spiritual resistance. Finally, forbidden any public activities whatever, in 1938, at the age of 60, he left for Palestine, where he became professor of social philosophy at the Hebrew University of Jerusalem, until his retirement in 1951. Remaining active in both scholarship and public affairs, he was the first president of the Israel Academy of Arts and Sciences, and helped found a college to train immigrants as teachers. His writing, in Hebrew as well as in German, also continued into his last years, and much of his work was translated into English.

Buber sought to remove both dogma and observance from religion, focusing instead on the relation between man and God and between man and man, between I and thou and between I and 'the Great Thou'. The fullest expression of the latter enables the fullest expression of the former. He constantly urged men to do the maximum good possible in concrete situations while doing the minimum of evil. (This might have been an attempt to combine the traditional core prescriptions of Judaism and Christianity: in brief, do not harm your neighbour (the former); love your neighbour (the latter). It clearly underlies his continued belief in a binational Jewish-Arab state, rather than the much more widely supported 'two-state solution'. He found it hard to give up on any relationship; as late as 1939, he rhapsodised about a German-Jewish symbiosis: 'It had been rudely interrupted by the Nazis, but it might be resumed again in the future'.[42] Buber has had a deep and continuing influence on Christian theology, and on the dialogue between Judaism and Christianity. And he presented Hasidism to enlightened Jewish and non-Jewish Germans as no one in the West had done before. Within Judaism, he opposed dry rationalism in favour of heartfelt prayer, song and dance. These are his enduring legacies, together with his concern for the Other.

Chapter Six

The Jews' Darkest Years: 1933 to 1945

Introduction

The years 1933 to 1939 were the run-up to – the preliminary act of – World War II, which began with the German invasion of Poland on September 1, 1939 and continued in its European phase until the German surrender on May 8, 1945.

World War II, the most awful war in history, recast the 20th century. It took its shape largely from a number of fateful choices made by the leaders of the world's major powers within a mere 19 months, between May 1940 and December 1941. The original catastrophe, of course, was World War I, which had shattered political regimes (the Russian, Austrian and Ottoman empires all fell in its wake) and destroyed economies. In obvious ways the Second World War was the unfinished business of the First. This second great conflict was not only even more bloody – costing upwards of 50 million lives, between four and five times the estimated death toll of the war of 1914-18 – and more truly global, it was also the more profound in its lasting consequences and its reshaping of the world's power structures.

Both in Europe and the Far East, previous power pretensions – those of Germany, Italy and Japan – collapsed in the maelstrom of destruction. A combination of national bankruptcy and resurgent anti-colonial movements put paid to Britain's world empire. Above all, the two new superpowers, the United States and Soviet Union, both relatively minor before 1939, now were locked in a Cold War that would last until the final decade of the century.

The Second World War also left mankind with a new term, since seen as a defining characteristic of the century: genocide. Within that term, what came to be known as the Holocaust – the planned attempt by Nazi Germany to wipe out a targeted 11 million Jews, a genocidal project unprecedented in history – left the most lasting and fundamental mark on future decades. The context for the killing of the Jews had been the Second World War, but the murder of the Jews had been an intrinsic part of the German effort. And more than anyone else the supreme architect of that genocide was Adolf Hitler.[43]

Hitler's rapid ascent to absolute power

On the 30th January 1933, Hitler was appointed to the Reich chancellorship by President Paul von Hindenburg. From then on, his views on foreign policy were no longer those of a fringe-party hothead, but carried the weight of the most important figure in the government, backed by a huge mass movement.[44]

Only four days after taking office, he addressed a meeting of his generals setting out the absolute priority of rearmament. This was a policy for which they had long been secretly planning. He also stated the importance of acquiring new living space in the East. Hitler's dominance of the German government was completed by the summer of 1933. He had at his disposal the well-honed bureaucratic state administration, as well as the ruthless use of the machinery of coercion and repression. Only a year later he had established total supremacy in the state. The brutal massacre of the 'brown shirts' leaders, in June 1934, removed the one remaining threat to his rule. And with the death of the aged Reich President Hindenburg, Hitler now became not just head of government, but head of state. The main beneficiary of the Hitler-orchestrated destruction of the rival 'brown shirts' had been the German army. This cemented its backing for Hitler, building on his support for a massive rearmament programme. Business and industry, drawn by the scope they were given to maximise profit, had also largely fallen in behind the new regime.[45]

The central philosophy of Nazism emphasised support for the strong and powerful, and encouraged unbridled competition and use of 'elbow power'. Positions on paper often meant little or nothing in reality; power resided with those individuals who could fight their way to the top and had immediate access to it. Heinrich Himmler, head of the SS, in control of the huge police and security apparatus from 1936 onwards, and Hermann Goering, head of the Four-Year Plan (to make the German economy ready for war) after 1936, were important examples.[46]

The big decisions of foreign policy from 1933 onwards, down to and including the decision to risk European war by attacking Poland in 1939, were Hitler's. His first major step in determining Germany's new, assertive course in foreign policy, the withdrawal from the disarmament conference and the League of Nations in October 1933, was fully in accordance with the wishes of the foreign ministry and army leadership. (The move was one which would probably have followed under any nationalist government of the time). Becoming more confident, in March 1935 he guessed correctly that the Western democracies would do nothing if he faced them with a major breach of the Versailles Treaty: he announced the existence of the German air force and the introduction of conscription to a mass army In early 1936 he again correctly presumed that the weakness of the Western democracies, laid bare by the Abyssinian crisis (the Italian dictator Mussolini's unopposed part in the "Scramble for Africa") offered an excellent opportunity to re-militarise the Rhineland – a further step that could well have been on the agenda of any nationalist government. Both moves were supported by the army and the Foreign Ministry alike.

Throughout the 1930s Britain had a government that followed a path of appeasing German ambitions and actions. Originally, Hitler had wanted Great Britain as a friend in the war he envisaged against "Jewish Bolshevism". But long before the final step of appeasement (Munich in 1938, which dismembered Czechoslovakia) Hitler had realised that he had to number Britain among Germany's foes. He also knew that Britain, with a world empire behind her and determined to defend it to the hilt, was starting, if rather late, to rearm with urgency. And across the Atlantic lay the vast potential of America, at that time locked in isolationism but potentially a future enemy to be viewed with the utmost seriousness (one whose intervention late in 1917 had sealed Germany's fate in the First World War). Clearly, then, time was not on Germany's side.

Hitler also had to consider that money for arms meant less for food. Guns *and* butter were possible only for a limited time. By the late 1930s alarm bells were starting to be heard across the economy; Hitler was under pressure to act, both because he felt Germany would be, before many more years, in a far inferior international position, and because an overstretched and overheated economy could not be indefinitely sustained.

By 1937, Hitler was expecting a major war within Europe in the next five or six years, and spoke of Bolshevism "as the danger that we will have to knock down sometime". (He never lost sight of the ideological aim he had developed in his wilderness years in the 1920s, even if practicalities required that it fade into the background for the time being.) In August 1939, he made the ultimate adjustment when he overturned the antagonism towards the Soviet Union embedded in Nazi ideology, to conclude a non-aggression treaty with the arch enemy. He stated: "Everything I undertake is directed against Russia; to beat the West I shall be forced to come to an understanding with the Russians, and then, after its defeat, to turn with all my concerted force against the Soviet Union".

In 1938, Britain and France had been so anxious to avoid war they had given in to Hitler's aggression against Czechoslovakia. He expected them to do the same in Poland. But he miscalculated. His action in occupying what remained of Czechoslovakia in March 1939 had destroyed the backing for appeasement. He thought, until the end of August, that Britain and France would still, at the last moment, yield – so that he could destroy Poland without their intervention. Two days after his troops invaded Poland, he finally – if not at the moment of his choosing – had his war with the West. The war he really wanted, with the Soviet Union, would have to wait

The German army crushed Poland in only three weeks. With Poland defeated, and the Soviet Union posing no danger for the time being, Germany was secure in the East; the Western front lay open. However, Hitler's generals made it clear to him that the Armed Forces were in no fit state for a full-scale, probably long drawn out, war against powerful enemies. Even the brief Polish campaign had left half the German tanks and motorised vehicles out of action. The generals argued that an immediate implementation of the war plan for attacking the West was unthinkable. The Western offensive was put off until the Armed Forces were, in the eyes of the generals, ready. They produced a bold and brilliant attack when least expected, through the Ardennes region of southern Belgium, and into lowland France, towards the coast. The offensive was a stunning success, greater than even Hitler had expected. The Dutch surrendered after five days. The Belgian army was also swiftly broken. And the French army, strong on paper but ineptly led and badly equipped as well as low in morale, proved no match for the Wehrmacht. On 14 June, less than five weeks after the offensive had been launched, German troops entered Paris. His self-glorification (embracing a sense of infallibility) was magnified by the plaudits of his generals, who had to concede not only the magnitude of what had been possible under Hitler, but also his extraordinarily successful strategic plan of attack. Only the British, Hitler thought, now stood between him and complete victory in the West. Surely, they would see sense and come to terms?[47]

The Jews of Europe: four regions

In the late 1930s, 10 million Jews lived in Europe. They were distributed among four regions that differed greatly – in history, conditions of life, and prospects for the future: in Western Europe, Jews had been emancipated for a century and felt relatively secure despite sometimes strong antisemitism, for example the Dreyfus Case in France, and the Aliens Bill in Britain; in Germany and the former Austria and Czechoslovakia (which had already been absorbed into the Third Reich), Jews were far along in the sequence of loss of citizenship and of professions, subjection to discriminatory laws and deprivation of possessions; and until the borders were closed on the outbreak of War on September 3rd, 1939, they were also under intense pressure to leave.

In a third zone, comprising all the states of eastern Central Europe, antisemitism was widespread among most of the population and in most countries was also part of government policy, which set out explicit anti-Jewish laws. Finally, in the Soviet Union, where the Jews had been emancipated in 1917, they did enjoy marked upward social mobility. However, *Jewish* life, secular or religious, was severely restricted. Stalin's murderous, paranoia-driven purges of the late 1930s fell particularly hard on Soviet Jewry

The Jews of Germany: from high culture to destruction

Immediately upon attaining power in January 1933, the Nazis launched their central programme: Jewish premises were destroyed; Jews were killed or beaten up in random street attacks;

almost all Jewish civil servants, including teachers and university professors, were dismissed; Jewish doctors and lawyers were restricted in their professions; state welfare support for Jews was limited; quotas were introduced for Jewish university students. As a direct result at least 300 German Jews committed suicide. In April 1933, just three months after Hitler seized power, Leo Baeck, who emerged as the German Jewish spokesman, declared, "The thousand-year history of German Jewry has come to an end". Of the half million Jews by religion in Germany about 40,000 fled the country within a year.

According to Elon,[48] the Jews in Germany had never ceased in their efforts to merge German and Jewish identity. (However, the vast majority never hid the fact that they were Jews.) A great many intermarried. Scores of thousands converted and disappeared within the majority.

'Their true home, we now know, was not Germany but German culture and language. Their true religion was the bourgeois, Goethean ideal of *Bildung* (high culture)'. The prominence of German Jews, and the contributions they made, became fully apparent only after they were gone. In 1933, in a last-minute attempt to counter the Nazi threat, the traumatised leaders of the Central Union of German Citizens of the Jewish Faith, the most representative organisation of the (culturally) assimilated German Jews, commissioned the compilation of a list of Jewish "achievers" and "achievements" in all fields. The project, pathetic only in retrospect, included Jewish luminaries in literature and the arts, in Jewish as well as Christian theology, in politics, warfare, industry, and the natural sciences. The result, entitled *Jews in the Realm of German Culture*, was a vast, meticulously detailed Encyclopaedia of Jewish Contributions to German Life and Culture, during the previous two centuries. The task was executed, with overwhelming thoroughness, by a committee of experts. The volume ran to 1,060 pages and comprised thousands of entries and names.[49] (Indeed, as late as 1939 Martin Buber, the leading German Jewish intellectual who moved to Palestine in the 1930s, spoke about a German Jewish symbiosis: it had been abruptly interrupted by the Nazis, he claimed, but it might be resumed again in the future.)

In the summer of 1935 the Nazi authorities passed the Nuremberg Laws which deemed that having one Jewish grandparent made a person Jewish. Several clauses banned Jews from all professions, schools and colleges, from owning factories, publishing houses, theatres and large stores. Jewish doctors could treat only Jewish patients, Jewish musicians could no longer play in orchestras or theatres. From that autumn every passport belonging to a Jew was stamped with a "J". Deprived of their citizenship and political rights, Jews were driven out of the state economy by relentless segregation

Starting in the early hours of 10 November 1938, and continuing until nightfall, violence against the Jews of Germany was unleashed in a whirlwind of destruction. Within a few hours about 70 synagogues were set on fire and destroyed in scores of Jewish neighbourhoods. Paramilitary stormtroopers – some in brown-shirt uniforms, others in civilian clothes – lit bonfires and threw furniture and books from synagogues and private homes into the flames. In the streets, Jews were chased and reviled. Thousands of Jewish shops and homes were ransacked. Jews were attacked in every German town, from the capital, Berlin, to the smallest towns and villages in which Jews lived. In 24 hours of violence, at least several hundred Jews were killed. Within those 24 hours, more than 30,000 Jewish men between the ages of 16 and 60 – one quarter of all Jewish men still in Germany – were arrested and sent to concentration camps There they were tortured and tormented for several months. More than 1,000 died in these camps The name given to the night and day of terror was Kristallnacht, the "night of broken glass". Kristallnacht was not a spontaneous response to the attempted murder of a German diplomat in Paris by a desperate Polish Jew, as was claimed by Goebbels, the Reich Minister for Propaganda, but was meticulously planned and executed; the attempted murder was simply the trigger.[50]

Hitler's War against the Jews – the Holocaust in Russia and Eastern Europe

Antisemitism was virulent, and endemic, throughout most of Europe in the decades preceding the Nazi genocide. As the "final solution" unfolded, long-standing hatreds ensured that the Nazi rulers, in the countries they conquered, never lacked willing helpers to carry out the deportations, then killings, of Jews. (There were also many who at great risk of their lives actively resisted. This should never be forgotten.) Sir Ian Kershaw, the leading biographer of Hitler and historian of the Second World War considers that 'the final solution itself could not have arisen anywhere other than Germany. It had to be a German creation'. And Adolf Hitler was its supreme architect. He never lost sight of the Jews as the main enemy of Germany.[51]

The antisemitic climate gradually worsened and, crucially, the state gave its backing to those who were making the lives of Jews difficult, even impossible. By 1939, removal of the Jews from Germany had advanced considerably. Nevertheless, at the end of 1938 over two-thirds of the Jewish population of 1933 still lived in the country. Almost as many Jews left in 1938-9 as in the previous four years of Nazi rule. Despite the terror of Kristallnacht, on the eve of war in September 1939 Jews in Germany still numbered not much less than half of the figure for 1933.

The Nazis were still far from achieving a complete solution to the Jewish question, even within the Reich. For most of the remaining German Jews, as the Nazi authorities concluded, there was nowhere to go – with the outbreak of war, emigration was not an option. Since 1937, the Jewish desk of the SS had been looking for ways to speed up their expulsion. A far-reaching idea was a "territorial solution": to ship the Jews out to some far-away, inhospitable place and dump them. (At the time, nothing came of such far-flung notions. But they recurred, in a different and even more dangerous setting.)

When units of the security police moved into Poland behind the invasion force in September 1939, Reinhard Heydrich occupied a key position dealing with the "Jewish question" in the newly conquered territories. It was a task that dwarfed any that he had taken on before the war. The job then had been to expedite the forced emigration of what remained of the German Jewish community. Now, with that initial aim still unfulfilled, the conquest of Poland had brought a further 2 million Jews within the

Nazi orbit (another million lived in Eastern Poland, seized by the Soviet Union, by agreement with Germany).

But a possible way out had been mentioned as early as January 1940, an idea first advanced by the German racist writer, Paul de Lagarde, in the 1880s, of settling millions of Jews in Madagascar, a French colony. The plan was that 4 million Jews – 1 million per year over the following four years – would be sent to the inhospitable island in the Indian Ocean, where they would be out of sight and out of mind. However, 'Madagascar' was a short-lived idea. A vanquished France could certainly have been compelled to cede Madagascar as a mandate under German control. But with Britain refusing to come to terms, the requisite shipping fleet and security on the seas were not available. The blueprint was left to gather dust; a different option was becoming more feasible.

The invasion by Germany of the Soviet Union, planned for the late spring or early summer of 1941, provided new opportunities for disposing of the millions of Jews already under German control, but also meant that millions more would fall into German hands. What to do with them? By the time the invasion was launched, plans were being compiled by the SS which anticipated the removal, mainly through deportation to Siberia, of no fewer than 31 million people, mainly Slavs, over the next quarter of a century or so. It was taken for granted that 5 to 6 million Jews would disappear as the first stage.

Of course, before this major transfer could take place, Germany not only had to invade the Soviet Union but win an overwhelming victory, which would give Germany total control over the whole Russian landmass. Well in advance of this, killing squads were dispatched to dispose of Jews in the newly conquered Poland and western Russia. Even now, however, not all Jews everywhere were immediately slaughtered. Manpower and logistics alone constituted a hindrance. But the killing squads went about their work, and by mid-August of 1941 their victims included Jewish women and children as well as men. As the German advance slowed and was then reversed, a continuation of the war into the coming year and even beyond became a probability; the prospect of territory into which to expel the non-Soviet Jews faded. The only solution was to kill them wherever they could be found, and the question of what should be done with the rising millions of

Jews gained great urgency. How was this to be solved? Poison gas was now starting to be recognised as an alternative method of killing

An important meeting was held on 20 January 1942 at Wansee, close to a beautiful lake on the outskirts of Berlin. Some weeks later, in March 1942, the gas chambers of Treblinka and Sobibor began operating. The largest death camp, Auschwitz-Birkenau, also began killing Jews in March of that year. The onslaught on the Jews of Europe, the vast majority of whom were now under Nazi control, continued over the next three years. More death camps were opened and operated, mainly in Poland. Jewish men, women and children were transported to them and killed. Cowed and starving, the Jews were able to mount only limited acts of resistance, but some did occur, to be put down ruthlessly. The best-known, and for a time the most effective act by the Jews, was the uprising of the Warsaw Ghetto in 1943. This received the most limited help from the Polish Underground Army but even considerable assistance would only have prolonged the inevitable end. (In turn, the Polish underground received no help from the nearby Soviet forces for its own uprising against the German occupation a year later).

The final year of the Nazi regime

'Even when it was faltering in every other respect, the Nazi regime managed to terrorize, kill and destroy to the last.'[52] By June 1944, Germany was militarily beset in the East by the devastating breakthrough of the Red Army, and in the West by the consolidation of the successful Allied landings in Normandy. A potentially decisive internal event took place in July 1944: a carefully planned attempt on Hitler's life, which was to be followed by a seizure of power. This failed, as had all previous assassination attempts on Hitler.

Despite the massive reverses suffered by the German forces – their collapse in the West, in September 1944, and the first incursion of the Red Army on to German soil in the following month, the catastrophe in the eastern provinces as they fell to the Soviets in January 1945 (all leading to an increasing escalation of terror directed against any expression of dissent by the German civilian population) – despite all this, the Nazi regime held out until early May, when Hitler and Goebbels committed suicide in the last redoubt of German resistance; Goering and Himmler were captured and Germany capitulated on 8 May 1945. The Nazi regime had finally crumbled, the agony for the German people having been prolonged by the very realistic awareness of the Nazi leadership, and lower echelons, that the impending Allied victory (which included the unconditional surrender of all German forces) would result in their being held to account. Surrender was postponed by a desperate hope that there would be a split in Allied unity between the West and the Soviets, and the hope of a secret, game-changing weapon that would destroy southern England and turn the war. The hoped-for split between the Allies did not materialise until some time after the war, with the development of the Cold War between East and West. And while the flying bombs caused considerable loss of life in the London area in the last months of 1944 and the early months of 1945, the launch sites were overrun and that hope was snuffed out.

In fact, although many leading Nazis were captured and put on trial (Nuremberg, in 1946, being the best-known example) a large number did manage to escape, using previously established routes and with assistance from elements of the Catholic Church, to the countries of South America, particularly Argentina.

The Jews of Western Europe, 1939 to 1945

In the spring and early summer of 1940, the German army rapidly overran first Holland and Belgium and then France. The Jewish communities of those countries were thus at grave risk. Only Britain and Sweden remained unoccupied; Britain because, having resolved to fight on, survived the German aerial onslaught and retained control of the English Channel, thereby nullifying the threat of seaborne invasion; Sweden because it remained neutral, a status convenient to both Germany and Britain.

France
In France, the period between 1940 and 1944 is known as the 'Dark Years'. After a catastrophic military defeat, an armistice was signed with Germany, and half of France, including Paris, was

occupied by German troops. In the other half, a supposedly independent French government, headed by Marshal Petain, was set up in the spa town of Vichy. The Vichy government liquidated France's democratic institutions, persecuted Freemasons, Jews, and communists, and embarked on a policy of collaboration with Germany. Thirty thousand French civilians were shot as hostages, many of them members of the Resistance; another 60,000 were deported to German concentration camps. Of the French Jewish community that had numbered 500,000, 72,500 perished in Auschwitz; only 2,500 returned. A sizeable French minority actively resisted the occupation, including several thousands who hid Jews, often for some years, particularly in rural areas.

A young Jewish boy was caught after curfew on the streets of Nazi-occupied Paris by an SS soldier. The soldier picked him up, hugged him, showed him a photograph of another boy and gave him money. After the war the boy, Daniel Kahneman, moved to Palestine and became a star of the Hebrew University's Department of Psychology before taking up a position in the United States. Many years later he was awarded the Nobel Prize for Economics for pioneering work on systematic human flaws in decision-making. It would have been shared with another Israeli psychologist, Amos Tversky, but he died before the award was made.[53]

Hungary

The one large remaining Jewish community on the European mainland by the beginning of 1944 was that of Hungary. In the preceding years successive Hungarian governments, whilst implementing harsh restrictions against the Jewish community, had resisted German pressure to eliminate the Jews physically. As the course of the war clearly moved against Germany, the Hungarian regime of Horthy was seen by Germany as readying to change sides in favour of the Allies. Germany decided to occupy Hungary. This took place on March 19, 1944. Adolf Eichmann, described by Himmler as "the master", went to Hungary to supervise and make more efficient the deportations which had already begun. Even when military materiel was desperately needed by the German army elsewhere, Eichmann still managed to get priority for his death trains to Auschwitz. When Himmler finally ordered the extermination process to be discontinued, he managed to organise the transportation of Jews from Hungary on foot. A high percentage of those on the death marches perished. International attempts were made to save Jews; a major figure among those doing so was Raoul Wallenberg.

Comment

At all crucial junctions of policy-making against the Jews, even in the 1930s – from the boycott of April 1933 to the pogrom of November 1938 – Hitler's authorisation had been needed and was given. By the Wannsee Conference, no further fundamental decision was needed. The task had become one of organisation and implementation. The decision to kill the Jews arose from an early aim, absolutely intrinsic to Nazism, to remove them. Hitler himself never lost sight of this from 1919. German military successes meant that increasing numbers of Jews were falling into the hands of the Third Reich. Without genocide, "removal" of the Jews was impossible.[54]

Germany's aggression was the main cause of Europe's second descent into war within a generation. It was also the crucial trigger, in the summer of 1940, to the spiral of events that, by December 1941, transformed conflicts at opposite ends of the world into a World War. That aggressively ideological mission was embodied by the figure of Adolf Hitler. And inherent in this mission was the removal of the Jews. In this way, the Nazi war on the Jews was a central component of, and inextricable from, the Second World War itself – the greatest slaughter the world has ever known.[55]

Yad Vashem ("A Memorial and a Name") in Jerusalem is devoted to commemorating Holocaust victims not only in aggregate (usually estimated at 6 million) but also as individuals, and thanks to digital analysis of the museum's millions of documents, the number has now reached 4.7 million names. Yad Vashem is racing against time to reach 6 million. Early in 2020, about 400,000 survivors were still alive, obviously all of very advanced years, and available to help the task.[56]

Could the effects of the Holocaust have been mitigated; could they have been even worse?

1. Stalin heeds warnings of German intentions and responds appropriately

On September 1, 1939, Joseph Stalin was in total control of the Soviet Union. This had been cemented by the purges of 1937: the first targeted the "Old Bolsheviks", and the second, the highest ranks of the armed forces. The Old Bolsheviks, many of whom were Jews, had played a leading part in Lenin's seizure of power in 1917. Their continued positions at the upper reaches of the Soviet hierarchy was seen by Stalin as a threat to his absolute power. They were therefore eliminated. He saw the same potential threat in the leadership of the armed forces. He removed no fewer than two of the four marshals, 14 out of 16 military commanders, and all eight admirals, as well as, on the civilian side, 75 out of 80 members of the Supreme Soviet – the highest political echelon.

All of this meant that only Stalin took key decisions concerning, for example, the meaning of intelligence information on the intentions and actions of potential foreign adversaries such as Britain and Germany. For many months, leading up to the stunning German attack on the Soviet Union on June 22, 1941, Stalin received a plethora of information concerning German troop movements, logistical build-up, and intentions. He ignored it all. His personal concept was that the Soviet Union's own military build-up would not be complete until 1943, even 1944. This then led to his conclusion that, while he fully expected Germany to attack the Soviet Union, this would not take place until his preferred date. (He had bought time for Soviet rearmament by the Soviet-German pact of August 1939, which included both mutual non- aggression and a carve-up of Poland, following a German attack.) Stalin really did think that he knew best.

"You must understand that Germany on its own will never move to attack Russia... If you provoke the Germans on the border, if you move forces without our permission, then bear in mind that heads will roll". (Reported comment by Stalin to his military leaders, mid-May 1941.)[57]

"Lenin left us a great legacy, but we, his heirs, have fucked it up" – Stalin's angry utterance six days after the German invasion had caught the Soviet Union astonishingly unawares.[58] Within days, the German army had advanced over 300 miles into Soviet territory at breakneck speed, capturing or killing huge numbers of Soviet soldiers, and destroying thousands of tanks and aircraft in the first wave of attacks. While the Soviet Union did fight back and eventually, after the loss of millions of the armed forces and vast expenditures of military materiel, totally defeated Germany, this took close to another four years.

We can speculate that, had Stalin responded to the overwhelming weight of intelligence – evidence of a planned German attack – and moved Soviet forces accordingly, the initial German thrust might have been blunted earlier, less Soviet territory captured, and the counter- thrust into western Russia and eastern Poland launched earlier. As concerns the Jews of Poland and the Soviet Union – the vast majority of European Jewry – the scale of the Holocaust might have been reduced. But Stalin's paranoia and appetite for absolute power ensured that events took the course that they did. By the time Soviet forces drove into Germany in the autumn of 1944, most of the Jewish victims of the Holocaust were already dead

2. What if Britain had sued for peace after Germany's stunning 1940s successes?

To consider this question, we need to look at the British situation in May 1940. The French army was on the brink of defeat; the Dutch and Belgian armies had already succumbed to German might. The British Expeditionary Force was falling back rapidly to the French Channel port of Dunkirk. The force of well over 200,000, together with French troops numbering over 100,000, looked as if they would be cut off from being brought back to Britain – in any event seen by Britain as near-unachievable.

Winston Churchill, who had become prime minister on May 10, was confronted with this seemingly impossible combination of unfavourable circumstances. Already 66, a considerable age for that period, his lengthy political history was very chequered and he was far from carrying the confidence of the Conservative parliamentary party. But he went on to become the most celebrated prime minister of the 20th century and arguably the most renowned British prime minister ever, an icon of modern history. But without World War II he might have been remembered as little more than a minor player in British political history.

During three days of intense discussion in the War Cabinet following Churchill's appointment as prime minister, two of the three Conservative members of the Cabinet, Neville Chamberlain, who had just resigned as Prime Minister, and Lord Halifax, the very influential Foreign Secretary, argued long and hard for some sort of peace negotiation with Germany, via Italy, so as to save at least something from the impending British defeat. But, having recognised that Churchill was far more suited to be a war leader than they were, as did the two Labour members of the War Cabinet, they gave Churchill their support. The task confronting him was clearly enormous. The British army was still on the wrong side of the Channel, the German army had the initiative, and the Royal Air Force was inferior to the German air force in numbers of planes and trained pilots. At that point, General Guderian's First Panzer Division was only 10 miles from the several hundred thousand exhausted Allied soldiers pinned down on the Flanders beaches. But he received a direct order from Hitler to halt. Despite his protestations, three days later the order was still in force. Meanwhile the Dunkirk perimeter was fortified, and over the next nine days over 300,000 Allied troops were evacuated to Britain in Operation Dynamo – an assemblage of Royal Navy ships and hundreds of privately owned vessels. Had the British troops been trapped on the French beaches, Britain would have lacked any sort of army to respond to the invasion then being prepared. Historians have long debated the reason for the halt order; the key point is that it allowed the Allied troops to escape, albeit without their heavy arms and exhausted, but nonetheless able to provide some sort of early concerted resistance to a German invasion. This never came, partly because Britain eventually won the Battle of Britain, which took place in the air in the Summer of 1940 (much assisted by the newly developed radar, which located oncoming groups of German planes even before they entered British air space) and partly because the commanders of the German Navy did not feel sufficiently confident in a seaborne invasion without German command of the air. So, Britain was able to fight on, in the eventual hope that America would join in. By turning away from the prospect of invading Britain to his massive attack on the Soviet Union on June 22, 1941, Hitler bought Britain further time – and once America had declared war, responding both to the Japanese attack on her base at Pearl Harbour in late December 1941, and Hitler's remarkably optimistic declaration of war on America immediately afterwards – the long-term trend was almost inevitable

But the halt order changed everything. Guderian himself always believed that the order was

"a mistake pregnant with consequence, for only a capture of the BEF [British Expeditionary Force]... could have created the conditions necessary for a successful German invasion of Great Britain". If Britain had lost the war there would obviously have been unpleasant consequences for the general British population, and particularly severe ones for the 450,000 British Jews, whose fate would have been similar to that of the Jews of France.

At the long-term strategic level, the United Kingdom would have been lost as an air base for the massive later bombing of Germany, there would have been no convoys of supplies to the Soviet Union to help in its protracted struggle with Germany, the UK would not have been a launch pad for the June 1944 invasion of Europe, or a support base for the various European resistance movements; no German forces would have had to be diverted from the assault on the Soviet Union to defend their western European conquests; the US would have been menaced from island bases in the Atlantic which Germany would have easily captured; and, despite America's massive resources, a full-scale war alone against Nazi Germany (as well as against Japan) might well have gone badly – and certainly would have been far more difficult than it actually turned out.

From the point of view of the Jewish people as a whole, had Britain not been able to stand firm in the late Spring and Summer of 1940 the Holocaust would have been even more complete than it actually was. The final outcome was bad enough, but without Churchill's indomitable and single-minded leadership, and the miscalculation of the halt order, it would have been even worse.

3. What if Germany had not declared war on America after Pearl Harbour, limiting America to a war with Japan?

Speaking on October 30, 1940, near the end of his campaign for election to an unprecedented third term in office, President Franklin Roosevelt made a pledge to his audience... "Your boys are not going to be sent to any foreign war."

He told his listeners what they wanted to hear. In late September, 83 percent of those asked in a public opinion survey had favoured staying out of the war against Germany and Italy. Only 34 percent supported doing more to help Britain fight Germany. Yet immediately after Pearl Harbour, only 15 months later, the United States entered the war against both Japan and Germany (in response to Germany's declaration of war against the United States). During that time, Roosevelt had gradually moved the United States closer to involvement on the side of Britain. He was constantly aware of the need to carry public opinion with him and it was likely that, but for the Pearl Harbour attack, an American declaration of war against both Japan and Germany would have been much delayed. At the very least, Roosevelt was spurred into decisive action by Japanese aggression and Germany's declaration of war. The consequences of delay would have been enormous: postponing America's massive rearmament and build-up of military forces would have meant delaying the D-Day invasion of Europe well beyond June 1944; it would have been the Soviet Union that eventually conquered the whole of Germany, rather than meeting American and British forces part-way. It is likely that the European Holocaust would have been fully completed by the time Germany surrendered. The Roosevelt counterfactual – a delay in America's full participation in the war – would have meant an even worse outcome for the Jews of Europe.

4. Might Hitler have been assassinated, allowing other, perhaps less fanatical forces, to take over German leadership?

Georg Elser, a skilled joiner, made his attempt to blow up Hitler on 8 November 1939. Nearly five years later, from a very different social class, Col. Claus Schenk Graf von Stauffenberg, made his attempt on 20 July 1944. Elser acted entirely alone. Von Stauffenberg was at the forefront of a very large and complex conspiracy among senior army officers and Foreign Office officials, nearly all from the aristocracy, long disdainful of Hitler's plebeian origins and angry at the disastrous consequences, for Germany, of the Nazi programme of conquest. Both plots were intended to have far-reaching consequences: Elser's to improve the conditions of German workers and to prevent a more extensive war; von Stauffenberg's to bring the war to an end before Germany was completely crushed. The first might just have averted the Holocaust (assuming power was seized by the generals and not by one of the leading Nazis); the second, even if successful, would have had little effect on the Holocaust, so far advanced was the German killing machine.

A. Elser

Elser had read in the newspapers that the next gathering of party leaders would be in the Burgerbraukeller in Munich on November 8, an annual celebration of the failed putsch of 1923 attended by many of the 'Old Fighters'. The security problems were not great. (Security for the event was left to the party, not the police). He worked out that the best method would be to place a time bomb in the pillar behind the dais where Hitler would be standing. Over the space of a month he stole explosives from the armaments factory where he was working, and designed the mechanism for his time bomb. His work at a quarry enabled him to steal dynamite. He constructed a model of the bomb in minute detail and carried out a trial explosion in his parents' garden. In the course of his preparations Elser hid overnight in the Burgerbraukeller more than 30 times, working on hollowing out a cavity in a selected pillar, and leaving by a side door early next morning. By 6th November 1939 the bomb was in place and set. Early on 8 November, he left Munich for Switzerland.

That evening, as always, the Old Guard of the Party assembled. Hitler had announced, the previous day, that he would give his annual address which usually lasted about two hours. He normally spent some time after his speech chatting to the Old Fighters. This time, escorted by a large number of very senior Party officials, he left immediately for the station, to take the 21:11 train back to Berlin. At 21:20, the pillar immediately behind the dais where Hitler had stood minutes earlier, and part of the roof directly above, were ripped apart by Elser's bomb. Eight persons were killed in the blast, a further 63 injured.[59]

Hitler had been gone no more than 10 minutes when the bomb went off. It was mere chance that the joiner did not succeed where generals had failed even to mount a serious attempt, despite many good intentions.[60] Had Elser's attempt been successful it is open to question whether the generals, with the object of their own abortive plans removed, would have seized power. But with Elser's failure, the possibility of more moderate forces taking over and pulling back from the brink of all-out war with the West, initially planned for late 1938, but then postponed until September 1939, had gone. So had any chance of averting the fate of several million European Jews.

B. von Stauffenberg

The plotters of the general staff had already made several abortive attempts on Hitler's life. By the summer of 1944, with the Allies well established in France and the Red Army driving towards Germany, they realized that even Hitler's death would have very little practical impact on the course of the war. But, as one of them, Major General Henning von Trescow, put it: It was no longer a matter of the practical aim, but rather to show "the world, and history, that the German resistance movement, at risk of life, has dared the decisive stroke... Everything else is a matter of indifference alongside that."[61]

All along, finding an assassin with direct access to Hitler had been a major problem for the plotters. Now, one was close at hand. Claus Schenk von Stauffenberg, from an aristocratic family, was aged 34. Like many young officers, he was initially attracted by aspects of Nazism – not least its renewed emphasis on the value of strong, armed forces and its anti-Versailles foreign policy. But he rejected its racial antisemitism and was increasingly critical of Hitler and his drive to war. Even so, he was enthusiastic about the German victory over Poland and even more so after the stunning successes in the West. However, the mounting barbarity of the regime appalled him. Hearing reports of massacres of Ukrainian Jews by SS men, he concluded that Hitler had to be removed. The plans to do so developed, but were dogged by bad luck – which was still on Hitler's side.

Then an opportunity presented itself. On 1st July 1944, now promoted to colonel, he had a job that gave him access to Hitler at military briefings relating to the home army. One such was scheduled at Hitler's headquarters for 20th July. On arrival, Stauffenberg and his aide prepared an explosive device and placed it in Stauffenberg's briefcase. Stauffenberg entered the briefing room and sat on Hitler's immediate right. His briefcase was placed under the table, against the outside of a solid right-hand table leg. He quickly made an excuse to leave the room and, together with his aide, arranged a car to take him to the nearby airfield to join the rest of the plotters in Berlin. At that point they heard a deafening explosion. They sped on their way to the airfield, convinced that Hitler was dead. In fact, though, while others had been injured, some seriously, Hitler had survived with no more than superficial wounds (someone, by chance, had moved the briefcase). His vengeance was terrible. Large numbers of the plotters were rounded up and executed. Hitler was still in power, even more hostile to the aristocratic members of the general staff and even more bent on pursuing the war to the end.[62]

5. What if Britain and the US had tried to save at least some of the Jews of Europe?

In 1939 Britain published a White Paper on Palestine which set a final figure of 75,000 for Jewish immigration to Palestine over a five-year period, at 15,000 per year. From the point of view of the Yishuv, and the Zionist movement in general, this was a death sentence. Britain understood the matter very differently. On the brink of war, it was vital to protect British interests in the Middle East, including the Suez Canal and the oilfields, as well as British military bases, all of which were in Arab lands. (In point of fact, the 15,000 per year figure was never reached; the actual annual average was about half that.)

Compared with these overriding British interests, the supposedly powerful international force of Jewry was of little consequence. Lord Halifax, then Foreign Secretary, expressed the British view in a letter to Weizmann in December 1939:[63]

'Let me assure you that I'm the last to underrate the value of Jewish sympathy and cooperation with the Allied war effort. But, highly as his Majesty's government appreciated Jewish offers of assistance on the outbreak of war, it must not be overlooked that these offers were made unconditionally and were welcomed on that footing. So far as this country is concerned, we are putting our whole energy into a life-and-death struggle with Nazi Germany, the persecutor of Jewry in central Europe, and by ridding Europe of the present German regime we hope to render a supreme service to the Jewish people'.

In other words, "you are on our side anyway, so you have nothing extra to offer and you can wait in the queue". This was, of course, in marked contrast to the British attitude to world Jewry which had led to the Balfour Declaration 22 years earlier: American Jewry was then seen as important in influencing an American decision to join the war on the British side; Russian Jewry, as influencing the Russian government to stay in the war on the British side.

Over a year earlier, in July 1938, an international conference was convened at President Roosevelt's initiative in the French spa town of Evian, to seek a solution to, or at least ameliorate, the refugee problem. In a series of speeches, the delegates of country after country declared the inability of his nation, notwithstanding the deepest sympathy and generosity towards Jewish refugees, to absorb further significant numbers of immigrants. The proceedings at Evian were a sort of dress rehearsal for a similar Anglo-American conference on refugees, in Bermuda, in April 1943. Well before that time, the Allies were fully aware that the Nazis were in the process of exterminating the Jews: "The German authorities, not content with denying to persons of Jewish race, in all the territories to which their barbarous rule extends, the most elementary human rights, are now carrying into effect Hitler's oft repeated intention to exterminate the Jewish people."(From a statement to the British Parliament in December 1942 by Foreign Secretary, Anthony Eden – *The Times of Israel*, 18.4.17.)

An article in the *Telegraph* on the Bermuda conference in April 1943 carried the headline: 'The Bermuda conference failed to save the Jews. The lilies were in bloom for Easter when British and American officials gathered beside the pristine beach on Bermuda's northern shore.... Their task was to find a way of saving as many Jews as possible from Hitler's gas chambers. As if to drive home the urgency, the Waffen SS stormed the Warsaw Ghetto on the same day as the conference opened. While the delegates pored over maps in The Horizons, one of Bermuda's most idyllic resorts, Jewish fighters were mounting a desperate resistance in the foetid alleys of the Ghetto'. According to the *Telegraph*, the Bermuda Conference was partly the result of an article which had appeared in that newspaper on June 25, 1942, almost 3 years before the liberation of Auschwitz. The *Telegraph* disclosed the murder of 700,000 Jews in Poland, amounting to the greatest massacre in world history: the detailed story revealed 'mobile gas chambers and the mass shooting of tens of thousands of Jews'. The *Telegraph's* story was the first result of a campaign by Shmuel Zygielbohm, a member of the Polish government in exile. He coordinated the efforts of a network of informers across occupied Europe who risked everything to smuggle eyewitness reports to London. The Bermuda Conference was seen by the *Telegraph* as 'The great missed opportunity to save many of Europe's Jews. Most shamefully of all, Britain and America turned down a plan to accept Jewish refugees. The central proposal was that the Allies should approach Germany, via a neutral intermediary, and offer to accept Jewish refugees. But on the second day of the conference the senior British delegate, Richard Law, warned: "If Hitler accepted a proposal to release perhaps millions of unwanted persons, we might find ourselves in a very difficult position... He might say all right, take 1 million or 2 million. Then because of the shipping problem we should be made to look exceedingly foolish".

'Put simply, the Allies feared that Hitler would land them with millions of Jewish refugees, forcing the diversion of ships away from the war effort to take the fugitives to safety. Nothing – not even the rescue of millions from concentration camps – would be allowed to steer resources away from winning the war... A wartime gathering, remembered only by specialists, amounted to the great missed opportunity to save many of Europe's Jews. Most shamefully of all, Britain and America turned down a plan to approach Nazi Germany with an offer to accept Jewish refugees. They did so not because this proposal might have been rejected – but because they feared its acceptance' (from an article by David Blair, Chief Foreign Correspondent of *The Telegraph,* 31.1 2015).

The *Telegraph* story takes us back to the letter from Halifax to Weizmann which began this section: Nothing would be allowed to distract from the central purpose of the British, and subsequently, American, war effort – to destroy Nazi Germany by all means possible. Once the War had begun, helping Jews to escape was, throughout, seen as a diversion of resources.

A plea by the Jewish Agency to bomb either, or both, the death camp of Auschwitz, or the railway lines leading to it, was considered in 1943 and 1944 but was eventually turned down, on technical, practical grounds.

The rewards of expulsion and genocide

Mark Mazower[64] points out: 'Genocide always offers spectacular opportunities for enrichment – abandoned factories, shops and properties, furniture and clothes – with which popular satisfaction may be purchased by the occupying power. After 1940, Eichmann extended the 'Viennese model of' Aryanization of Jewish property to Amsterdam, Paris, Salonika, and Europe's other major cities, while Rosenberg's agents [Minister for the Occupied Eastern Territories] alone plundered the equivalent of 674 trainloads of household goods in Western Europe. Seventy-two train loads of gold from the teeth of the Auschwitz victims were sent to Berlin. If most of this went into German homes or Swiss bank vaults, a considerable sum lined the pockets of unscrupulous collaborators, informers and agents of every nationality. Yet it must be said that approval of the Final Solution was not a common phenomenon. In response to the horrors of occupation, most people living under Nazi control had retreated into a private world, trying to ignore everything that did not directly concern them. With traditional moral norms apparently thrown to the wind, the unusual cruelty of the Germans towards the Jews created a more general alarm among non-Jews... Most Germans appear to have accepted that the Jews were no longer part of the community'. The gains resulting from the expulsion from Germany and the killing of Jews throughout Europe were not confined to the material goods listed above; legal, medical and other practices, were available to be taken over by non-Jewish professionals). So were businesses:

'In 1933, nearly 2,700 Jewish-owned clothing companies – mostly in the ready-to-wear line – existed in Berlin, accounting for an overwhelming 85 percent of the industry and employing some 90,000 workers. By 1939, only about 150 remained.... The industry was completely and utterly destroyed and robbed with the help of German banks, which refused to give loans to Jewish businesses, and insurance companies which refused to issue Jewish businesses with policies to protect exports – and this was an industry largely based on exports.' (From an interview[65] with Uwe Westphal, who for 30 years has investigated the Nazi takeover of the Jewish-dominated clothing industry, and whose findings have since served as evidence in numerous restitution claims.)

Many thousands of artworks owned by the Jews of Europe, including some of the most iconic paintings and sculptures in private hands, were simply stolen by leading Nazis or were 'sold' under duress at absurd prices. Many decades later, their descendants are still struggling to regain possession, often after exhausting and financially draining legal battles.

Reserve Battalion 101

Middle-aged policeman took part in mass executions; university professors, lawyers and doctors commanded the *einsatzgruppen* (killing squads) which operated throughout Eastern Europe in the wake of the advancing German army. They were much assisted by local participants, particularly in the Baltic countries and the Ukraine. By mid-April 1942, they had killed precisely 518,338 people: the vast majority were Jews.[66] Based on an extraordinary study by Christopher Browning,[67] Ferguson gives the following description of Reserve Battalion 101 on 13 July 1942. 'The Battalion was given their orders on arrival at the Polish village of Jozefow. They were to round up the local Jews, numbering about 1,800, picking out the able-bodied young men who could be used as forced labour... about 300 of them. They would then drive the rest – the sick, the elderly, women and children – to a quarry in the nearby forest, where they would shoot them all'.

Reserve Battalion 101 was not a hardened group of Nazi fanatics. Most of its 486 men came from working class and lower middle-class neighbourhoods of Hamburg. 'Over half were aged between 37 and 42. Very few were members of the Nazi party, although their commanding officer, Major Trapp, had joined in 1932. They were, without a doubt, just ordinary Germans ...but also willing executioners. They were not merely following orders. Before the killings began, Trapp made an extraordinary offer to his battalion: if anyone did not feel up to the task that lay before them, he could step forward and be assigned to other duties. Only 12 men did so.' Ferguson points out: 'We should not forget the obvious impulsion of self-preservation.... In the midst of a full-scale war, killing Jews was a soft option compared with front-line duties. Old men, women and children could, after all, be relied on not to shoot back'[68].

Relevant psychological studies and concepts

1. Orders and instructions

Anyone who has served in the Armed Forces has experienced behaving aggressively, either in reality or in mock battle, in response to orders from superiors. Immediate obedience to instructions is expected, disobedience is punished. Such newly trained habits rapidly increase the probability of acts which, prior to military service, might have seemed unthinkably aggressive. The process is assisted by the gradual escalation of aggressive behaviour, as well as lack of direct contact with the victim, derogation of the victim and the approval of a superior for aggression in response to orders. All of these processes, combined, led part of the way to the Nazi concentration camps, as well as to other large-scale murders, such as those carried out by Reserve Battalion 101.

A striking series of researches by Stanley Milgram[69], summarised by M.P. Feldman,[70] studied the relationship between aggression and verbal orders mediated by 'obedience'. The basic situation consisted of an experimenter, an unaware subject and a confederate. The subject was always assigned to the role of 'teacher' in a learning task, the confederate to the role of 'learner'. The assignation of roles, apparently at random, was prearranged. The task of the teacher was to inform the learner of his 'errors', again pre-planned, by inflicting electric shocks from an impressive looking but simulated apparatus, the range of shocks available being marked from low to highly dangerous; the voltage levels represented were also clearly visible. The teacher was instructed by the experimenter (firmly, rather than in the peremptory manner of a military superior) to raise the level of shock in response to errors as the experiment proceeded.

In the first study there was no face-to-face contact between teacher and learner; the only feedback of the learner's distress received by the teacher was when the learner pounded on the wall or emitted an occasional moan. In later studies, proximity between the two was varied, as was the closeness of the contact between experimenter and teacher, and the presence of other (confederate) teachers who were either responsive to the experimenter's requests, defied them or made no comment. The two response measures recorded throughout were the percentage of participants (teachers) who obeyed orders to give shocks as opposed to walking out of the situation, and the mean level of shock used. After the first study, undergraduates, not themselves participants, were asked to estimate what percentage of people like themselves would obey orders in the situation used in the first study (experimenter present, no face-to-face contact between teacher and learner, and a single teacher). The consensus was that only a very small number would do so. In fact, almost 70 percent of the teachers (Yale undergraduates) both remained in the situation and used the maximum level of shock.

To check against the possibility that this was due to undergraduates failing to disobey a prestigious professor, the study was repeated in the local town, in an innocuous office, using participants recruited by a vaguely worded advertisement. The results were similar, underlining that obedience to an order to inflict pain on another person is a rather frequent response, displayed by a substantial number of the population at large, given the appropriate set of stimulus conditions. Milgram also varied the degree of proximity between teacher and learner, from the learner being heard banging on the wall but not seen, heard crying out, but again not seen, to being both seen and heard and in the same room as the teacher. The greatest proximity was provided by the situation which the teacher had to hold the learner's hand onto a 'shock' plate in order to inflict punishment. The percentage obeying orders (defined as using the maximum level of shock) was 66 percent, 62 percent, 40 percent and 30 percent in the above four levels of proximity, respectively. In a further study, obedience was significantly less when the experimenter was on the end of a telephone than when he was in the same room. Finally, the presence of compliant peers resulted in markedly greater obedience than when the others present defied orders or made no comment.

Elms and Milgram[71] compared the 20 participants who were obedient in the two closer proximity situations (heard and seen) with the 20 who were defiant in the two lesser proximity (heard but not seen) situations, on a number of tests and questionnaires. No marked differences were found in a then widely used test of personality (the MMPI), but the obedient group was more authoritarian in personality (respectful to authority, derogatory towards subordinates and social and ethnic minorities) on the California F scale (Adorno, 1950). The obedient group described themselves as being less close as children to their fathers and as being less well disposed towards him currently than the defiant group. A finding of particular relevance is that almost the same number (10 obedient versus 8 defiant) had done active duty while on military service, but eight of the obedient versus only two of the defiant had actually shot at an enemy, suggesting, in the context of Reserve Battalion 101, the importance, for behaviour, of previous training and experience in obeying orders to perform highly aggressive acts.

2. A simulated prison experiment
Haney and colleagues[72] began by noting two current explanations of 'documented evidence' on 'the deplorable conditions of our penal system and its dehumanising effects upon prisoners and guards'. The first is the disposition hypothesis, which implies that confinement with irredeemably bad criminals damages those who

are remediable; hence isolate the former. A corollary is that it is initially cruel persons who are more likely to seek jobs as prison guards. In this case the remedy is more careful selection. The second hypothesis implies that the fault lies in the prison environment, which 'brings out the worst' in people.

In order to test these competing hypotheses (the authors regarded the general charge of "dehumanization" as proven), a simulated prison situation was set up in the cellars of the Psychology Department at Stanford University for an intended period of two weeks. From 75 undergraduates who responded to an advertisement for 'volunteers for an experiment on prison life' to be paid at the rate of $15 per day, 24 were selected on the basis of several personality questionnaires and interviews as being the most stable and mature, and as having the least severe histories of antisocial behaviour. All were college-educated, middle-class and white, and strangers to each other. They were randomly assigned to serve either as guards or prisoners and given a battery of personality measures. The prison consisted of three small cells, containing a cot for each prisoner and a closet. Each cell was occupied by three prisoners for 24 hours a day. Other rooms were used as guards' quarters; guards worked eight-hour shifts in rotation throughout each 24-hour period, going home when not on duty. The prisoners received contracts guaranteeing them adequate diet, clothing, housing and medical care. They were told that as they were under surveillance some civil rights would be lost, but that there was to be no physical abuse. The assigned task of the guards was to 'maintain the reasonable degree of order in the prison necessary to its effective functioning.' How this was to be done was not specified but the details of the administrative system were laid out. The guards were told that the purpose of the experiment was to study the behaviour of the prisoners and that they were not to use violence of any kind. They were issued with uniforms and batons. The prisoners were clothed only in smocks (without underclothing) and a nylon cap, and were allowed no personal belongings, the combined purpose being to reduce the prisoners sense of individuality, power and masculinity.

To increase the realism of the study, the prisoners were arrested at their homes by genuine policemen, who first informed them of their rights, and then fingerprinted, searched, stripped, deloused and photographed them. They were placed in their cells, given work assignments, and told they would have two visiting periods during the two weeks, as well as daily exercise periods, and would be counted three times a day.

The data available for qualitative and quantitative analysis included videotape recordings of meals, visits and all other regular events, and audio recordings of conversations between prisoners and guards, both separately and together. The guards made daily reports, experimenters kept informal diaries, and all participants were interviewed one month after the end of the study.

The experiment was stopped after six days, eight days sooner than the two weeks intended, because of the growing distress of the prisoners, five of whom had to be released, even before six days had elapsed, mainly because of 'extreme depression and anxiety'. Whereas the remaining prisoners were delighted when the experiment ceased prematurely, the guards were not. During the 6 days, all guards came to work on time, and some worked overtime without extra pay. Despite the attempt to exclude deviant individuals, the behaviour of the guards varied widely, some being 'tough but fair' others 'cruel', still others 'passive'. Only one described himself as 'upset' by the prisoner's distress; he made no attempt to ease their situation.

Most of the behaviours of guards towards prisoners were negative, consisting of threats, physical aggression and insults. As time passed, the prisoners initiated fewer exchanges with the guards and became more passive. There were considerably more negative than positive statements about themselves by both guards and prisoners, particularly by those prisoners who sought an early release. Ninety percent of the conversations of both groups, even in the guards rest-room, consisted of prison topics. Prisoners were frequently uncomplimentary and deprecating towards each other. The major findings from the personality tests were that the early release prisoners were more extrovert and less empathic, conforming and authoritarian than those who stayed until termination. The final interviews yielded a number of striking statements: 'looking back, I'm impressed by how little I felt for them, and 'acting authoritatively can be fun, power can be a great pleasure'. Prisoners' comments included: 'my prison behaviour was often less under my control than I realised... I was operating as an isolated self-centred person... rational rather than compassionate, and I learned that people can easily forget that others are human'.

The authors concluded:

1. Prisoners' rights, including even eating and sleeping, were rapidly redefined by the guards as privileges and were subject to withdrawal.
2. Prisoners sided with guards against 'trouble-making' prisoners
3. The most hostile guards served as social models for the less hostile ones, rather than the reverse.
4. The experimenters witnessed the transformation of 'ordinary American students' into 'cruel guards and passive self-deprecating prisoners'.
5. The abnormality in the situation resided in the institution (i.e. in the demands of the situation) and not in those placed in the situation, a conclusion similar to that drawn by Milgram.

The Milgram and Haney studies were widely criticised at the time as unethical and there is no doubt that their protocols would not pass muster with current research ethics committees, but they do serve as salutary evidence that 'psychopathic' behaviours are much more potentially widespread than it is comforting to believe. This is particularly the case when they are modelled and rewarded by those in positions of power. When the *regime* in power, *orders* behaviours that are the obverse of those previously illegal, and there are no independent legal restraints, we reach the situation which obtained in Germany from 1933 to 1945 and in the countries conquered by Germany, from 1939 to 1945, as well as in the Soviet Union and its satellites for many decades.

Without Jewish sovereignty, in an independent homeland (and transportation) there was little to be done to save the Jews of occupied Europe except by semi-official initiatives, in rather less pressured times, to accept highly desirable immigrants and. sometimes, children.

Chapter Seven

Hitler's Bounty: A Talented Remnant Escaped to the West

Several years elapsed between Hitler's accession to power and the closing of frontiers in September 1939 (Eastern Europe) and June 1940 (Western Europe). In the interim, many leading German and Austrian Jewish figures in the sciences and the arts found havens on safer shores within their areas of expertise, often with much success, to the lasting benefit of the host countries.

1. Britain

In pre-Nazi Germany, Jews comprised only 1% of the population but won 25% of German Nobel prizes in literature and the sciences (of 100 prizes in science, up to 1933, Germany won 33, Britain, 18, and the US, 6). This was in spite of considerable obstacles in the way of advancement, obstacles that led many German Jews to convert to Christianity. In the decade before 1933, nearly half of all German Jewish marriages were mixed and there were 500 conversions annually.[73] German Jews sought acceptance, not only *Bildung* but in many ways to be more German than the Germans; 100,000 served in the German army in World War I, of whom 12,000 were killed.[74]

German Jews were also very prominent in the professions, well beyond their population share, particularly in law and medicine, despite obstacles to entry. In addition to their continuing attachment to high culture, German Jews, as well as their Austrian counterparts, were at the forefront of the break with the past; they embraced "modernism".

Shortly after Hitler's accession to power there were wholesale dismissals of Jewish academics from German universities. These amounted to 20 percent of academic appointees in physics and maths. At the Gottingen Institute of Advanced Physics and Mathematics more than 30 percent were dismissed.[75]

The British Cabinet discussed what could be done for the Jewish academics, and adopted the following broad view:

'We should try to secure for this country prominent Jews exiled from Germany who had achieved distinction in pure and applied sciences, in medicine, in technology, music or art. This would not only gain for this country the advantage of their knowledge and experience but will also create a very favourable impression in the world, particularly if our hospitality were offered with some warmth'.[76]

In contrast, Lord Dawson of Penn, head of the Royal College of Physicians, believed that "The number of useful doctors could be counted on the fingers of one hand". (At a time when German medicine led the world, with Jews occupying a very prominent place.) As late as 1940, a British Nobel prize winner for Physiology and Medicine, A.V. Hill, commented rather bitterly (in the context of attempts to get German Jewish doctors released from internment as 'enemy aliens' on the Isle of Man): "the strict trade union attitude of the British Medical Association and the royal colleges has meant that they have done nothing at all. The Home Office is terrified of the BMA."[77] Impecunious foreigners were granted entry pre-1939 if they were prepared to work as domestic servants. One senior German Jewish doctor applied for entry as a tutor. He was told by the British visa officer in Paris: "a tutor is not a domestic servant." The doctor said that he was ready to work as a butler, but the official retorted: "That is absurd, butlering requires a lifetime of experience."[78].

The situation was much more favourable in the leading British universities: Oxford and Cambridge and the London School of Economics (LSE). The key movers in the establishment of the Academic Assistance Council (AAC) on May 22nd, 1933 were William Beveridge (later the main figure in the post-war establishment of the welfare state in Britain), Lionel Robbins, a senior academic at the LSE, J.M. Keynes, the most distinguished British economist, Prof. Gilbert Murray (philosophy), Prof. G.M. Trevelyan (historian and Master of Trinity College, Cambridge), and seven Nobel laureates in science and medicine. All were signatories of a letter to *The Times*, describing the establishment of a fund 'to maintain and find work in the universities, for displaced teachers and investigators'.[79] The fund was housed in two small rooms at the

Royal Society. By the end of the war, 2,541 refugee scientists had been registered with the AAC or its successor. The entire enterprise owed a great deal to the work of 'the untiring Tess Simpson'.[80]. ('Ms. Simpson' had in fact been born Esther Sinovich, in 1903, in the Leylands district of Leeds, the heart of the Jewish area settled by Lithuanian Jews in the previous quarter century, nearly all of whom were extremely poor. When she was 21, Esther managed to obtain a place at Leeds University, where she took a First Class honours degree in French and German. At the time of her appointment to the AAC she had been working in Geneva as an assistant to the director of the YMCA in that city. The salary was about one-third of what Tess Simpson had been paid in Geneva, but she straightaway took the job as assistant to Walter Adams, who left a lectureship at University College, London, to become the AAC's full-time secretary.

While Oxbridge and the LSE seized the opportunity to appoint some of the world's leading scholars, this was not always the case. For example, Prof. Erwin Rosenthal applied for the chair in Semitics at Cardiff soon after he came to Britain in the 1930s. Although he had all the qualifications he was turned down. He was told: "We can't have a Jew teaching Hebrew at the professorial level in Wales, because he would be teaching the clergy."[81]

By 1992, 74 displaced central European scientists or their children had become Fellows of the Royal Society, the pre-eminent scientific body (8 percent of the total membership), and 34 had become Fellows of the British Academy (the equivalent leading body in the humanities). Seven of those displaced were already Nobel laureates, 20 received the award later. Of the post-war science Nobelists, six won the award while still living in Britain, including E.B. Chain (a joint discoverer of penicillin), and Sir Hans Krebs, a leading figure in the study of human metabolism. In all, 18 of the scholars were knighted. The second generation included Lord Krebs, Hans Kreb's son, who had come to Britain as a schoolboy in 1936 and became the government's chief scientific advisor, and Claus Moser (later Lord Moser, born in Britain in 1945 to refugee parents), who founded and developed the British government's use of statistics.

For more detail, we can look at Physics. Göttingen University, which before 1933 had been one of the world's three leading centres, was devastated. Three of the four heads of the institutes of physics and maths were Jewish; of the total of 33 academic staff, 11 were exiled. Elon[82] recounts the story of a visit by the Nazi Minister of Education to Gottingen. He asked a non-Jewish mathematician, Hilbert: Had the Institute suffered from the expulsion of Jews? Hilbert answered: Suffered? It hasn't suffered, minister; it no longer exists. Hitler had got his wish: "If the dismissal of Jewish scientists means the annihilation of German science, we shall do without science for a few years!" (The loss was felt for more than a "few years"; whereas British Nobel prizes for science increased from 18 in the years 1900 to 1932, to 21 in the years 1933 to 60, German science Nobel prizes fell from 33, in the earlier period, to eight in the later one.

The loss to Germany of the Jewish scientists is further illustrated by the story of the nuclear bomb. Rudolf Peierls, who had left Germany in 1933, became Prof. of Theoretical Physics at Birmingham University in 1937. In March 1940 he met Otto Frisch, another refugee, then Chair of Physics, at Cambridge. They discussed recent work on atomic fission and realised that the new phenomenon could be used to devise an enormous explosion. They decided that only a few pounds of uranium would be needed, and wrote a three-page memorandum to Prof. Oliphant, head of the Department of Physics at Birmingham[83].

It was astonishingly prescient: setting out methods, implications and costs, as well as the risks of fallout and the moral implications. Contact followed contact; eventually the memorandum reached Lindemann, chief scientific adviser to Winston Churchill, who had just become Prime Minister. In a memo to Churchill, Lindemann wrote: "although personally I'm quite content with the existing explosives… I must not stand in the path of improvement". The work developed fast. Jewish emigrés – physicists and mathematicians – were available (they were not allowed to work on the key scientific development of the day, radar, as they were enemy aliens).

Meanwhile, there were parallel developments in the USA. Three Jewish emigré physicists gave a letter to Einstein ("I had not thought of that"). Einstein told President Roosevelt on 2 August 1939: "an atomic bomb is a possibility". By the end of October, Roosevelt had set up a group with $6,000 in hand to buy uranium. (By 1945, the bill to test a bomb came to $2 billion and 200,000 people were involved.) Development proceeded in the United Kingdom, but financial resources were limited and there was always the risk of air attack. In 1942 the work was transferred to the United States. The so-called Manhattan Project was under way. Most of the scientists involved were German and Austrian Jews. The engineers, responsible for translating the design into an actual bomb, were mainly native Americans. The head of the project was Robert Oppenheimer, whose Jewish family had immigrated from Germany early in the 20th century. Few of those involved had doubts at the time. One of them, Otto Frisch, recalled: "We were at war, the idea was reasonably obvious, no doubt German scientists had the same idea and were working on it."

The contributions of emigre biologists were equally important. After being released from internment on the Isle of Man, together with other enemy aliens, Max Perutz took up a position at Cambridge. His work on haemoglobin led to the award of the Nobel Prize for medicine/physiology in 1962. Along the way he set up the Medical Research Council Molecular Biology Unit at Cambridge.[84] He attracted young researchers, among whom were Francis Crick and Jim Watson. Their double helix model of DNA – the key genetic building block of life – earned them the Nobel prize. Major assistance was given by a Jewish woman, Rosie Franklin (not a refugee), mentioned in Chapter 1. To this day, Cambridge is a world leader in molecular biology.

One of Churchill's senior advisers, General Sir Ian Jacob (not Jewish) said: "One of the main reasons we won the war was that our Germans were cleverer then their Germans!"

1. Some important Jewish refugee figures in the arts in Britain

Musicians and conductors
The Amadeus Quartet, the leading British string quartet for several decades, was formed in an internment camp in the Isle of Man, where three of its members spent some time. Ida Haendel was a prominent violinist of the day, and Walter Susskind and Walter Goehr were major conductors. There were also numerous orchestral players. Somewhat wryly, Vaughan Williams, a famous British classical composer of his time, wrote in an essay: 'The problem of home-grown music has lately become more acute owing to the friendly invasion of these shores by an army of distinguished German and Austrian musicians... They have great musical traditions behind them... In some ways they are more musically developed than ours and therein lies the danger'. Hans Keller was a major musicologist, as was Erwin Stein who, on arrival in the UK in 1938, joined the leading music publishers, Boosey and Hawkes, and was a key figure in the development of Benjamin Britten.[85]
Writers
Given the difficulty of leaving behind one's native language, few writers succeeded in making the transition. Their number included Arthur Koestler, who like George Orwell was a leading political journalist; Judith Kerr, who produced well-regarded novels for adolescents; and the novelist Eva Figes. There were several important figures in book publishing, including George Weidenfeld, and Bela Horovitz who established the Phaidon Press, a major publisher of art books.[86] Jewish immigrants also made their mark in journalism. David Astor, publisher of the *Observer* gave a home to such distinguished emigrés as Isaac Deutscher, Sebastian Haffner, and Koestler. W. Clark, himself an *Observer* journalist, said of his first editorial board: "More than half was German or Central European". Astor's guiding ethic was: try to do the opposite of what Hitler would have done.[87]

The BBC also employed Jewish refugees: the actor Marius Goring became a script editor and head of feature programmes. Others worked on what was called "black propaganda". Some monitored German broadcasts.

It was very hard for actors, except when playing parts that required foreign accents. Most went to Hollywood, as did most writers and directors, organised almost single-handedly by Varian Fry. Two refugees who came to Britain in their youth, Peter Brook and Tom Stoppard (ex-Prague), became key figures in directing and playwriting, respectively.

Other fields
Notable German Jewish historians included Geoffrey Elton (Ehrenberg), the great master of the detail of Tudor politics; Ernst Gombrich, who became a leading art historian, and Niklaus Pevsner, who pioneered and popularised the historical study of British architecture.

In philosophy, Karl Popper (ex-Vienna) was described by Peter Medawar, himself a Nobel prize winner for science, as incomparably the greatest philosopher of science there has ever been. Initially, on leaving Vienna, the only university job that Popper could get was in New Zealand; however, after the war, he was appointed to the LSE, where he had a huge influence.

Finally, in the field of cultural entrepreneurship, emigré Jews were to the fore: Rudolf Bing was one of the main founders of the Edinburgh Festival (1947), and Karl Ebert and Fritz Busch were instrumental in the establishment of the Glyndebourne Opera Festival (1934).

2.The Kindertransport
Almost up to the last minute before war was declared by Britain against Germany in September 1939, 10,000 German Jewish children were allowed into Britain, between December 1938 and September 1939. The British government agreed to allow them in provided that the funding involved was entirely private. (Six hundred children from Prague were brought to Britain through the personal initiative of Nicholas Winton, a young English stockbroker.) It was a dramatic rescue that involved great parental sacrifice and brought the mostly unaccompanied children across Europe and the Channel by train and boat, to security in Britain. (A parallel American agreement, drawing on the vastly greater numbers and resources of American Jewry, would have saved many

thousands more Jewish children. Although the idea might have been approved by President Roosevelt, and especially by his wife Eleanor, who was known for her humanitarian views, the isolationism and virulent antisemitism prevailing in America would have made such an idea a non-starter.)

In 2007 the Association of Jewish Refugees sent out a comprehensive questionnaire to 1,500 known Kinder in the UK, USA, Israel and continental Europe. The aim was, among others, to register their ultimate achievements in life. The return rate was 70 percent.

Sixteen percent of the sample attained university degrees; 22 percent achieved some kind of higher education. These figures are several times higher than the proportion going to university at the time – the late 1940s and 1950s. (Many only had the means to attend evening classes after work, so as to supplement an elementary education.)

One of the Kinder was John Grenville (originally Hans Guhrauer), whose obituary appeared in the *Guardian* on 23 March 2011. He arrived in Britain at the age of seven. His mother died in a concentration camp, while his father, a high-ranking judge in Berlin, managed to emigrate and worked in an English munitions factory, but had limited means to support his son. John studied for two years at a good preparatory school and one year at a technical school, which he left at 14. Four years of manual labour culminated in a gardener's job at Peterhouse College, Cambridge. Grenville gained access to its library on condition that he did not seek admission to the college; he was encouraged to think of himself as a future head porter. However, he combined daytime school teaching with evening classes at Birkbeck College, University of London, where one of his history teachers was the young (and later celebrated) Eric Hobsbawm, a very early refugee from Nazi Germany. Thanks to a London County Council grant he was able to move to the LSE, where he graduated with a First. He gained his PhD under a distinguished historian, Sir Charles Webster, and his thesis, on Lord Salisbury and foreign policy, established him as a serious diplomatic historian. There followed a lectureship and readership at Nottingham, and a Harkness Fellowship at Yale. In 1969 he was appointed professor of Modern History at Birmingham University. Grenville produced a series of major works on diplomatic history, and finally a World History of the 20th Century, synthesising a large body of knowledge.

Turning perhaps belatedly to the events of his own traumatic past, he became associated with the Leo Baeck Institute in London and, from 1991, acted as editor of its yearbook, a position he held until shortly before his death in March 2011. (Another product of his acceptance of his past, *The Jews of Hamburg: The Death of a Civilisation from 1790 to the Holocaust,* appeared later that year.)

3. United States: Varian Fry[88]

An able, multilingual student, Fry scored in the top 10 percent in the entrance exam to Harvard. While working as a foreign correspondent for the American journal, *The Living Age,* he visited Berlin in 1935 and on more than one occasion personally witnessed Nazi abuse of Jews. This turned him into an ardent anti-Nazi. Ten years later he said "I could not remain idle as long as I had any chance at all of saving even a few of [Nazism's] intended victims".

After his visit to Berlin, Fry wrote about the savage treatment of Jews by Hitler's regime in *The New York Times* and helped to raise money to support European anti-Nazi movements. Following the occupation of France, in August 1940 he went to Marseilles (a port city of the Unoccupied Zone) as an agent of the newly formed Emergency Rescue Committee, in order to help those wishing to flee the Nazis, and to circumvent the opposition of the Vichy French authorities, who would not issue exit visas. Fry had $3,000 and a shortlist of refugees under imminent threat of arrest by agents of the Gestapo. Clamouring at his door came anti-Nazi writers, avant-garde artists, musicians and hundreds of others desperately seeking any chance to escape France. Most were Jewish.

In 1940, despite the attentions of the collaborationist Vichy regime, he and a small group of volunteers in Marseilles began to hide people at the Villa Air-Bel until they could be smuggled out. More than 2,200 people were taken across the border to Spain and entered the safety of neutral Portugal, from where they made their way to the United States.

Especially instrumental in obtaining the visas that Fry needed for the artists, intellectuals and political dissidents on the list, was Hiram Bingham IV, an American vice- consul in Marseilles, who fought against State Department opposition and was personally responsible for issuing thousands of visas, both legal and illegal. Fry relied on the Unitarian Service Committee in Lisbon to assist the refugees he sent there. The USC helped refugees to wait in safety for visas and other necessary papers, and to gain safe passage from Lisbon. Fry was forced to leave France in September 1941 after both the Vichy authorities and the State Department disapproved of his covert activities.

Among those whom Fry aided were distinguished writers, including Hannah Arendt, Heinrich Mann, Lion Feuchtwanger and Franz Werfel, and artists Mark Chagall, Marcel Duchamp and Jacques Lifshitz, as well as the noted film director Max Ophuls and the leading authority on social anthropology, Claude Levi-Strauss.

Back in the United States, Fry wrote and spoke against US immigration policies, particularly with regard to the Jews in Europe. His writings included a scathing article in the December 1942 issue of *The New Republic*, titled 'The Massacre of the Jews of Europe'.

Comment

After the war, most non-Jewish refugees returned to Germany and Austria. But almost all their Jewish counterparts (the great majority of those who left because of the Nazi rise to power) stayed where they were. One scientist wrote: 'Before 1933, science spoke in German; afterwards in English with a German accent'.

Many of those who went to Britain and the US represent a record of success achieved by remarkable people who were able to transfer their talents to friendly shores. But a fuller picture is more nuanced. There were many suicides, some at the time, like the social philosopher, Walter Benjamin, and some in later years. Depending on their age and where they ended up, many of the children probably never recovered fully from their interrupted education.[89] It is likely that many suffered from post-traumatic stress disorder and that this affected both their social and their working life, well into the future.

The plight of most German and Austrian Jewish adults – small businessmen, minor professionals, office workers and manual workers – was well caught by W.H. Auden (Elon 2002, p. 400) in "Refugee Blues":

The consul banged the table and said,
"If you've got no passport, you're officially dead"
but we are still alive, my dear, but we are still alive.

Saw a poodle in a jacket fastened with a pin,
Saw a door opened and a cat let in.
But they weren't German Jews, my dear, but they weren't
                German Jews.

Several consuls, other government representatives and self-elected people helped many tens of thousands of ordinary Jews to escape. A sample of those individuals follows.[90]

The consuls

1. Sempo Sugihara

Mr Sugihara, the Japanese consul in Kovno (now Kaunas) was not what he seemed. His government had sent him, as a Russian language teacher, to the Lithuanian capital at the end of 1939 because, with the signing of the German-Soviet pact, Tokyo was anxious to monitor all Soviet-German relations. (The Japanese were looking ahead to their own potential pacts with Germany and Italy.) Hence, Sugihara was a spy. Until 23 July 1940, he issued not a single visa, but over the next month signed hundreds a day – all for Jews fleeing neighbouring Poland which had been invaded by the Nazis. At the end of each working day Sugihara's hands were so stiff his wife had to massage them back to life. Three times his government ordered him to stop, three times he defied instructions. By his own count, Sugihara saved 4,500 Jews. (However, a member of Japan's small Jewish business community put the number at 10,000). Whatever the true figure, no one disputes that Sugihara put his career in jeopardy.

2. Aristide de Souza Mendes

Over five weeks in the early summer of 1940, the Portuguese consul general in Bordeaux, and his family, signed entry visas for 30,000 refugees fleeing the Nazi occupation of France. About 10,000 of them were Jews, mainly from Belgium. Without Portuguese visas, they would not have been allowed to cross the border to the safety of neutral Spain. The leading Israeli Holocaust historian, Yehuda Bauer, rated this as perhaps the largest rescue operation by a single individual during the Holocaust. The Portuguese paid with his career, his pension, and his not inconsiderable fortune. It took his family nearly half a century to shame the Portuguese authorities into rehabilitating him. Mendes, a devout Roman Catholic, whose Jewish ancestors had converted to Christianity 400 years earlier, told his family that he felt driven by a divine power: visas would be issued free to all who needed them.

3. Georg Ferdinand Duckwitz

On 19 September 1943, the German shipping attaché in Copenhagen wrote in his diary: "I know what I have to do". This was to thwart plans to deport Denmark's 7,700 Jews to the concentration camps. He did so with such persistence and conviction that all but 472 of the Jews escaped one jump ahead of the Gestapo. Between 26th September and 12th October, about 6,000 full Jews and 1,300 part Jews, were smuggled by fishing boat across the sound to neutral Sweden. It was a victory for the people of Denmark, who had resisted all discrimination against its Jewish minority and were ready to risk their lives for them. But without Duckwitz's early warning they would not have been able to mobilise in time. A special SS unit had already arrived; a small fleet of German transport vessels was on its way to ferry the entire Jewish population to the camps.

4. Frank Foley

Officially, until the outbreak of war in 1939 he was the British passport officer in Berlin. Unofficially, he was the local head of MI6. He therefore ran the risk of his life twice over, first because of his undercover job as the top British spy in Berlin, and secondly because he worked tirelessly to issue visas to some 10,000 German Jews, saving them from the Holocaust. He not only bent the rules by giving visas to Jews trying to flee mounting persecution, he even went to concentration camps to plead for prisoners, and sheltered many in his home. As an undercover agent, Foley had no diplomatic immunity and put his life in danger with his actions. A reliable estimate is that he saved 10,000 Jews otherwise unable to obtain a visa to enter Mandatory Palestine. On returning to Britain on the outbreak of War, Foley resumed his distinguished career with MI6. His story is told by Michael Smith in *Foley: The Spy who Saved 10,000 Jews.*[91] Many years after his death, Foley's rescue work was recognised by Yad Vashem, and his work as an agent by the head of MI6.

5. Raul Wallenberg, Swedish diplomat and scion of one of the wealthiest Swedish families

In July 1944, the Swedish Foreign Ministry, at the request of Jewish organisations, sent him on a rescue mission to Budapest, as attaché to the Swedish embassy. By that time, 476,000 Hungarian Jews had already been deported to death camps, a major role in this being played by Adolf Eichmann. Wallenberg distributed Swedish 'certificates of protection' and applied pressure on the Hungarian government; his department employed 300 Jews. When the pro-Nazi party, Arrow Cross, seized power from the relatively moderate Hungarian leader, Horthy, in October 1944, Wallenberg initiated the establishment of the 'International Ghetto'. About 33,000 Jews, 7,000 of whom had some links with Sweden, thus found refuge in houses flying the flags of neutral countries.

In November 1944, thousands of Budapest Jews, including women and children, were forced on a death march to the Austrian border. Wallenberg, together with the embassy secretary, followed after them with a convoy of trucks carrying food and clothing which they distributed to the marchers. Through huge efforts he managed to free some 500 persons and return them to Budapest. He had earlier saved several hundred members of a Labour Detachment from the deportation trains. In Budapest he organised 'International Labour Detachments' and even a 'Jewish Guard', consisting of 'Aryan looking' Jews dressed in SS or Arrow Cross uniforms, as well as establishing two hospitals and soup kitchens. Eichmann threatened to kill him.

During the liberation of Budapest by the Soviet army, Wallenberg was ordered to report to Soviet army headquarters. He was last seen on January 17, 1945. Some years later it was learned that he was in a forced labour camp in the Soviet Union. The Soviet authorities claimed that he had died of a heart attack. Just a few years ago, it was discovered that Wallenberg had spent many years in forced labour in the Soviet Union, before dying, still in prison, sometime after 1987.

Others who helped

1. Oskar Schindler, a German businessman and Nazi Party member

Soon after the Nazi invasion of Poland, Schindler, then aged 31, went to Kraków, bought a confiscated Jewish factory and transferred it to Germany. He employed Jews who would otherwise have been sent to their deaths; working for Schindler saved their lives. In all, about 1,200 people worked in Schindler's factory. Interviewed many years later by an Israeli journalist, Eric Silver, Moshe Bejski, Schindler's master forger who became an Israeli Supreme Court judge, summed up: "Schindler was a very complex person: a drunkard, a womaniser, but a good human being... If Schindler had been a normal man, he would not have done what he did.... he could have done much less, and still qualified as one of the righteous".

After the war, Schindler failed in numerous business ventures, and was heavily criticised by many Germans when his story came out. For the rest of his life, he would spend some months every year in Israel, being well looked after by the survivors.

In 1982 Thomas Keneally, an Australian writer, published a novel, *Schindler's Ark*, which won the Booker Prize, the most prestigious and lucrative competition for novels; the book was also made into a highly successful film, *Schindler's List*.

2. Charles Coward, a British professional soldier and German prisoner of war

Sgt Major Coward spent the years 1940 to 1945 in a POW camp, about a mile from Auschwitz. His involvement as a British prisoner representative with the Red Cross and as the British POW spokesman, gave him access to the Auschwitz inmates. Well aware of the bribery value of the POW food parcels, Coward plotted a particularly ghoulish rescue operation: the trade of corpses for contraband, the dead for the living. For the dead, he struck a bargain with a corrupt German sergeant major who was in charge of an emaciated gang of Jewish workers. On agreed dates, the German delivered the bodies of three Jews who had died of disease and exhaustion, being paid in cigarettes and chocolate, coffee and soap, donated by the POWs. Coward's Jewish resistance contact then briefed three inmates to prepare to escape. (Coward had noticed that batches of labourers, starved and no longer fit to work, were marched every night from Auschwitz to the gas chambers in the twin Birkenau camp). With the help of another POW, 'Tich' Keenan, Coward hid the three stiffening corpses in a ditch. The three condemned men, chosen by the Jewish contact, then dropped out, according to plan, from the centre of the 200 or so marchers, and hid in the ditch. Coward scattered the three bodies along the roadside for the Germans to find. The escapees were given clothes to replace their striped pyjamas and went into the nearby forest. This was repeated many times over the next few months until Coward was made aware that the Gestapo was on his trail.

How many of the Auschwitz Jews saved by Coward survived the war? His biographer put the figure at nearly 400; the Israeli son of Yitzchak Perski, one of Coward's fellow POWs, put the figure as high as 700.

All of those listed above, with many thousands of others who helped Jews during the Nazi years, are memorialised as Righteous Among the Nations in Yad Vashem, a Jerusalem institute devoted to the study of the Holocaust.

Chapter Eight

Post-war Jewry: Eastern Europe

By the time the war in Europe ended, with Germany's unconditional surrender on 8th May 1945, the Jewish population had been transformed. Over half of the 10 million Jews living there in 1939 had been murdered. By 2020 Europe's Jewish population was further depleted by emigration and a surplus of deaths over births, dropping by more than two-thirds to about one and a half million. By contrast, the Jewish population of the United States was on a slow increase before peaking; that of Palestine would again slowly increase up to the Declaration of the State of Israel in 1948, from which point, it has increased more than tenfold, to the present time.

Displaced Persons (DPs)

On 27th January 1945, Russian forces captured the Nazi mass murder centre at Auschwitz. More than 1.1 million people had been killed there, nearly one million of them Jews. Only about 3,000 were still alive. In April and early May 1945, as American and British forces advanced from the West, other concentration camps were liberated one by one. The Western allies were totally unprepared for what they found in the camps in the West. The survivors were a remnant of the large pre-war Jewish communities of Eastern and Central Europe. In Poland, home of some 3.2 million Jews in 1939, nearly 90 percent had been murdered by the Nazis and their local collaborators during the German occupation. The same was true of the former Baltic states, Belarus and the Ukraine – even before the Nazis arrived.

With their liberation, those of the camp inmates who were physically able to move were free to go. But in many cases, former deportees discovered that their homes had been occupied by other people who were unwilling to move. In Poland, the Ukraine, Slovakia, and elsewhere, returning Jews were often met with hostility or violence. (At Krasnik, in Poland, the 300 Jewish survivors, of the pre-war community of 5,000, were ordered out of town within 24 hours by the mayor).

The conduct of the Red Army in the areas of Eastern Europe that it occupied was often both rapacious and brutal. Many Jewish survivors from the East joined the general westward stampede of millions of people fleeing to the safer Western occupation zones The Jews found themselves back in camps, but as refugees; the British and American forces were protectors. These were the 'displaced persons', a new term that became widely used – a major headache for the occupation forces in post-war Germany and Austria. The Western governments avoided the term 'refugee', which could imply acceptance that returning "home" was impossible. The DPs soon became a major problem for the Allies.

The Jews of the United States numbered more than 5 million and, as now, were heavily Democratic in a Democratic administration. The Holocaust had left them by far the largest and most important Jewish community in the world. Most were immigrants or children of immigrants from the lands of the Holocaust, to which many had lost relatives. For years they had been told that the only way to help the Jews of Europe was to win the war as soon as possible. Now it was won; their representative bodies were anxious to help the surviving remnant.

The most important of these organisations was the American Joint Distribution Committee (the 'Joint'). Its initial attempts to conduct welfare work in the Western Zones of occupation were hampered by the military authorities, who objected to independent activities.

The newly elected British Labour government's response to pleas for help was not sympathetic. The Prime Minister, Clement Attlee, stated that the Jews were to be treated in the same way as everybody else, rather than as a special category. British policy on the issue was dominated by Palestine; under the 1939 White Paper the British authorities had limited Jewish immigration in the hope of damping down Arab hostility throughout the Middle East. Britain had become increasingly dependent on Middle East oil and was less able to maintain large forces in the area, to hold down local populations whether Arab or Jewish. Moreover Britain was near-bankrupt. It decided that the Jewish DPs should return to their countries of origin, in common with the rest of the displaced populations of Europe. (A flurry of enquiries into various far-fetched proposals for Jewish settlement in remote corners of the

Empire, or the globe, revealed a host of obstacles – as had similar investigations before the War and for several decades earlier.)

President Truman, however, was both more sympathetic and practical. He appointed Earl G. Harrison to investigate the problem and report back. He did so, within six weeks stating: 'The first and plainest need of these people is a recognition of their actual status, and by this I mean their status as Jews... As matters stand, we appear to be treating the Jews as the Nazis treated them except that we do not exterminate them. They are in concentration camps in large numbers under our own military guards instead of the SS troops.'

The US zonal authorities established 12 all-Jewish camps, dismantled barbed wire and watchtowers, recognised the Jews as a separate, favoured category and increased their standard food ration. Direct administration of the camps was taken over by the United Nations Relief and Rehabilitation Administration (UNRRA); the 'Joint' was enabled to carry on its welfare work with relative freedom. The British were compelled to follow the American example. Similar measures were taken in the French zone and in all three Western occupation zones in Austria.

In the latter part of 1945, the number of Jewish DPs began to increase. This was because many Jews were leaving Eastern Europe, particularly Poland, after repeated outbreaks of anti-Jewish violence. It is estimated that 353 Jews were killed by Poles between May and December 1945.

A clandestine organisation of Palestinian Zionists, the Mossad l'Aliyah Bet, was instrumental in channelling the movement of Jews out of Eastern Europe and towards Palestine. In June 1945, members of the Jewish Brigade of the British Army stationed in Italy, mainly Palestinians, had begun moving boatloads of illegal Jewish immigrants to Palestine. The British embassy in Warsaw, closer to the realities, reported that it was 'nonsense to imagine that there was any prospect for the revival of Jewish life in Poland; the remaining Jews there would leave *en masse* whatever his Majesty's government or anyone else may say'. A poll taken in a Bavarian DP camp, in early 1946, showed that of 22,000 people, 13 wished to stay in Europe, 596 hoped to go to the USA, the British Commonwealth or Latin America, while almost all the others said they wanted to go to Palestine. In

May 1946, UNRRA carried out a poll of DPs in assembly centres in Germany and concluded that the Jews 'expressed a unanimous desire' to emigrate, 'the majority of them either to Palestine or the US.'

In October 1945 an Anglo-American Committee of Enquiry was established. Its report, in April 1946, pleased almost nobody. It angered the British, and the Arabs, by calling for the immediate admission to Palestine of 100,000 Jewish refugees from Europe. At the same time, it infuriated the Zionists by rejecting their demand for a Jewish state, and recommending the disbandment of the Jewish underground armed forces in Palestine.

Meanwhile the Jewish position in Eastern Europe deteriorated. By mid-1947, the Jewish death toll in attacks in post-war Poland had risen to over 1,500. About a quarter of a million Jewish refugees fled Eastern Europe between 1945 and 1948, about four-fifths of whom were brought out under Zionist auspices. Many of these were then moved to Palestine aboard boats sailing from a number of Mediterranean ports. In all, 65 of the rickety vessels set sail; most were intercepted and boarded by the British, who interned the passengers, first in camps in Palestine, and from August 1946, in Cyprus. Despite the obstacles the Jewish populations in Poland and elsewhere in Eastern Europe needed little persuasion. Only too aware of the mounting hostility of the surrounding non-Jewish populations towards them, most resolved to leave.

Eastern Europe

Of the victorious allies, by the end of the Second World War the Soviet Union had made the greatest sacrifice, in percentage terms, of human lives lost, but had also made the greatest gains: all the countries of Eastern and south-eastern Europe were now satellites of the Soviet Union. This effectively meant that Soviet Jewish policy would determine the Jewish policies of the newly empowered communist regimes in those countries.

Soviet policy towards Jews had been contradictory from the beginning of the regime: Jewish emancipation had been one of its earliest legislative acts; but its hostility towards all expressions of religion included the observance of traditional Jewish practices. At the same time, Jews were heavily over-represented in both the pre-revolutionary Bolshevik leadership and in the Soviet government. This was also the case in the newly acquired Soviet satellites.

Their Jews were the best educated element in the largely peasant societies of the eastern European satellites, and their leadership was disproportionately Jewish. This was an important source of antisemitism, as the masses struggled economically (hard hit by the war they were further impoverished by the Soviet authorities' widespread practice of removing major physical assets to the Soviet Union). Someone had to be blamed; the Jews were a safe target.

The Soviet Union

The Jews were the most successful group in the post-war Soviet Union: the best educated, most urbanised, most professionalised. They were also among the least liked. Their success notwithstanding, many were discontented; a quarter of a century on, they formed a movement of peaceful resistance They repeatedly sought to leave, a demand much stimulated by their pride in Israel's successes.

By the late 1960s, the demographic patterns of Soviet Jewry closely resembled those of Jews in Western Europe and the United States. Jewish births had fallen far behind the already low rate for the general population – by 1969, to less than a half. Jews married later and tended to limit their families by using reliable birth control methods. The Jewish age profile was significantly older than the rest of the population: more than a quarter of Soviet Jews were 60 or older. As a result, Jews had an unusually high death rate. The combined effects of a low birth rate and a high death rate produced an annual natural *decrease* in population.
As a result, the Jewish population of the USSR declined even faster than that of Western Europe – to only 2.15 million, according to the 1970 census.

Many traditional customs faded away, amongst them circumcision and bar mitzvahs. As in the West, the rate of intermarriage with non-Jews increased rapidly – to a third by 1979. Yiddish was no longer the lingua franca of Soviet Jews. In

1959, fewer than a fifth of them declared it as their mother tongue. (It is a reasonable supposition that the use of Yiddish was greater among the older section of Soviet Jewry.)

Yet Jews were not absorbed into Soviet society. Their social circles were heavily Jewish – again similar to Western Europe. Despite considerable evidence of anti-Jewish discrimination in admissions to higher education, Jews were much better educated than the general population. According to the 1970 census, 47 percent of adult Jews in the Russian Federation had some form of higher education. The Jews were also heavily concentrated in the professions. This feature was even more marked in the USSR than in Western Europe or the USA, where a large part of the Jewish population was involved in business – simply not allowed in the Soviet Union. In Moscow in 1960, more than one in three physicians and two-fifths of lawyers were Jews – reminiscent of pre-1933 Berlin. Soviet Jews were particularly numerous in the arts, above all in music, and in scientific research. In the early 1970s Jews constituted 14 percent of all the holders of the highest science qualification in the USSR.

In sharp contrast, their participation in politics had declined. In the early years of Soviet power, Jews had been disproportionately over-represented among the political elite; by the 1950s, few Jews remained in prominent positions. Of the 1,443 members of the Supreme Soviet in 1964, only eight were Jews. The same was true at lower political levels – all despite their being much more likely to be members of the Communist Party, the entry ticket to political office.

The Soviet dictator Josef Stalin died in 1953. His passing was marked by a relative thaw in Soviet society in general. Past episodes of antisemitism, such as the 'Doctors' Plot' (a group of Jewish doctors was arrested on false charges of attempting to murder Stalin), were disowned and regretted. Jewish writers and cultural activists were released from prison camps. Beginning in 1956, those who had been the victims of purges, and were executed or died in captivity, were 'rehabilitated' under Kruschev's leadership of the Soviet Union – too late, of course, for the doctors, and for the Yiddish writers executed in the late 1940s on trumped-up charges of 'cosmopolitanism'.

However, the most controversial issue concerning the Jews was emigration. Until the 1970s the departure of Jews (like that of every other citizen) was almost completely banned in the USSR. One of the main reasons was the government's fear of a 'brain drain' of highly qualified professionals, particularly scientists. But in 1965 a modest exit to Israel began – to go into sharp reverse when Israel's 1967 victory, a source of enormous pride among Soviet Jews, caused the authorities – faced with the possible loss of hitherto considerable influence in the Middle East – to launch a massive propaganda campaign against Israel, equating Zionism with fascism and racism. Jewish emigration was abruptly halted. Pressure for emigration only increased.

In the spring of 1971, the Soviet government performed a remarkable about-turn: for the first time, Jewish emigration to Israel was permitted on a large scale. Over the next decade a quarter of a million Jews left the country. Brezhnev, by then the Soviet leader, may have been persuaded that the shift would help to secure the agreements he sought with the Nato countries. A long and skilful campaign by Western Jewry is also likely to have played a part.

Anatoly Shcharansky, the best-known Soviet Jew seeking departure, was unusual in playing a significant role in both the Jewish emigration movement and the general human rights movement in the USSR. He was singled out for especially harsh treatment by the Soviet authorities. In 1978, he was found guilty of trumped-up charges of spying for the USA and sentenced to three years in prison, plus ten in a hard-labour camp. He was not released until February 1986, as part of a complicated East-West deal. He emigrated to Israel where, as Natan Shcharansky, he became a leader of Soviet Jewish immigrants.

About 40 percent of emigrants from the Soviet Union in the 1970s went to the United States, particularly towards the latter part of the decade – it is likely that the uncompromisingly Zionist segment left for Israel in the earlier years. It is also the case that there was a massive disparity in economic attractiveness between the USA and Israel, which was obviously perceived by Soviet emigrants. American standards of living were far higher and job opportunities much greater, and the heavy loss of life in the 1973

Yom Kippur War cast a pall of gloom over Israelis, let alone potential Soviet immigrants.

Six-year-old Sergei Brin was one of those who went to the United States together with his parents, both computer scientists. Many years later he was one of the two founders of the Google search engine. He is now among the 20 wealthiest Americans.

The large-scale emigration of the 1970s had accentuated the process of Soviet Jewish demographic decline. The 1979 census counted only 1.8 million Jews in the USSR, while the departure of many young people left behind an ageing community. By 1986, the median age of Jews in the Russian Federation was estimated at 50. In 1982, the departure gates were virtually closed once again, and this remained the situation for the rest of the 1980s (in spite of the reforms of the *perestroika* period under Mikhail Gorbachev, between 1985 and 1991).

Gorbachev was succeeded by the unpredictable and unstable Boris Yeltsin, before the rise to power of Vladimir Putin, a former senior KGB officer in East Germany. To date, the 21st century has seen Putin in effective power in the former Soviet Union, whether his job title was that of president or prime minister. Putin and his colleagues bitterly regretted the breakaway of the Soviet Union's satellites between 1989 and 1991, with the fall of the Berlin Wall opening the way for the reunification of the two Germanys. Under Putin, the Russian Orthodox Church became an integral part of the regime, as it had not been since before 1917, adding its traditional antisemitism to the pattern that already existed. Putin much regretted not only the breakup of the Soviet Union, which he described as the greatest tragedy of the 20th century, but also the decision to allow the Jews to emigrate in very large numbers.

The new emigration regime had come into effect in October 1989; essentially, the gates were thrown wide open. Over the next decade about 1 million Jews left for Israel, nearly 200,000 for the US, and approaching 100,000 for other destinations. The result was a major transformation of the social make-up of Israel.

Poland

As a result of the wave of emigration that followed the Kielce pogrom, the Jewish population of Poland fell sharply. In June

1946, there were 241,000 Jews registered in the country. By 1948, the number registered had fallen to 88,000. Antisemitism brought the new communist ruling class closer to its hostile and suspicious subjects. Restitution of Jewish property was highly contentious. Jews soon discovered that an alliance of right and left combined to oppose them on this issue. The right opposed restitution on familiar antisemitic grounds; the communists, on the other hand, often did so out of a wish not to enrich people they regarded as belonging to the former 'possessing classes'. Communist economic policies affected Jews, more directly and more damagingly, than almost any other group. The Jews in Eastern Europe had been overwhelmingly concentrated in small commerce and the professions. In many places, including Poland, they had dominated these spheres in the inter-war period, often encountering bitter nationalist hostility as a result. Under the communist regime, the old Jewish commercial middle class was effectively eliminated. Many Jews were virtually ruined. By 1950, not only representative bodies, but all subsidiary Jewish institutions, such as newspapers, synagogues, schools and theatres, had been either closed or deprived of their last shreds of autonomous existence.

An attempt to reform Polish communism, in 1956, was suppressed. At the time Soviet party officials expressed support for the elimination of Jews from senior positions in the party, government and press. "You already have too many Abramoviches" – the remark, attributed to Khruschev, was widely quoted. The surge in antisemitism in this period led many Polish Jews to leave, some for Israel. Among the latter was the small daughter of a distinguished economist, in whose footsteps she followed. In 2013, Karnit Flug became Governor of the Bank of Israel.

A further wave of Polish antisemitism, in 1968, was led by the Minister of the Interior, perhaps ambitious to replace the Polish Prime Minister. The few Jews who still occupied prominent political positions were dismissed. Intellectuals were also prime targets. The result of all this was another, this time final, wave of Jewish departures from Poland. Between 1968 and 1972, more than 10,000 Polish Jews were assisted by HIAS to go to the United States and elsewhere. Another 4,000 went to Israel. The total number of Jews who left Poland in this period was probably about 20,000. By the early 1970s the country's Jewish population, which had been over 200,000 even after the war, was reduced to no more than 8,000 mostly elderly people, mainly in Warsaw and Kraków.

Since 1970 Kraków has hosted an annual Jewish Culture Festival spanning the full range of pre-war Polish Jewish culture – and beyond. (Most recently it included Yemeni singing.) The event is attended by several tens of thousands of people, largely non-Jewish tourists, but many Israelis also visit, and it is clearly an important source of foreign currency for Poland. Commenting on the Festival, a distinguished Israeli author, Aharon Appelfeld (since deceased), a Holocaust survivor, said "Jewish life in Poland could have stood a chance, had the Poles not murdered Jewish survivors after the war".

At the same time as official Poland turns a benign eye on the Jewish past, the past is still very present in Poland. A *New York Times* piece[92] by Jan T. Grosz, chronicler of the Jebwabne massacre in 1946, described an event a few days earlier: 'Tens of thousands of people... flocked to the Polish capital to celebrate Independence Day in a march organised in part by two neo-fascist organisations. They waved white and red Polish flags, they brandished burning torches, wore white power symbols.... and they screamed "Sieg Heil" and "Ku Klux Klan".... Though the Polish president condemned the march, saying Poland has no place for sick nationalism, the interior minister called it a "beautiful sight"... Ever since the Law and Justice party won both the presidential and parliamentary elections in 2015, Poland has been undergoing a disturbing political transformation. Law and Justice is an Orwellian name for a party that constantly violates the law, breaks constitutional provisions, and is hell bent on subjecting the courts to its control.... A year ago, a quarter of Poles opposed accepting anyone fleeing the ravages of war in the Middle East; after months of relentless propaganda, 75 percent are now opposed. This year, the country has let in only 1,474 asylum seekers, nearly all of them from Russia or Ukraine.... Their animus, which carries Polish nationalism into such an aggressively xenophobic articulation, springs primarily from a deep pool of ethnic-cum-religious hatred, which is indigenous to Poland and has historically been aimed at Jews. Antisemitism is a deeply entrenched and historically rooted element of this Polish nationalist world view." Finally, Grosz reminds us that half of the 6 million Jewish victims of the Holocaust were Poles.

Another *New York Times* piece,[93] by Maya Vinokur, also concerns the pernicious influence of nationalist politics on historical memory, this time at the Auschwitz-Birkenau Memorial and Museum. She points out that, 'most of its million plus annual visitors eschew the do-it-yourself approach, and trust themselves to trained guides. Instead of impartially describing what happened at Auschwitz, tours drift into nationalistic bias. They pay tribute to the preponderance of Poles at Yad Vashem's Holocaust Museum, But, even as righteous Poles are glorified, their less than righteous counterparts – perpetrators of atrocities like the Jedwabne massacre and the Kielce pogrom – are simply ignored... The history of World War II becomes a chronicle of Poland's victimisation by Russia and Germany... This script espouses a version of history in which no Poles collaborated with the Nazis of their own free will. In rejecting even the term 'Polish antisemitism', Memorial officials fail to acknowledge that half of all Jewish Holocaust victims died not in German-controlled extermination camps, but in occupied territories where locals, including Poles, often participated in the killing... Attempts to "tame" the Holocaust, in order to transform it into a new national myth, have been under way for years, with measurable effect. According to a 2005 public opinion poll, 51 percent of respondents believed that the majority of the victims of Auschwitz were Jewish. A poll from January 2015, revealed that only 33 percent of Poles currently associate Auschwitz with Jewish deaths, with 47 percent believing it to be primarily a site of Polish suffering'.

Hungary

The communist regime in Hungary proceeded as elsewhere in the Eastern European Soviet satellites. In the first phase of communist rule nationalisation was mainly confined to the heavy industrial sector, in which Jews were less involved. But from about 1949, most light industry in Hungary, as elsewhere, was nationalised and retail trade too was brought under state control. Of 1,721 retail stores nationalised in Hungary in 1949, 1,400 were Jewish-owned. The old Jewish commercial middle class was effectively eliminated. Many Jews were virtually ruined. In formerly free professions, such as medicine and law, communist rule made it increasingly difficult to earn a livelihood. Many Jewish lawyers were disbarred. Jews once again encountered restrictions on entry to universities – in effect a revival of the old *numerus clausus,* this time, allegedly based not on racial or religious origin, but on class background. The teaching of Hebrew was suspended in 1949; nearly all Jewish schools were taken over by the government. As in other East European states, antisemitism and anti-Zionism coalesced between 1949 and 1951.

The Hungarian Revolution of 1956, led by the communist Imre Nagy, produced a resurgence of nationalist xenophobia that found its target not only in the Russian overlords, but also in the Jews. The Revolution was crushed; Western, particularly American opposition to this was muted by the distraction of the forced take-over of the Suez Canal by Britain and France. In 1967 Hungary was the last of the East European satellites to break off relations with Israel, following the Six Day War. In the years that followed, anti-Zionist propaganda remained mild by comparison with the fierce denunciations coming from Moscow.

By the 1980s Hungary was the only country in east Central Europe that still harboured a substantial Jewish population, and Hungarian Jewry, exceptionally, was allowed to maintain a rabbinical seminary. Nevertheless, the Jewish population steadily declined: from 145,000 in 1946, to 55,000 in 1996, and to around 45,000 at the present time. The community still lives with undisguised verbal expressions of antisemitism, which are, to say the least, not discouraged by the current right-wing nationalist government of Victor Orban. The Hungarian-born Jewish American billionaire, George Soros, is a well-established hate-figure for Hungarian nationalists, ostensibly because of his consistent support for Hungarian human rights organisations, but much play is also made of his Jewish origins.

Romania

By the end of the war, the remaining Jewish community had shrunk to about 420,000, half its pre-war size. But even in Romania, whose Jewish community was one of the most backward, culturally and economically, in Europe, Jews were significantly better educated than their fellow countrymen: in 1956 8.2 percent of Jews had a higher education, as against only 1.6 percent of the general population. Romania also distinguished itself from the rest of the communist bloc in the post-Stalin period by seeming to show a special solicitude towards Jews. This was due, in large part, to the Chief Rabbi of Romania, Moshe Rosen, a person of genuine distinction, and a shrewd and gifted negotiator, who established a mutual understanding with the megalomaniac communist dictator Nikolai Ceausescu. Even before his ascent to power, Romanian Jews were permitted, in 1958, to emigrate to Israel, and several tens of thousands did so. Under the new dictator, a system of state-to-state bribery was instituted, whereby Israel paid approximately $3,000 per person for each Jew allowed to emigrate to Israel. By 1989, when the Jewish population had dwindled to fewer than 30,000, most of them elderly, Moshe Rosen could look back on a job well done.

Chapter Nine

Post-war Jewry: Western Europe

Immediately upon the end of the war, the victorious allies had divided Germany into four zones of occupation: American, British, French, and Soviet. Before long, the first three formed themselves into the Federal Republic of West Germany; the Soviet zone became the Democratic Republic of East Germany.

In 1947, President Truman appointed as his Secretary of State, George Marshall, who had been head of the U.S. Army in the war. He rapidly became aware that something drastic had to be done to help Western Europe back on its feet. Because the mood in Paris, Rome, Berlin and elsewhere was resigned, even doom-laden, he decided that the initiative would have to come from Washington.

Marshall's plan for a European Recovery Program was made public in a famous Commencement Address at Harvard University on June 5, 1947. It was both dramatic and unique. But it did not come out of nowhere. Between the end of the war and the announcement of the Marshall Plan, the United States had already spent many billions of dollars in grants and loans to Europe. No country had been excluded. But these monies had served only to plug holes and meet emergencies. They were not used for reconstruction, or for long-term investment. And they came with strings attached. Marshall's proposals were a clean break with past practice. It was to be left to the Europeans to decide whether to take American aid, and how to use it, although American experts would play a significant role in the administration of the funds; and assistance was to be spread over a period of years. From the start, it was a strategic programme of recovery and growth rather than a disaster fund.

Crucial to the logic of the Marshall plan was the lifting of all restrictions upon West German production and output, so that the country could once again make an important contribution to the European economy. Indeed, Marshall made it clear from the outset that his plan meant an end to French hopes of war reparations from Germany – the point, after all, was to develop and integrate Germany, not make it a dependent pariah, in order to avoid a tragic rerun of the events of the 1920s, in which frustrated efforts to extract war reparations from a prostrate Germany had led, it seemed in retrospect, directly to French insecurity, German rearmament and the rise of Hitler. The Marshall Plan would only work as part of a broader political settlement, in which French and Germans alike saw real and lasting advantage. Post-war settlement in Germany was the key to Europe's future. So, the Marshall Plan assisted the future development of the European Union, which was initially based on Franco-German economic cooperation.

A corollary was that initial efforts at denazification were fairly soon scaled down. It became obvious that almost the only people capable of running matters in Germany, in the early years after the war, had been equally active under the Nazi regime. German administrators had to become as acceptable as German rocket scientists. In the words of General Lucius Clay, the American military commander: "Our major administrative problem was to find reasonably competent Germans who had not been affiliated or associated in some way with the Nazi regime... all too often, it seems that the only men with the qualifications... are the career civil servants... a great proportion of whom were more than nominal participants... in the activities of the Nazi party."[94]

Many of the major German industrialists, who had been heavily involved in building up the German military machine in the pre-war years, were also rehabilitated and played important parts in the spectacular economic revival of Germany in the post-war years, to which bankers and economists also contributed.

In a series of trials, the four Allied occupying powers in Germany prosecuted leading Nazis and their collaborators for crimes of war, crimes against humanity, murder and other felonies committed in pursuit of Nazi goals. The International Military Tribunal in Nuremberg, which tried the major Nazi leadership between October 1945 and October 1946, is the best-known. It included a new concept in international law, 'crimes against humanity', under which heading was included the mass murder of Jews. The first big trial, of 24 major war criminals, among them Goering, Hess, and Ribbentrop, ended with the conviction of most of the defendants. Twelve were sentenced to death, among them

Goering, who cheated the executioner by swallowing a cyanide pill in his jail cell. The rest were sentenced to varying terms of imprisonment. (In all, the Western occupation powers tried, and convicted, about 5,000 Germans; 806 received the death sentence, of which 486 were carried out.) But detracting from the huge importance of the series of trials was a deficiency in the proceedings, which arose from the restriction of the indictment to events during the war. Nazi persecution of the Jews between 1933 and 1939, in the form of economic boycotts and confiscations, the Nuremberg racial laws of 1935, the Kristallnacht arsons and pogroms of November 1933 were all excluded from the purview of the court.

Many leading Nazis were able to escape to South American countries on the 'rat line' from Germany to Italian ports of departure – with the Catholic Church playing a significant part. This episode has been fictionalised by Frederick Forsyth in *The Odessa File*.[95] Angered by the escape from justice of many of those who had played active roles in the Holocaust, a number of survivors, aided by Palestinian Jews, set up an organisation to seek out and kill such persons. It is well described by Michael Elkins, a long-serving BBC correspondent in Israel, in *Forged in Fury*[96] and in a fictionalised account, *The Final Reckoning*,[97] by Jonathan Freedland (writing as Sam Bourne), a leading columnist for the *Guardian* newspaper.

France

The main dividing line among West European Jews, after 1945, was between those who had experienced Nazi occupation and those who had not. Of the latter, by far the largest group was in Britain. In formerly occupied Western Europe in 1945, the largest surviving Jewish community was that of France, about 225,000 strong. French Jewry had been deeply scarred by their wartime experience, in which 75,000 Jews had been murdered in the death camps. The readiness of the collaborationist Vichy regime to assist in the deportation of foreign-born, mainly East European Jews, divided the remaining community.

Post-war French Jewry remained stratified along lines of geographical origin. An old Sephardi element – mainly descended from the wealthy Jewish merchant community of Bordeaux, the first to be emancipated by the French Revolution – had partially assimilated in the course of the 19th century. However, some remained Jews, among them a future prime minister of the fourth Republic, Pierre Mendes-France. In the 1960s, they were augmented by large numbers of Mizrahi immigrants from North Africa. A second group consisted of long- established Ashkenazi elements, most notably the French branch of the Rothschilds. Some of them, like Simone Veil, had survived the war in concentration camps.

Deportation to Auschwitz, Simone Veil said, shaped her life – as a magistrate, a civil servant and a politician. She was infuriated by selective French amnesia. Reconciliation trumped justice. Members of the anti-Nazi resistance were honoured, but in what she called Gallo-Communist France, nobody seemed willing to believe that the Germans – and their local accomplices – had persecuted people simply for being Jewish. The silence was mixed with mockery. At a diplomatic reception, a senior French official jokingly likened the tattoo on her arm to a cloakroom ticket. She wept, and thereafter wore long sleeves.

For years she was France's most popular politician. She could – and, many thought, should – have been prime minister or even president. Instead, her political career peaked in 1979 as president of the first directly elected European Parliament. She delighted in the post's symbolism – of reconciliation among wartime foes, and that a Jew and a woman could hold the continent's highest elected office.

She was interred, alongside Victor Hugo, Voltaire, and Emile Zola, in the Paris Pantheon. Her previous great honour was to become a member – one of five women among 40 – of the Académie Française, guardians of the language's purity and precision. On appointment, each 'immortal' is given a ceremonial sword. Hers bore the mottos of the French Republic and the European Union. A third engraving was the number from her arm: 78651.[98]

A third stratum of French Jews, by far the largest, consisted of the masses of East European Jews, immigrants or the children of immigrants from Russia and Poland. In the case of France, unlike Britain, such immigration, particularly from Poland, had continued throughout the inter-war period, with the result that Yiddish was still spoken in France on a significant, albeit diminishing, scale in the early post-war period.

In general, French Jews remained much more at home, politically, on the left than on the right in the Fourth, as in the Third, Republic. Mendes-France assumed office in mid-1954. His Jewishness proved to be a lightning-conductor for hostility from the right, a hatred that was personal, not merely political. A populist demagogue, Pierre Poujade, led a protest movement of small shopkeepers that won short-term electoral support with an appeal which included a strong element of antisemitism. Following Mendes-France's fall from power in 1955, there were three years of acute political crisis, dominated by the Algerian War of Independence which divided French Jews, as it divided the French nation as a whole. There was also a Jewish dimension in the form of the 140,000 Jewish inhabitants of Algeria. Most were French citizens, thanks to a law of 1870. When Algeria won independence in 1962, nearly a million Europeans moved to France. Unlike the Moroccan and Tunisian Jews, many of whom, particularly the poor, had gone to Israel, few Algerian Jews felt attracted to the Jewish State; not more than 10,000 settled there permanently. As French citizens, they felt much more at home in French society and French culture. At least 80 percent chose to move to France. In all, some 145,000 Jewish immigrants from North Africa settled in France in the 1960s. Together with the earlier arrivals from Tunisia and Morocco, they roughly doubled the size of the French Jewish community.

In formerly Yiddish-speaking Ashkenazi areas of Paris, the new lingua franca was Judeo-Arabic. The Algerian Jews tended to settle in the outer suburbs or *banlieues* of Paris, and in the provinces. Many provincial Jewish communities were reinvigorated by the influx; the Jewish population of Marseilles rose from 12,000 in 1955 to over 65,000 by 1968.

The influx also changed the demographic outlook for French Jewry, but only in the short term. The fertility of North African Jewish women was much higher than that of the native French Jews, and the average family size of the immigrants was much larger. But in North African Jewish families, as in French families, the number of children steadily declined. Jewish fertility in the 1960s fells rapidly. By 1967-71 the average Jewish woman in France had 1.4 children – well below the replacement level.

Whereas more than a third of French-born Jews had been to university, only a small proportion of the immigrants had done so. Nevertheless, the newcomers integrated very easily and quickly. Within a few years the new immigrants displayed a marked upward social mobility. Following the pattern of the Ashkenazi Jews, they tended to move, between generations, from the ranks of artisans and small businessmen into the professions. The extent of social movement between generations was indicated by the fact that, of those born in France, 28 percent were in the liberal professions as compared with only 14 percent of those born in North Africa. By 1988 no less than 42 percent of economically active Jews in France were estimated to belong to professional and managerial groups. Many North African Jews, particularly the Algerians, moved swiftly up the social ladder, some attaining positions of importance. One became head of French state television, another created the Club Mediterranée. Algerian-born Bernard-Henri Levi began a distinguished career as one of France's leading public intellectuals. Like earlier waves of Jewish immigrants, many shed some of their religiosity after settling in France. As early as 1963, half of those surveyed said they were less religiously observant in France than they had been in North Africa.

Jews in France, like those of the rest of Western Europe, had grown used to basking in the reflected glory of Israel's successes and unique institutions such as the kibbutz. They suddenly faced a new and disturbing situation in which Israel was transformed from an object of pride into a worrying source of insecurity. The rise of international terrorism, notably targeting Jews, was also a source of great distress. Palestinian terrorists, sometimes assisted by European ultra-leftists, hijacked aircraft and attacked airports and airline offices, particularly those of the Israeli airline, El Al.

There were two especially dramatic terror attacks in Europe, one of which ended well, the other badly. The first was the hijacking, in the summer of 1976, of an Air France plane to Entebbe, Uganda. A German member of the terrorist group ordered the separation of Jewish from non-Jewish hostages.

Israeli special forces stormed the airport and secured the release of the passengers. The second was a terrorist attack on the members of Israel's Olympic team in Munich, in 1972. Local special forces failed to free the hostages and many were killed.

In France itself, the threat from Palestinian and ultra-left terrorism was compounded by similar violence from the far right. In 1976 there began a series of bombings of Jewish institutions in France, attributed to the extreme right. Synagogues, schools, kosher butcher shops, memorials, communal buildings, Jewish-owned businesses and a day nursery were among the targets. In 1978, the neo-fascist French National Liberation Front claimed responsibility for three explosions at the Paris offices of the Club Med. In March 1979, a bomb in a kosher restaurant in Paris injured 33 students, several seriously.

Israel's invasion of Lebanon in June 1982 and a massacre perpetrated by Israel's Christian Lebanese allies, shortly afterwards, in the Palestinian refugee camps of Sabra and Shatila, took anti-Israel feeling in Western Europe to a new level. In a new series of terrorist attacks the targets were often Jewish as distinct from Israeli. For example, on 9th August 1982, a machine-gun attack on Jo Goldenberg's kosher restaurant in the heart of the old Jewish district of Paris killed six people and injured 22. The government took vigorous countermeasures, placing armed guards at Jewish institutions, particularly schools and synagogues.

Terrorist attacks in France became more frequent from 2015 onward, and were all claimed by the terrorist organisation, Islamic State (IS). Several attacks on the Ile de France, on 7th January 2015, killed 28 and injured 22. A series of attacks in Paris on 13th November 2015 killed 137 and injured 368. On 14th July 2016, a truck attack on passers-by on the seafront at Nice killed 87 and injured 434. An attack on a kosher supermarket in Paris on the same day killed four Jews; in 2006 a young Jewish man, Ilan Halimi, was kidnapped and murdered in the Paris suburbs. This was followed by a shooting in a Jewish school at Toulouse. Terrorist attacks throughout Europe in the second decade of the 21st century were mostly either claimed by or attributed to IS.

As far as French Jews were concerned, the result was a marked rise in emigration to Israel: 7,231 left in 2014, followed by 7,900 in 2015, and 5,000 in 2016. A total of over 40,000 have emigrated since 2006. (Over the preceding years, the average was around 1,000 per year.) However, the predominantly middle-class French immigrants face considerable difficulties in their absorption: the lack of availability of jobs in their particular skill-set; and the problem, particularly for older people, of learning and working in a new language. The result was that many, variously estimated at between 10 and 35 percent, returned to France.

Britain

British Jews were divided not only by class but also by a four-part stratification based on the successive waves of Jewish immigration to Britain. The smallest, most select group had come mainly from Amsterdam, following the readmission of Jews in 1660. A century later they had been joined by other Mediterranean Jews, such as the Montefiores and the Disraelis. The second group was Ashkenazi, the descendants of immigrants from Germany in the 18th and early 19th centuries, many of whom had prospered in finance; the most notable of these families was the English branch of the Rothschilds. All belonged to the close-knit group known as the 'Cousinhood', among whose members were Edwin Montagu and Herbert Samuel. Although both were part of the Cousinhood, they diverged widely on Zionism. Montagu was a member of the cabinet that issued the Balfour Declaration – which he strongly opposed; Samuel was the first High Commissioner for Palestine under the British Mandate, and an enthusiastic Zionist.

At the base of the social pyramid were Jews of Russo-Polish origin who had immigrated between 1881 and 1914, and whose descendants formed the overwhelming majority of Anglo-Jewry. By the early post-war years, the old Jewish proletariat was seeking to move into the middle class. Its offspring benefited hugely from the 11 Plus examination, a type of intelligence test, selecting on grounds of potential and not of attainment. Among Jewish children, the pass rate was at least twice that of their non-Jewish social counterparts. The 11+ transformed the lives of tens of thousands of Jewish children, propelling them from their working-class origins to good schools and then on to universities and the professions.

A fourth stratum consisted of Jews, mainly from Central Europe, who had arrived in Britain as refugees from Nazism. About 50,000, including 10,000 mainly unaccompanied children (the Kindertransport), reached the country between 1933 and 1939. They included many notable scholars brought to Britain by the Academic Assistance Council. Although Ashkenazi, they had little in common, culturally or socially, with the East Europeans.

In general, leadership positions in the community were still the preserve of the old Sephardi and Ashkenazi Cousinhood. However, in 1939, under the unusual conditions of wartime, something of a palace revolution brought Selig Brodetsky to the presidency of the Board of Deputies of British Jews. Born in a Ukrainian shtetl, in 1893 he moved to London with his family as a five-year-old and received his early education at the Jewish Free School, rather than one of the great public schools that educated the Cousinhood. He displayed an early, outstanding ability in mathematics and earned a place at Cambridge, where he won the title of Senior Wrangler – meaning the best performance for mathematics in his undergraduate degree finals. A PhD in Leipzig followed in 1913. In 1920 he became a professor at the University of Leeds, where he remained until 1949, specialising in theoretical aerodynamics, a field that was vital for the development of the aeroplane.

From his earliest youth, he was an ardent Zionist. In 1928, he became a member of the Executive Committee of the Zionist Organisation of England and served as the head of the Political Department of the Jewish Agency in London, a key position in the struggle against declining British government support for the idea of a Jewish homeland in Palestine. When Weizmann became President of Israel, Brodetsky succeeded him as President of the British Zionist Federation. In 1949 he became President of the Hebrew University, making his home in Israel. He resigned this position, in part on account of ill-health, and returned to England in 1952. For a period he was President of the (British) Association of University Teachers.

British Jewry was the one Western European community of significant size that had survived the war intact (aside from substantial material damage caused by the German bombing, and the loss of life of civilians and serving soldiers). It attained its demographic peak of about 410,000 in the early 1950s. A trickle of immigration did not compensate for natural population decline. As early as 1950, the average number of children in an Anglo-Jewish family was estimated at 1.4, or less. A significant fact in Britain, as elsewhere in the Jewish world, was increasing out-marriage, rising to between 40 percent and 50percent by the late 20th century.

The children and grandchildren of the immigrant generation abandoned the characteristic Jewish trades such as tailoring and cabinet making, and moved into larger-scale businesses and the professions. Major fortunes were made by the founders of department store empires such as Marks & Spencer (the Spencer half of the partnership had departed half a century earlier) and the Great Universal Stores (Sir Isaac Wolfson). Property magnates such as Charles Clore and Jack Cotton flourished. A 1967 listing of 110 British millionaire property developers found that 70 were Jewish. A 1961 analysis of the Jewish population of England and Wales suggested that 44 percent of Jews fell into social class I (professional: doctor, accountant, university teacher, etc.) or class II (mostly self-employed), as compared to 19 percent of the general population in these two classes.

British Jews' involvement in everyday political activity began in the middle of the 19th century. In contrast to the Cousinhood, the great mass of British Jews were on the left. In the general election of 1945, which saw a massive victory for the Labour Party, with a majority in the House of Commons for the first time, 27 Jewish MPs were returned: 26 for the Labour Party and one Communist. This reflected the overwhelming preponderance of the Jewish vote at the time, which was well to the left. By contrast, in the election of June 2017, of the 21 Jewish MPs, nine were Labour and 12 Conservative. Yet even this evidence of a shift in political beliefs did not fully reflect the Jewish vote, which was only 26 percent for the Labour Party.

To an extent, the massive loss of Jewish support for Labour was linked to repeated accusations of antisemitism among the 'hard left' wing of the Labour Party. However, the explanation lies more substantially in the rapid and considerable increase in affluence among British Jews. The 'Jewish vote' plays a very small part in British elections: of the 650 constituencies in the House of Commons, no more than three or four have significant numbers of Jewish voters, reflecting the declining Jewish population. The Moslem vote is far more important: the Moslem share of the population is about 7 percent (as compared to the Jewish share of under 0.5 percent) and plays a decisive role in some 31 parliamentary seats – a figure likely to rise as the Moslem population is increasing by about 10 percent per year. Many Moslems have shifted their political allegiance to the Conservative side as they become more prosperous. The Labour Party cannot afford to alienate Moslem voters, and its leadership, until 2020 in the hands of the left of the party, stated its 'opposition to all forms of racism', of which antisemitism was only one.

The sharp leftward turn of Labour, based on the unexpected rise to the Labour leadership of Jeremy Corbyn in 2015, owed a good deal to the activities of the highly organised Momentum group, founded and led by Jon Lansman, a Left ideologue from a conventional Anglo-Jewish background. The question as to whether the Labour Party – or at least its left wing – is antisemitic has continued to exercise both the more politically moderate Jewish members of the Labour Party and official Jewish bodies such as the Board of Deputies. Several major Jewish donors to the party have announced that they will no longer give it financial support.

Concluding a trenchant analysis of the Labour Party and antisemitism, *The Economist* Bagehot column states: '… Mr Corbyn has devoted much of his life to protesting against racism. But for him, racism is linked to class and exploitation. It is about privileged people doing down the marginalised, and saintly activists like Mr Corbyn riding to the rescue. But the Jews are perhaps the world's most successful ethnic minority. They have almost always succeeded by the sweat of their brow rather than the largesse of activists or government programs. They are often hated precisely because they have succeeded where other marginalised groups have failed. The danger is not that Mr Corbyn will continue to ignore antisemitism ... It's that he doesn't understand what antisemitism is.'[99]

Quite out of the blue, inserted into a speech on a different topic, Corbyn stated "British Zionists have no sense of English irony, no matter how long they have lived here." He invited to Parliament a Palestinian who had suggested that Jews were absent from the World Trade Centre when it was attacked. In 2014 he appeared at a wreath-laying ceremony in Tunis that appears to have honoured those associated with the 1972 Olympics massacre of Israeli athletes, stating that although he was present, he "was not involved in the wreath-laying" (rather like the politician who denied smoking cannabis "because I didn't inhale").

His political travails with Labour Party antisemitism continued, and intensified into 2019. A Jewish Labour MP, Luciana Berger, left the party because of repeated antisemitic experiences in her constituency (held by Labour with a large majority). She had to endure "pictures of Stars of David superimposed on my forehead, and my face imposed on a rat or many rats. There are pornographic images, violent images, oversize features like a witch".[100] By December 2019, the severe harassment had led to two prison sentences; more trials are pending. In leaving the Labour Party Ms Berger was joined by eight other Labour MPs, none of them Jewish. Jon Lansman, stated: "There is a major problem [in the Labour Party] with hard-core antisemitic opinion". In autumn 2019 Ms Berger joined the Liberal Democratic Party and was adopted as their candidate for a London constituency with a significant Jewish population. There was no happy ending; Ms Berger performed creditably but did not win the seat.

Shortly before the General Election of December 12th, 2019 the Chief Rabbi, Ephraim Mirvis, made an unprecedented intervention, denouncing antisemitism "at the head of the Labour Party" and advising British Jews to vote for other parties; the story received front-page coverage across the dailies. In a TV interview, pressed to apologise for Labour antisemitism, Corbyn did so only at the fourth time of asking.

In March 2019, the Equality and Human Rights Commission launched a formal enquiry into British antisemitism in general. On past form it would not report its conclusions for many months. However, tension mounted further when, in July 2019, three peers – two of them Jewish, Lord Turnberg, an eminent physician, and

Lord Treisman, a former general secretary of the Labour Party – resigned the Labour whip. They were joined by another eminent doctor of Armenian origin, who referred to the World War I Turkish massacre of his people. A few days later, a full-page advertisement in the *Guardian,* signed by 64 Labour peers (one-third of all Labour peers, of whom a minority was Jewish), charged that "in Jeremy Corbyn's Labour Party: all are welcome but Jews". This was immediately followed by a BBC documentary which gave a detailed account of the harassment suffered at the hands of very senior Labour officials, by more junior Labour employees, when they attempted to explore and combat antisemitism within the party. Finally, after a long period of totally denying any antisemitism in the party, Jeremy Corbyn issued a somewhat restrained apology to Jewish Labour members who had "been hurt".

The Labour antisemitism issue had disappeared from the media in late July, eclipsed by the Conservative Party choice, as leader and prime minister, of Boris Johnson, an ebullient Old Etonian and Oxford classicist, and the prospect of a general election in the near future. This took place in December 2019. The result was a Conservative landslide, a majority of 83 over all other parties and the worst Labour performance since 1935. Corbyn returned to the obscurity of the back benches, to be succeeded as Labour leader by Sir Keir Starmer, relatively more centrist, and much more able. From the point of view of British Jewry, Starmer is a vast improvement on Corbyn: genuinely determined to uproot antisemitism from the Labour Party. On July 22[nd,] 2020 the whistle-blowers and the Panorama programme presenter were all awarded massive damages against the Labour Party, and also received a fulsome apology from the party.

The Equality and Human Rights Commission issued its report at the end of October 2020. Its conclusions were damning: under Jeremy Corbyn, the Labour Party had become seriously antisemitic. The Party now led by Starmer immediately suspended Corbyn's membership and withdrew from him the Labour whip in Parliament. The great majority of Anglo-Jewry welcomed the Report and the Party's response. Corbyn and his allies, including Momentum, vigorously rejected both the Commission's conclusions and the response of the party's current leadership. A schism in the Labour Party loomed. Jewish membership, votes and donors, might all return over the coming years.

Antisemitism in Britain

Interviews conducted in 2016 and 2017, with a combined sample of 7,156 Jewish respondents, found that 37 percent had been concealing, in public, signs that would indicate they are Jewish. Just under 60 percent said that they felt welcome in Britain; 17 percent that they felt unwelcome. Only 39 percent of respondents said they trust justice authorities to prosecute perpetrators of antisemitic hate crimes. Three-quarters of those interviewed said they felt that recent political events had resulted in increased hostility towards Jews; 80 percent believed that the Labour Party is harbouring antisemites in its ranks. Finally, almost a third said they had considered leaving the United Kingdom over the past two years, on account of antisemitism. A poll published early in 2019 reported that the number seriously considering departure had risen to nearly 40 percent and that the possibility of a Corbyn-led Labour victory in a future general election played a major part in their thinking. A similar poll in January 2015, before Corbyn became Labour leader – conducted after two major terrorist attacks in Paris – found that only 11 percent of British Jews were considering leaving the UK.[101] (In 2020, the figure remains around 500 annually emigrating to Israel – less than half the number leaving France for Israel, allowing for the difference in the sizes of the respective Jewish populations.)

So, there is a marked sense of unease among British Jews, though perhaps not much more. It is striking that whereas terrorist attacks in France have included specifically Jewish targets, this has not been the case in Britain, where there was an increase in such attacks in 2016 and, particularly, 2017. (Despite the security services 'foiling 20 plots in the past four years', five terrorist attacks succeeded in Britain in 2017, killing dozens of people; they have all been claimed by IS.) In a rare public statement, Andrew Parker, the head of MI5, Britain's domestic intelligence service, warned that the country was contending with an intense terrorist threat from Islamic extremists that was evolving rapidly and becoming harder to detect. Mr Parker said the threats were increasing at the fastest rate he had seen in his 34-year career.

There may be yet more, as British-born jihadists return following the defeat of IS in the Middle East.

A 2016 poll of British Moslems lent support to Mr Parker's concerns: four percent of the sample said they sympathised with people who took part in suicide bombings (1 percent said they completely sympathized, 3 percent sympathised to some extent); a further 4 percent sympathised with people who committed terrorist actions as a form of political protest generally. (These percentages may appear small, but as proportions of the total Moslem population, estimated at 4.1 million in 2017, they give cause for concern. It is likely that attitudes sympathetic to terrorism are held by young men rather than women or older people. Almost half of British Moslems are under the age of 24 and one-third are under 15, making it the fastest growing group among young Britons.)

Moreover, commenting on the detailed results, Trevor Phillips (of Afro-Caribbean origin), a former head of the British Race Relations Board, stated: "On specific issues – families, sexuality, gender, attitudes towards Jews and on questions of violence and terrorism – the centre of gravity of British Muslim opinion is some distance away from the centre of gravity of everyone else's opinion. One in 6 Muslims say they would like to live more separately; a quarter would like to live under sharia law. It means that as a society we have a group of people who basically do not want to participate in the way that other people do.... There is a correspondence between this desire to live separately and sympathy for terrorism. People who want to live separately are about twice as likely to say that they have sympathy for terrorist acts."[102]

Jewish insecurity may be particularly felt among university students. Baroness Ruth Deetch, a cross-bench peer who formerly held the highest national office dealing with student complaints, and a former principal of St Anne's College, Oxford, enquired into a series of high-profile incidents at top universities where Jewish students claimed that they were verbally abused or physically attacked. In an interview with the *Telegraph*[103] she stated that institutions may be failing to combat hatred against Jews as they are "afraid of offending" their potential benefactors from Gulf states. "A handful of universities are now gaining reputations as institutions where Jews are unwelcome. Amongst Jewish students, there is gradually a feeling that there are certain universities that you should avoid."

It is certainly the case that nearly two-thirds of Jewish students study at just six out of the 140 UK universities. They include Oxford (about 8 percent of undergraduates are Jewish) and Cambridge, as well as several other, second-tier but still prestigious universities. More surprising, at first sight, is that the six do not include any of the London universities, some of them among the world's top 20. However, this likely due to the almost universal preference among students to leave home (at least two-thirds of UK Jews live in London).

How many Jews are there in Britain? After many years of decline, from a peak of around 410,000 in 1950, there was a very small uptick between 2001 and 2011 to about 270,000. The decline was due to the usual factors: a high average age, and a generally low birth rate and a rate of intermarriage approaching a half of all marriages involving one Jewish spouse; the slight increase overall was clearly due to the rapid expansion of the Strictly Orthodox (or ultra-Orthodox, in Israel termed Haredi) section of the Jewish population. According to a study by the Institute of Jewish Policy Research (JPR): 'The British Jewish population is on the verge of significant demographic change. This is fuelled by a birth rate of seven children per woman in the Strictly Orthodox community, which is growing at nearly 5 percent per year, while the number of secular and moderately religious Jews was declining, annually, by 0.3 percent'. The report estimates the Strictly Orthodox population in 2015 to number about 40,000, and that the high birth rate means that their children will reach 50 percent of all Jewish children by 2031. It adds: 'Strictly Orthodox Jews are expected to constitute a majority of the British Jewish population, long before the 21st century is over'.[104]

The long-term decline in the Anglo-Jewish population, apart from the Strictly Orthodox, may be slowed by the success of Jewish day schools – perhaps a half of non-Strictly Orthodox Jewish children attend such schools. They aim to inculcate a strong Jewish identity, as well as achieving excellent results in national examinations. In 2015, of the top five non-selective schools in the country, two were Jewish. The same was true of the results in 2018: Yavneh College, in Hertfordshire, was the top performing non-selective school in the country, measured by results of public examinations at the ages of 16 (GCSE) and 18 (A level). The long-established JFS (Jewish Free School) was third among non-selective schools. Yavneh placed 52nd when measured against selective schools – which have a much higher average intellectual calibre of pupil at entry. It is a reasonable speculation that Jewish parents, now mainly middle-class, seek entry for their children to the selective (and fee-paying) schools. It is well established that these are the schools which are most likely to produce Oxbridge entrants. Finally, an Oxbridge degree opens the way to the most sought-after careers. The Jewish proportion of Oxbridge undergraduates (about 5 percent, according to the nationwide Union of Jewish students) far exceeds the Jewish share of the university age population (about 0.3 percent), even allowing for the Anglo-Jewish population being more affluent than the overall UK population.

The children of the Strictly Orthodox section, particularly the boys, are not exposed to much, if any, secular education; this may change, due to both parental and government pressure (the public funding of a school is conditional upon the provision of a minimum of secular education).

Germany and Austria

On 11 May, nine days after the fall of Berlin, Jewish religious services were again held in the German capital. By autumn of that year more than 7,000 Jews were living in Berlin. About 1,000 had survived in concealment in the city; in the following weeks they were joined by 1,628 people who returned from concentration camps. In addition, there were several thousand Jews who had been spared by the Nazis because they were married to a non-Jewish spouse.

To most of the Jewish world, however, the idea of reconstituting Jewish communities in Germany was anathema: post-war Germany was a land in which self-respecting Jews should not live. Figures in the arts, such as Kurt Weill, Arthur Schnabel and Richard Tauber, who had made Berlin and Vienna world-class centres of musical life, remained in the USA or Britain. The leaders of German Jewish scholarship had settled in Israel (including Gershom Sholem and Martin Buber) or the United States, and cinematic directors and writers such as Fritz Lang, Ernst Lubitsch and Billy Wilder remained in Hollywood. The absence not only of those who had died but also of these exiles impoverished German cultural life and irreversibly changed its character.

The only large, organised, group of German Jews who returned came in the late 1940s from Shanghai: about 18,000 German and Austrian Jews had immigrated there in the late 1930s, it being the only place on earth, at that time, for which immigrants did not have to obtain entry visas. Most settled in Israel, the USA or Australia, but about 2,500 returned to West Germany.

The government of the new state of West Germany well understood that its conduct towards the Jews would be a touchstone of its rehabilitation in the world. It therefore took energetic measures to help provide a legal and financial basis for the reconstitution of Jewish communities throughout Germany. In 1955, a law was passed offering 6,000 marks to any returning Jews who had left the country because of persecution under the Nazis. As a result, a few thousand more German Jews returned from Israel. But the demographic make-up of the German Jewish community in the 1950s and 1960s seemed to offer little hope of its survival; the returning Jews were predominantly elderly, the annual death rate seven times the birth rate.

The exit from the USSR in the 1970s brought new life to the community of West Germany. By the end of the decade more than half of the Jews in Berlin were Russian immigrants. They also brought a more normal age structure. In 1986, a Jewish school, the first since the war, opened in Berlin and was an immediate success. But the school, like every Jewish institution in Berlin, and most in Germany, operated with round-the-clock armed guards.

The German Chancellor Konrad Adenauer visited Israel in 1966 and diplomatic relations were established between the two countries. In May, 1985, the Federal President Richard von Weizsacker, son of a convicted war criminal, invited his fellow countrymen to 'look truth straight in the eye'. He rejected the frequently heard excuse that the German people had not known what was being done to the Jews.

The Russian zone of Germany, the east of the country, had become the German Democratic Republic. The secret police (Stasi) were omnipotent in the 1950s and 1960s. Several thousand people of Jewish extraction still lived in East Germany, most choosing not to register as members of the Jewish community. But, unlike in the Federal Republic, no more than vague hints were dropped of reparations to Jews. By the time of the fall of the Berlin Wall in 1989 and the collapse of East Germany in 1990, followed by the unification of the two parts of Germany, its Jewish community was on the brink of dissolution.

Austria, the third German-speaking state, behaved very differently from the western zone of Germany, which made substantial efforts to acknowledge and deal with the legacy of Nazism. Instead, the leadership promoted the convenient myth of Austria as Hitler's first victim, which enabled successive governments to avoid any serious confrontation with the past. Nor was there, at first, any official public readiness to accept the return of substantial numbers of Jews as fellow citizens. However, by the early 1980s about 12,000 Jews lived in Austria, most of them in the capital – all that remained of the great cultural hothouse of Viennese Jewry.

By the time the Berlin Wall fell, Germany's Jewish community, had only 30,000 ageing members and was dwindling rapidly. But within a decade and a half it had become the third largest Jewish population in Western Europe, after France and Britain, and the fastest growing. Between 1991, when the country was unified and immigration rules relaxed, and 2005, more than 200,000 Jews from the former Soviet Union emigrated to Germany as part of the massive exit of Russian Jews. Many moved on elsewhere, and many of those who remained in Germany neither knew nor cared about Jewish rituals and traditions. Most of the running costs of Jewish institutions, from synagogues to nursing homes, were met by the German authorities. Compared with the former Soviet Union, their material conditions were vastly superior. What was now the minority of originally German Jews had to accept that the glory days of sophisticated German Jewry, from Einstein to Weill, were gone forever.[105]

However, perhaps a new influx, this time from – of all places – Israel, might do something, however limited, to produce a facsimile of those days? This was the hope expressed by a German cabinet minister: "We would like Germany to become a world centre of the arts, as it was before 1933, but can we do it without the Jews?"

Between 2000 and 2015, 33,321 Israelis were granted European Union passports because their grandparents had been German citizens before 1939; approximately 13,000 Israelis without such a connection now live in Berlin. The latter are mostly young, well-educated and working in the arts, though not exclusively. Why the move from Israel? There seem to be a number of factors: Berlin offers considerable economic advantages, including a lower cost of living than Tel Aviv, as well as lower-cost rentals and virtually free university tuition. For its size, Israel has a large number of colleges providing training in the arts, from photography, via film making to classical and jazz music, painting and sculpture. Germany offers a much bigger population of potential consumers of the arts. In addition, for many of the mainly left-wing young Israelis now living in Berlin, they have removed themselves from the constant political tension over the Palestinian issue. It remains to be seen whether they will partner, have children, and generally put down roots there.

Before the German election of September 25, 2017, the familiar 'grand coalition' of the Christian Democrats and the Social Democrats seemed likely to continue. But the election results meant that while the CDU remained in power as the largest single party, despite losing a significant share of the vote, the Social Democrats, which also lost votes, initially decided to go into opposition in order to rebuild. However, after several months of tortuous negotiations, the grand coalition was reconstituted, with Angela Merkel, once more, as Chancellor. The major new development was that the far-right Alternative for Germany party (AfD) tripled its previous vote to 13.6 percent, meaning that it entered Parliament for the first time, with over 90 seats. Its main emphasis in the elections was on its opposition to immigration (i.e. Moslems) and to the European Union, which it sees as exploiting German prosperity to subsidise the more feckless members of the EU. On the face of it, then, a conventional populist party of the kind familiar both throughout Europe and in the United States. However, both before and after the election, its leaders argued for an end to German apologising for the persecution of the Jews, which one of them attributed solely to the SS and not to the German Army, and of which another said: 'We should allow ourselves to feel proud of the Army's successes in two world wars and earlier, just as Britain and France feel proud of their armies' successes.' In June 2018, Alexander Gauland, a co-leader of AfD, said "Hitler and the Nazis are just a speck of bird shit in over 1,000 years of successful German history." It is, of course, still a long way from the prospect of neo-Nazis rampaging through the streets of Berlin, or even mounting a sober procession. And it is even further from the possibility of young Israelis, because of AfD's relative success, returning to Israel.

So, for Jews living in Germany there are concerns arising from parties of the extreme right; there are also potential problems from the German Moslem population (largely Turkish in origin and ensconced in Germany for at least two generations). In a representative survey conducted by the University of Münster in 2016, 47 percent of Turkish immigrants and their descendants said it was more important for them to abide by religious commands than by the laws of the country they lived in. Some 32 percent said that the Moslems should try to re-erect a social order like the one during the lifetime of the Prophet Muhammad. Commenting on the results, Jochen Bittner, a political editor at *Die Zeit,* stated: 'These are troubling figures.... The apparent longing of so many Moslems for an authoritarian rather than an open society is shocking.'[106]

An Austrian populist party, Freedom, has tilted that country's politics to the right, with the party emerging as coalition king-maker after the elections of mid-October 2017. The Freedom party is led by Heinz-Christian Strache, who became the first European politician with a neo-Nazi background to sit in government since the Second World War. His party finished in third place behind the winning centre-right Austrian People's

Party and took control of several key ministries, including Interior and Foreign Affairs. (Strache was arrested by German police as a 20-year-old for taking part in a march organised by a banned neo-Nazi movement modelled on the Hitler Youth.) The Freedom party has repeatedly been linked to articles claiming that George Soros was the shadowy instigator behind the refugee crisis, and behind the sanctions against Russia. Once again, the Austrian situation is a far cry from its Nazi past, but as with Germany, it will bear watching.

Antisemitism in Europe

A Pew Survey on antisemitism, the Global 100, conducted in 100 countries in 2014 and 2015 to develop an index of antisemitism, has produced a wealth of data.[107] The main instrument was a list of 11 statements about Jews; those who checked 'probably true' to 6 or more statements were considered antisemitic. The statements ranged from: 'Jews are more loyal to Israel than to this country [the countries they live in]' to 'Jews are responsible for most of the worlds' wars.' The first of these was endorsed by 44 percent of respondents worldwide, the latter by 15 percent of respondents. The second most commonly-held stereotypes were that 'Jews have too much power in business' and 'Jews still talk too much about what happened to them in the Holocaust' (both endorsed by 38 percent of all respondents). Looking at the results worldwide, Moslems were more likely than the general population, sometimes massively so, to endorse antisemitic statements.

The results for Europe, generally, of index scores of antisemitism, varied from Greece, with a score of 69 percent (i.e. the percentage of adults self-reported as agreeing with at least six of the 11 classical antisemitic statements) to Sweden (4 percent). For France, the percentage was 37, for Germany, 27, and for Britain, 8 – almost the lowest score of the 17 Western European countries surveyed.

The survey also covered 17 eastern European countries. Index scores of at least six ranged from Poland (45 percent) to the Czech Republic (13 percent). Neither have significant Jewish populations at the present time. Scores for the Ukraine and Russia – both of which still have sizeable Jewish numbers – were 38 percent and 30 percent, respectively, indicating still serious levels of classical antisemitic beliefs.

The Pew Global 100 survey also found, in the wake of antisemitic violence in Europe, that there had been a significant drop between 2014 and 2015 in index scores in France and Germany, and that in those countries there was, respectively, a 20 percent and 33 percent increase in concern over violence.

French Moslems have a slightly lower index score than those residing in Germany or the United Kingdom, though it is still quite high: 49 percent of the Moslem population (compared to 56 percent and 54 percent for Germany and the United Kingdom, respectively). In France, Germany and the UK, the Moslems surveyed had significantly higher percentages endorsing all 11 index statements at the 'probably true' level, than the general population. For example, regarding the statement 'Jews have too much power in the business world', in all three countries Moslems endorsed the statement at least twice as often as the general population.

An earlier Pew survey concerned Moslem views of Jews as people in general.[108] For the European countries studied, much the lowest score for unfavourable views was obtained by the Moslems of Great Britain (6 percent, followed by those of the Netherlands with 11 percent), and France (16 percent). The two Eastern European countries with the highest scores for unfavourability were Poland (27 percent) and Russia (26 percent).

One of the 2006 survey's most striking findings was that majorities in Egypt, Indonesia, Jordan and Turkey – all Moslem countries with fairly strong ties to the United States – said they did not believe that Arabs carried out the September 11 attacks in the United States. In not one of the Moslem populations polled did a majority believe Arabs were responsible.

The Moslem populations of Europe are far from being solely, even largely, the authors of antisemitic incidents, particularly those involving physical violence, which rose sharply across Europe in 2018 and have continued since. Adherents of far-right political parties or beliefs are largely responsible for the more serious attacks.[109]

A particularly horrific attack on two mosques in far-away New Zealand resulted in 49 deaths. Brenton Tarrant, charged with their murder, is a white supremacist whose self-appointed targets included Jews living outside Israel ('acceptable as long as they stay there [in Israel]'). The Anti-Defamation League draws a clear link between this ideology and the American Alt Right.

Brief Lives

4. Isaiah Berlin (1909-1997)

Isaac Wolfson gave his name and some of his fortune to found two colleges, one at Oxford and one at Cambridge. The moving spirit of the Oxford Wolfson College, and later its first president, was Isaiah Berlin.

Berlin was born in Riga, the only child of comfortably off, traditionally Jewish parents. In 1917, with the family now removed to Petrograd (later St Petersburg), he was a witness to the Russian revolution. Educated at home, he left with his family for the security of England in 1921, arriving with almost no spoken English. He adapted quickly, however, first to school and then to Oxford University, where he spent most of his career. After a First Class degree, Berlin was awarded a Prize Fellowship at All Souls College, only the third Jew to have been elected a fellow of any Oxford college, and the first to All Souls – making him, at 23, a member of the most exclusive club in English life, along with cabinet ministers and the leading intellectuals of the day. The next six years were the happiest of his life. He was free to read, to think and to develop his approach to philosophy – a liberal, distinctly un-Marxist, political philosophy, strongly influenced by his sense of what lay at the heart of the 'Englishness' he had come to love. This involved a decent respect for others, toleration of dissent and a belief that liberty is often to be preferred over mere efficiency.

In September 1939, Berlin immediately volunteered for the war effort. As a 'foreigner', however, he was rejected for any but the most humble positions. Salvation came with his appointment, early in 1941, to the New York office of the Ministry of Information. His job was to provide a weekly report on American public opinion, then mainly isolationist. Churchill was desperate for American involvement in the war; Berlin's work pitched him into the real world. He had to meet all kinds of people, including prominent Jews, from the Zionist leader Chaim Weizmann, to such assimilationists as Walter Lippmann, one of the most influential columnists of the day, and Arthur Hays Sulzberger, publisher of the *New York Times*. Weizmann became Berlin's hero, in contrast to the 'trembling, amateur Gentiles', as they were described by another eastern European Jewish academic, Lewis Namier.

In April, 1946, Berlin returned to Oxford. He had made a reputation in the outside world. Now it was time to get back to his real work. He found the 'one big thing' that was to dominate his work, and thereafter: the theme of freedom and its betrayal. In a series of lectures and essays he explored the distinction between negative and positive liberty.

Along the way, he was tempted successively by two of the great men of Zionism. Chaim Weizmann, shortly to be Israel's first president, invited him to be his chief of staff, and David Ben-Gurion, its first prime minister, offered him the directorship of the Israel Foreign Office. Berlin was deeply attached to what he called his 'tribe', and would always remain a friend of Zionism, albeit a critical one. While acknowledging 'that it might seem a kind of levity to choose Oxford in an hour of crisis for our own people', that was nevertheless what he chose. After nearly 30 years of anglicisation he would not have coped easily with the hard provincial realities of the new state. Moreover, he did enjoy the pleasures and opportunities of Oxford, and the steady flow of distinctions that accrued over the years. These included a knighthood in 1957 (suggested by a 'waspish' friend as being 'for services to conversation'), presidency of the British Academy, and membership of the Order of Merit (reserved for 24 living individuals whose unusual distinction had added greatly to the lustre of the nation), as well as numerous honorary degrees. Long before his death in 1997, he had become Britain's leading public intellectual, discoursing brilliantly on a very wide range of topics. Berlin had a wonderful ability both to expound conflicting points of view with remarkable clarity and to inform the discussion with his constant insistence on the need to tolerate dissent. His political philosophy is at the very heart of Western liberal thinking.[110]

Surprisingly, Berlin was never raised to the peerage as a member of the House of Lords. He would have enjoyed the ceremonial and ornamental aspects of that House, the political power of which has been progressively whittled away over the past century. (Nevertheless, the House of Lords does provide a useful source of expertise on many topics and sometimes serves as a check on the policies of the House of Commons.) The great majority of its members are peers for life, rather than hereditary aristocrats as in the past. Of its approximately 800 members, about seven percent are Jewish: 23 Labour, 18 Conservative and 16 'Cross Benchers' (belonging to neither main party). Many have risen from humble origins. One, Lord Alf Dubs, was a Kindertransport child.

Chapter Ten

Post-war Jewry: the US

Introduction

The United States emerged from the Second World War, in which it had first engaged with Nazi Germany and then with Japan, with a vastly enhanced role on the world stage. It was the only major combatant whose physical territory was unscathed by military action (apart from the initial attack on Pearl Harbour, which had precipitated America's entry into the war), although it lost several hundred thousand personnel. In addition to having total control over Japan, it was the senior Western partner in the takeover of Germany after its unconditional surrender. From then on, it would be impossible for any major initiative to take place without the central role of the United States, in the Far East, Europe, or the Middle East, where Britain had to surrender pre-eminence to the United States. This last point was of particular importance to American Jewry: not only was America now the key player in the reconstruction of Europe, but nothing could happen in the Middle East, either, without America's involvement. This meant that both in Western Europe and the Middle East, American Jewry played an important role.

Demography

By 1945 there were around 5 million American Jews by religion, perhaps 3 percent of the total population. Some 70 years later, in 2015, a major survey by the Pew organisation reported on the situation.[111] It found that about 4.2 million American adults said they were Jewish by religion, representing 1.8 percent of the US adult population. However, the figure was approximately 5.3 million (2.2 percent of the population) if the total also included 'Jews of no religion, a group of people who say they are atheist, agnostic or nothing in particular', when asked about their religion, but who were raised Jewish or have a Jewish parent, and who still consider themselves Jewish aside from religion.

Two other groups were not counted as Jews in the report: an additional 2.4 million adults in the 'Jewish background' category – that is, people who were raised Jewish or had at least one Jewish parent, but who now either identify with a religion other than Judaism (most are Christian) or say they do *not* think of themselves as Jewish, or partially Jewish, by religion or otherwise. In addition, there are about 1.2 million adults in the 'Jewish affinity' category – people who were not raised Jewish, do not have a Jewish parent, and are not Jewish by religion, but who nevertheless consider themselves Jewish in some sense.

According to the Pew survey, the respective shares of the major denominations within Judaism are: Reform, 35 percent; Conservative, 18 percent; Orthodox, 10 percent; other (such as Reconstructionist), 6 percent; no denomination, 30 percent. The trend over time is a move from Orthodox, to Conservative, to Reform, to no denomination. Within the Orthodox community, its younger members seem to be retained rather more than the older ones, who left in earlier decades. This is associated with full-time attendance at Jewish day schools – which are seen as expensive, so that attendance is a struggle for parents, particularly when there are several children in the family.

Estimating the number of Jewish children presents another challenge. About 1.8 million children live in a household with at least one Jewish adult (not necessarily a parent). Among those, roughly 900,000 are being raised exclusively Jewish by religion; 100,000 are being raised with no religion, but as Jewish aside from religion; and another 300,000 raised partly Jewish and partly in another religion. About 400,000 children are not being raised Jewish at all, despite living in a household with at least one Jewish adult. The Pew survey, cited above, was reviewed by Michael Lipka, a senior editor at the Pew Research Centre. It conveys a sense of an overall decline in the total number of US Jews, of a decrease in the total number of Jews by religious observance and of a community in flux.

Two main factors are responsible for the reduction in total size: intermarriage and a low birth rate; the Strictly Orthodox community is an exception to the general trend (as is the case in Britain). A national survey by the Council of Jewish Federations in 1990 found that 52 percent of the Jews who married between 1985 and 1990 married non-Jews (and another 5 percent married converts to Judaism). The exogamy rate climbed dramatically from decade to decade, from the comparatively low and stable level characteristic of the period before the 1960s.[112] Recent figures suggest a continuation of the trend. As indicated by the Pew data, the children of mixed marriages tend not be raised Jewish.

A survey by the Jewish Federation of Greater Washington found the intermarriage rate in the DC area to be about the same as it is nationwide – 44 percent of all Jews are married out, including about 60 percent of younger Jews. However, 61 percent of intermarried couples in and around DC are raising their children Jewish, as opposed to about a third of intermarried couples nationally.[113]

Three waves of post-war Jewish immigrants have somewhat counteracted the downward trend in the American Jewish population: European Holocaust survivors in the early post-war period; former Israelis (some rather briefly of that status, with Israel serving as a waystation), and Jews from Russia. In all, these three groups comprised well over a million people. (As it is now over 70 years since the arrival in America of the first group, those who still survive are likely to be very elderly.)

There are currently an estimated 200,000 Israelis in the US, though the figure is probably much higher. Between 1995 and 2016, about 150,000 Israelis became US citizens or legalised permanent residents.[114]

A significant number of Russian Jews preferred the United States to Israel when the exit barriers were lifted in the 1970s and 1990s. According to a survey by the American Jewish Committee[115] about 700,000 Russian-speaking Jews live in the United States. It found that the Russian-speaking Jewish immigrants of the 1970s and early 1980s integrated relatively quickly into American society because they were classified, for the most part, as refugees or the relatives of refugees. The immigrants of the 1990s, on the other hand, left home primarily because of economic collapse, the fear of possible pogroms and the disintegration of the state. Their number included large numbers of non-Western Jews, such as Bukharans and Georgians. In general, Russian Jews retain strong links with Russian-origin family members in Israel. Perhaps the most distinctive feature of Russian Jews in America is the emphasis they place on education, particularly in science and mathematics (likewise a major preoccupation among Russian Jews in Israel). Virtually all young Russian Jews who graduate from high school go to college. In fact, according to the AJC survey, Russian-speaking immigrants comprise the best educated group in US immigration history.

For Russian Jewish immigrants, as for former Israelis, Jewish identity is based less on religious belief or practice than an attachment to Israel. Only 6 percent of the Russian Jewish population consider religion 'very important' and another 35 percent 'somewhat important.' By contrast, 88 percent of those surveyed agree that caring about Israel is 'very important' for being a Jew.

Education

After the war, US army veterans took full advantage of the GI Bill of Rights to enter higher education in large numbers. Over the years, there was an increase in the proportion of Jews with both a first degree and then a second. At the present time, some 60 percent of American Jews have at least a first degree, and a half of those hold a postgraduate degree.[116] (However, it is striking that American Jews are only the second most educated religious group in America, after Hindus of whom 77 percent have a first degree.)

In the 1950s, an acceptance to America's "big three" universities (Harvard, Yale, and Princeton) was based solely on examination performance. Jews were admitted at record rates, and this led to a policy of limiting their number. In the wake of World War II, rank antisemitism waned, but institutional imperatives, primarily the need to keep alumni happy, meant that Jews still found it hard to gain admission to the big three. The differing acceptance rates for students from the best big-city public high schools, who tended to be Jewish, and for students from exclusive private schools, who tended not to be, illustrates the continuing difficulties. For example, from 1950 to 1954, Yale enrolled just seven students from the heavily Jewish Bronx High School of Science, one of the nation's top performing schools. During that same period, Yale took in 275 students from a single prep school, Philips Academy Andover.

At all three universities, the preference for private school graduates continued into the 1960s, even though admissions directors knew the public-school graduates performed better once in college.

A Cold War-inspired pressure to excel in the sciences, legislative moves to outlaw discrimination, and the changing cultural environment of the 1960s, finally loosened the Protestant establishment's grip on the big three. At Yale, a new admissions director, with the support of the president of Yale, determined that scholastic excellence would be the primary criterion for admission. The proportion of Jews rose from one-tenth to one-third within one year. Co-education and a greater enrolment of racial minorities have also made the big three more diverse institutions, although the preference for alumni children, athletes and even certain private school graduates has continued. Overall, enrolment increased.[117]

At the present time there are estimated to be 350,000 Jewish students in American universities – and about 10 percent of faculty members are Jewish. The numbers seem to be even higher in medical schools. Whereas the proportion of PhD students who are Jewish males peaked around the middle 1960s and has since declined, the picture for women is rather different, with a continuous rise to the present time. This may be associated with male students leaving the humanities and social sciences in favour of STEM (science, technology, engineering and maths) subjects in which female students are under- represented, as compared with the humanities and social sciences, in which a PhD at the present time seems to be a prerequisite for university employment. It is certainly possible to obtain a non-university job in one of the STEM subjects with only a first degree, for example in the rapidly burgeoning high-tech field. It may be that in the US, as in European countries, men are more motivated by financial considerations than are women. Jobs with tech companies tend to be relatively short-term and subject to renewal – but this is also the position in the universities, where tenure, for the majority of university teachers, is a distant prospect, with the reality a succession of short-term appointments, and not very well paid at that. They can be seen as a contemporary version of the wandering scholars of mediaeval Europe.

Occupations

In the post-war years, as in Europe, American Jews left the proletarian, labouring classes as the generation of immigrants from Eastern European died off. Instead, Jews moved into professional and managerial occupations. The increase in the number of Jewish doctors and lawyers was not surprising – these were the traditional Jewish occupations. What was less expected was the expanding number of Jews working in organised and institutional professional life, not only in college faculties, but also in government bureaucracies, as state and private school teachers and as engineers and accountants for industrial firms. The number of Jewish managers, executives, officials and independent proprietors also increased. This last group was now less likely to be in distinctively Jewish trades. Instead, they established themselves in construction, rapid transit, real estate, transportation and communications.[118] The trend has continued more recently, so that Jews are less concentrated in the previous big city locations, and instead spread more widely across the country. They are more likely to be found in the full range of occupations, except for unskilled and semi-skilled manual work. The pattern, clearly evident among Russian immigrants, is that once a family has made it into the middle class, this is seen as a launching pad for even further progress by the next generation.

Cultural Life

As in the pre-war years and continuing to the present day, American Jews are major patrons of the arts both as audiences and as donors.

The novels of Philip Roth (long expected to win the Literature Nobel, but who died in June 2018), Bernard Malamud, and particularly Saul Bellow, have long been in the first rank of American literary achievement; they have been joined by several of the younger generation, such as Jonathan Franzen, Jonathan Safran Foer and Nicole Krause. Major post-war American playwrights are headed by Arthur Miller and include David Mamet, Neil Simon and Tony Kushner. For sheer productivity, as well as quality, Woody Allen, Steven Spielberg, the Coen brothers and Billy Wilder, among several others, rank very high among film makers. In musical theatre, the lyrics of Stephen Sondheim are probably pre-eminent on Broadway.

Antisemitism

Amid the glittering prizes, antisemitism – often disguised in accusations of dual loyalties, or claims to be anti-Zionist, not anti-Jewish – has rarely been very far from Diaspora Jewish life. This has also been true, at least intermittently, of America. Regarding the dual loyalty issue, on one side are the vital interests of the United States itself, as interpreted by the government of the day. The other, over the years, has taken two forms: one is loyalty to the Soviet Union, or at least to the ideal of a better world, as represented by the Soviet Union, and the other, loyalty to Israel. From the time the Soviet Revolution of October 1917, led by Lenin, the Soviets made considerable use of admirers in other countries – described by Lenin himself as 'useful idiots'. They were either overt members of the local Communist Party, for example, of the United States, or else active sympathisers, known as 'fellow travellers', or covert assets, operating under cover. Idealistic Americans, both Jews and non-Jews, responded to clever Soviet propaganda, which negated the evidence of the ruthlessness of the Soviet Union's leadership, both in causing the deaths of millions of Soviet citizens, by draconian internal policies, and in single-mindedly advancing the interests of that country, rather than the pursuit of a better world, benefiting all citizens.

In the immediate post-war period the Soviet Union sought to obtain American atomic weapons secrets, sometimes through financial inducements, at other times through the actions of high-minded individuals with no pecuniary motive, but a deeply held belief that the Soviet Union acted not only in its own interests, but in those of oppressed people everywhere.

The accusation of loyalty to Israel, rather than to the United States, is well represented by a talk on October 10, 1976, by General George S. Brown, Chairman of the Joint Chiefs of Staff, at Duke University Law School. His antisemitic remarks were taped by a student and published by the *Washington Post*. Brown spoke about Jewish influence in the United States and said: "It's so strong you wouldn't believe it... We have the Israelis coming to us for equipment. We say we can't possibly get the Congress to support a program like that. They say, don't worry about Congress. We'll take care of the Congress. Now this is somebody from another country, but they can. They own, you know, large banks in this country, the newspapers, you just look at where the Jewish money is in this country."[119] (Four decades on, Israel is one of a number of countries in receipt of American military aid to the tune of several billion dollars a year, and there is a very close collaboration between Israel and the United States in the development of weapons, the mutually beneficial sharing of intelligence, and the advancement of international policies in the interests of both countries.)

The Pollard Affair, which began 35 years ago in a very different world of US-Israeli relationships, exemplified that world.[120] Jonathan Pollard, who served as a civilian intelligence analyst for the US Navy, was arrested by the FBI on November 21, 1985, together with his wife, and charged with providing a contact at the Israeli Embassy in Washington with classified security information involving scientific, technical and military data; specifically, intelligence information on Arab and Soviet weapons development. This took place over the course of a year and a half, in exchange for $45,000.

In June 1986, Pollard and his wife pleaded guilty to all charges, with the understanding that the plea bargain and their cooperation with the United States Justice Department would result in a reduced sentence. Nevertheless, in March 1987 Pollard received a life term in a US federal prison and his wife was sentenced to five years, also in a US federal prison, as an accessory.

In defence of his actions, Pollard declared that he committed espionage only because 'the American intelligence establishment collectively endangered Israel's security by withholding crucial information'. Israeli officials, American-Israeli activist groups, and some American politicians, who saw his punishment as unfair, lobbied for the reduction or commutation of his sentence. The Israeli government acknowledged a portion of its role in Pollard's espionage in 1987, and issued a formal apology to the US; but did not admit to paying him until 1998. Over the course of his imprisonment, Israel made repeated, unsuccessful attempts, through both official and unofficial channels, to secure his release. He was granted Israeli citizenship in 1995.

Opposing any form of clemency were many active and retired US officials, including Donald Rumsfeld, Dick Cheney, former CIA director George Tenet; several former US secretaries of defence; a bipartisan group of US congressional leaders; and members of the American intelligence community. They maintained that the damage to US national security, due to Pollard's espionage, was far more severe, wide-ranging, and enduring than publicly acknowledged. Though Pollard argued that he only supplied Israel with information critical to its security, opponents pointed out that he had no way of knowing what the Israelis had received through legitimate exchanges, and much of the data he compromised had nothing to do with Israeli security. Pollard revealed aspects of the American intelligence gathering process, its 'sources and methods'. He sold numerous closely guarded state secrets, including the National Security Agency's ten-volume manual on how the US gathers its signal intelligence, and disclosed the names of thousands of people who had cooperated with US intelligence agencies. While Benjamin Netanyahu argued that Pollard worked exclusively for Israel, Pollard himself admitted marketing his services – successfully, in some cases – to other countries. Pollard was released on November 20, 2015, in accordance with federal guidelines in place at the time of his sentencing.

In October 2017, Dennis Ross, a retired senior US foreign service officer, revisited the dual loyalties issue in an opinion piece in the *New York Times*[121]. He began by referring to 'the former CIA officer Valerie Plame Wilson' who, in her twitter account on the first day of Rosh Hashana, 2017, shared an article that said "America's Jews are driving America's wars: shouldn't they recuse themselves when dealing with the Middle East?"

Ross stated that she was repeating the well-worn narrative that Jewish neo- conservatives promoted the invasion of Iraq – and were beating the drum for a conflict with Iran. He went on to point out that 'of course most Jews are not neo-conservatives, and most neo-conservatives are not Jewish'. It was, he said, two influential non-Jews – Vice President Dick Cheney and Secretary of Defence Donald Rumsfeld – who played the central role, with President Bush, in deciding to invade Iraq in 2003. He then recalled memories of how Jews were long perceived within the national security apparatus. 'When I began working in the Pentagon during President Jimmy Carter's administration, there was an unspoken but unmistakable assumption: if you were Jewish, you could not work on the Middle East because you would be biased. Under later secretaries of state, the presumption of Jewish bias was no longer made, and being Jewish was no longer a disqualification from working on Arab-Israeli issues.'

Nevertheless, Ross recounted a personal experience of being asked by an investigator making background checks on a person under consideration for a position: If this person had to choose between America's interests and Israel's, whose interests would be put first? Ross realised that there was nothing subtle about this presumption of dual loyalty. "Why would you ask that question? I asked... He answered. Because he is Jewish". Ross asked: "If the person of interest was Irish and had to work on problems related to Ireland, or if he was Italian and had to work on Italy, would you ask that question... he suddenly realised that I was Jewish. And at that point he changed the subject.... The idea that Jewish Americans might have dual loyalties was not challenged or questioned, it was assumed... It is the definition of prejudice. How can it not be when you label a whole group and ascribe to all those who are part of it, a particular negative trait or threatening behaviour? It is the same today with those who single out all Moslems as dangerous extremists. It is just as unacceptable".

Charlottesville

The report in *Time*[122], was terse but clear: Clashes broke out between white nationalists and counter protesters; the 'Unite the Right' rally at a park once named for Confederate General Robert E Lee, was deemed unlawful... A vehicle drove into the crowd of counter- protesters marching through the downtown area before speeding away, resulting in one death and leaving more than a dozen others injured... President Trump addressed the violence in televised remarks, condemning "A display of hatred, bigotry and violence on many sides" and calling for a swift restoration of law and order... Senator Ron Wyden of Oregon stated: "What happened in Charlottesville is domestic terrorism... The President's words only serve as cover for heinous acts". The night before Saturday's violence, hundreds of white nationalists marched through the University of Virginia campus while carrying burning torches.

The Alt Right (Alternative Right): a recent cause for concern

The Charlottesville violence falls under the general heading of Alt Right. According to the Anti-Defamation League CEO, Jonathan Greenblatt, in an appearance on MSNBC, "People who identify with the Alt Right regard mainstream or traditional conservatives as weak and impotent, mainly because they do not sufficiently support racism and antisemitism.... Though not every person who identifies with the Alt Right is a white supremacist, most are, and 'white identity' is central to people in this milieu. In fact, Alt Righters reject modern conservatism, explicitly, because they believe that mainstream conservatives are not advocating for the interests of white people as a group. However they define themselves, Alt Righters reject egalitarianism, democracy, universalism and multiculturalism. A number of Alt Righters are also blatantly antisemitic and blame Jews for allegedly promoting anti-white policies such as immigration and diversity. Alt Righters mock conservative support of Israel as anti-white".

According to Greenblatt: "The number of people who identify with the Alt Right is growing... It has a loud presence online. The intellectual racists who identify as part of the Alt Right also run a growing number of publications and publishing houses that promote white supremacist ideas. Their goal is to influence mainstream whites by exposing them to the concepts of white identity and racial consciousness".

The Anti -Defamation League (ADL)
Founded in October 1913, the ADL is an international Jewish non-governmental organisation based in the United States. It states that it 'fights anti-Semitism and all forms of bigotry, defends democratic ideals, and protects civil rights for all', doing so through 'information, education, legislation, and advocacy'. The ADL has 29 offices in the United States and three in other countries, with its headquarters located in New York City. Abraham Foxman was its national director since 1987. In July 2015, Jonathan Greenblatt succeeded him.

Of all the countries surveyed in the Global Pew survey of antisemitism, described earlier, the results for the United States were among the least unfavourable towards Jews, as well as having among the lowest Index Scores; very unusually, this was true both for the Moslem and for the general population. They may indicate a relatively successful current outcome of many decades of work by the ADL. Nevertheless, the statement 'Jews are more loyal to Israel than to this country' evinced 'probably true' responses from 33 percent of the US general population, by far the most believed stereotype in the United States sample.

Ascending the Heights: American Jewish achievements in Public Service and in the Private Sector.

The Supreme Court has nine associate justices; in 2018 three of them were Jewish: Ruth Bader Ginsburg (deceased in late 2020), Elena Kagan and Stephen Breyer.

Both the recently retired Chairman of the US Federal Reserve (Janet Yellen) and her predecessor (Ben Bernanke) were Jewish, as was the vice-chairman of the Federal Reserve Bank, Stanley Fischer, who retired in September 2017.

In the Congressional Elections of 2020-22 there were, overall, 9 Jewish Senators, out of the 100 members (all Democrats, or allies) and 27 members of the House of Representatives, 25 Democrats and 2 Republicans, out of the 435 members. These numbers are about three times the Jewish share of the general population. It is also of note that the minority leaders of both components of Congress were Jewish: Diane Feinstein in the House and Charles Schumer in the Senate.

The top 10 names in the US Forbes rich list for 2020 include three Jews: Larry Ellison (Oracle) at number four; Mark Zuckerberg (Facebook) at number five; and at 10, Larry Page (Google; his co-founder and co-owner, Sergei Brin, is at 11). All three are in the information technology software or hardware fields. Two of them: Zuckerberg (age under 40) and Page (under 50) are much the youngest of the top ten.

Michael Bloomberg (currently out of the top 10) is of particular note among the Forbes billionaire listing, being both highly successful in the private sector and very active in public service, having been mayor of New York for a decade.

George Soros, a Holocaust survivor, is an intriguing combination of extreme wealth and a lifetime involvement in liberal causes. He is both one of the world's most successful investors (as of 2020, he ranked among the 30 richest people in the world) and also a well-known supporter of American and European progressive and liberal political causes. He dispenses his largesse through his Open Society Foundations. Between 1979 and 2011, Soros donated more than $11 billion to various philanthropic causes. By 2017, his donations on 'civil initiatives to reduce poverty and increase transparency', and on scholarships and universities around the world, totalled $12 billion. He played a significant role in the peaceful transition from communism to capitalism in Eastern Europe in the late 1980s and early 1990s, and provided one of Europe's largest higher educational endowments, to the Central European University (its President, Michael Ignatieff, is a distinguished Canadian former Liberal politician), based in his home town. (In 2018 the CEU was expelled from Hungary by order of its right-wing government).

Born in Budapest in 1930, he survived Nazi-occupied Hungary and emigrated to England in 1947, beginning his business career, after degrees in philosophy at the London School of Economics, by taking various jobs with merchant banks in England and then the United States, before starting his first hedge fund in 1969. In October, 2017, he transferred about $18 billion, the bulk of his estimated fortune, to his Open Society Foundations, making them the second largest philanthropic grant-making group in the United States. (Only the Bill and Melinda Gates Foundation is currently larger.) Now aged 90 (2020), Soros's life-long work will be continued by the Open Society Foundations, with which his children are closely involved. In 2018 the *Financial Times* named Soros 'person of the year' for 'the values he represents'.

US Jewry and Israel: A selection of organisations

AIPAC
The American Israel Public Affairs Committee is a lobbying group that advocates pro- Israel policies to the Congress and Executive Branch of the US. It states that it has more than 100,000 members, 17 regional offices, and 'a vast pool of donors'. AIPAC is one of the most effective lobbying groups in

the United States (though it probably pales in comparison with the NRA).

Its critics have charged that it acts as an agent of the Israeli government with a 'stranglehold 'on the Congress. It has also been accused of 'being strongly allied with the Likud party of Israel, and the Republican Party in the US.' It is reasonable to conclude that AIPAC has the support of the overwhelming majority of Republican Jews – but they are in the minority of American Jewry, which is heavily Democratic. However, AIPAC's yearly policy conferences are addressed by leading figures from both major parties.

J Street.

A liberal advocacy group based in the United States, its stated aim is to promote American leadership to end the Arab-Israeli and Israeli-Palestinian conflict peacefully and diplomatically. J Street describes itself as 'the political home for pro-Israel, pro-peace Americans who want Israel to be secure, democratic and the national home of the Jewish people... advocating policies that advance shared US and Israeli interests, as well as Jewish and democratic values, leading to a two-state solution to the Israeli Palestinian conflict'. It would be fair to characterise J Street as being close to the moderate left of Israeli politics. It will be more prominent during the Biden than in the Trump administration.

Jewish Voice for Peace.

JVP is a left-wing activist organization in the US, focused on the Israeli-Palestinian conflict. It describes itself as 'a diverse and democratic community of activists, inspired by Jewish tradition to work together for peace, social justice and human rights... [It] supports the aspirations of Israelis and Palestinians for security and self-determination and seeks an end to the Israeli occupation of the West Bank, Gaza Strip, and East Jerusalem'. Its critics say 'it musters Jewish opposition to, and works to undermine, public support for Israel'.

Boycott, Divestment and Sanctions (BDS)

This is a global campaign to increase economic and political pressure on Israel to end what it describes as violations of international law. The stated goals of BDS: the end of Israel's occupation and settler colonisation of Palestinian land and the Golan Heights, full equality for Arab Palestinian citizens of Israel, and acknowledgement of the right of return of Palestinian refugees. (While BDS is an international organisation, its activities in the US have achieved the most publicity, particularly on American campuses and via American pop artists and so it is appropriate to consider it here.)

Supporters of BDS compare the movement with the 20th-century anti-apartheid campaign and view their actions as similar to the boycott of South Africa during its apartheid era, comparing the situation in Israel to apartheid. In response, critics of BDS vehemently repudiate the charge that Israel is an apartheid state, pointing out that outside of the West Bank – in Israel proper – Jews and Arabs mix reasonably freely, particularly at university level, Israeli Arabs have full voting rights to the Knesset and work together in the same settings, for example in hospitals.

As to the effectiveness of BDS, its activists cannot be criticized for lack of effort, but thus far achievements have been meagre: a number of pop artists have withdrawn from Israeli venues, but few Israeli academics have been barred by overseas conferences; investors at all levels, from governments to private individuals, have rarely divested for political, as opposed to commercial, reasons, and joint research projects between Israel, the EU and the US are thriving. Whatever the emotional appeal of the BDS movement to some, its practical impact has been miniscule, a conclusion driven home by a July 2019 (non-binding) resolution condemning BDS, which was passed by the US House of Representatives by 398 votes to 17.

US and Israeli Jewries: Quantitative data

A Pew survey published in June 2018,[123] illustrates the divide between American and Israeli Jews on issues ranging from the US embassy move to Jerusalem to egalitarian prayer at the Western Wall. The survey, conducted in April and May that year, was based on a representative sample of 1,000 Israeli Jews and 1,001 American Jews. Significantly, that year's big annual American Jewish Committee conference was held in Israel for the first time in its 112-year history. During previous decades the AJC was distinctly anti-Zionist.

The majority of the sample identified with the Democratic party, voted for Hillary Clinton and are less identified with the Jewish people and more favourable to religious pluralism, than the minority who are Republicans and report that they voted for Donald Trump. There was little change in future voting intentions. (A finding of particular interest to the US Jewish community was that 55 percent of the sample said that the status of Jews in United States is less secure now than it was a year ago.)

American Jews are much more disturbed than their Israeli counterparts by the Orthodox monopoly on religious life in Israel. For example, whereas 80 percent of American Jews support having non-Orthodox rabbis perform weddings, divorces and conversions in Israel, slightly under a half of Israeli Jews support non-Orthodox rabbis doing so. Whereas only a small majority of Israelis – 55 percent – support the introduction of civil marriage and divorce in Israel, among American Jews, support is overwhelming, with 81 percent saying they favour such a move; and while almost three-quarters of American Jews support the plan to establish a mixed gender prayer space at Jerusalem's Western Wall, Israelis are split on the matter, almost equally. (An increasing proportion of Israeli Jews circumvent the rabbinical monopoly on marriage and divorce by marrying outside the country.)

On the question of the establishment of a Palestinian state there was a relatively small difference: 51 percent of American Jews favoured such a development, as opposed to 44 percent of Israelis. While 44 percent of American Jews said they would be willing to evacuate some of the settlements, the proportion of Israeli Jews was 35 percent.

A large majority in both communities (78 percent of Israeli Jews and 69 percent of American Jews) agreed that a thriving Diaspora is important for the long-term future of the Jewish people. An even larger majority (79 percent of American Jews and 87 percent of Israeli Jews) agreed that a thriving State of Israel is vital for the long-term future of the Jewish people. Two-thirds of American Jews said they regarded Israeli Jews as part of their family, while an even greater share of Israeli Jews – 78percent – said they viewed American Jews as part of their family.

However, a more recent Pew poll[124] gave rise to much concern in Israel's liberal media. While 64 percent of the 10,000 Jewish respondents had a favourable view of Israelis as a people, only 41 percent had that view of the government of Benjamin Netanyahu. The disparity was much greater among Democratic voters (34 percent) than among Republicans. Younger Democrats were even more negative about the Netanyahu-led government than the older generation. A positive view of Israel, irrespective of the Israeli party in power, political affiliation and age, has been a constant among American Jews for decades; this is in the process of change.

Brief Lives

5. Julius Robert Oppenheimer (1904-1967)

Oppenheimer – always called Robert rather than the more foreign sounding Julius – was born in New York to German Jewish immigrant parents. The home was wealthy and cultivated. As a Harvard undergraduate, he excelled in the classics, physics and chemistry, wrote poetry and studied Oriental Philosophy. Next came Oxford, where he worked with the great Lord Rutherford, a pioneer in the study of atomic structure, and then Gottingen, where he received his doctorate. He was soon part of an international collaboration of scores of scientists pursuing the great questions of atomic physics, in which national interest was scarcely involved. For some years he taught physics at Berkeley and the California Institute of

Technology. Oppenheimer trained and was the intellectual leader of a generation of American physicists. In the 1930s he became interested in politics, much affected by the rise of Nazism in Germany and the Spanish Civil War – in which he sided with the Republic, as did many young American intellectuals, whose sympathies were with the left in general. His political associations and contacts at this time came back to haunt him in the McCarthy years, when he was investigated for treason in his conduct of the Manhattan Project.

Oppenheimer was appointed Scientific Director of the Project, and brilliantly orchestrated a huge team of physicists and mathematicians – native British and American as well as emigré Jewish. Many of them were conspicuously eccentric and some, like Edward Teller, had high aspirations of their own. It was Teller, a Jewish refugee from Hungary and viscerally anti-Communist, who was to be Oppenheimer's nemesis.

The Manhattan team was racing to complete the bomb for possible use against Germany, still thought to be working on its own version. The many Jews in the project, including Oppenheimer, were additionally concerned about the safety of their European brethren, and hoped that their work on the bomb would shorten the war. The common imperative was to develop and test a bomb before Germany did so. In the event, the European war ended before the successful test in New Mexico, and attention switched to the war still raging in the Pacific. The American Administration, by now headed by Harry Truman, sought unconditional surrender from the Japanese, along the lines of that imposed on Germany. The Japanese were adamant in their refusal; without some dramatic new development, the war of attrition would have continued for a year to 18 months with huge losses on both sides. In August 1945, a few days after a second bomb was dropped, Japan surrendered on American terms.

Oppenheimer, then at the height of his career, was appointed Chairman of the Advisory Committee of the Atomic Energy Commission – in effect, the most important scientist in the West and a key player in the rapidly heating Cold War with the Soviet Union. But he opposed the development of the next generation of nuclear weapons – the hydrogen bomb – the particular project of Edward Teller that was strongly favoured by the US military as likely to confer a crucial advantage over the Soviets. Oppenheimer was inclined to some sort of sharing of atomic secrets with the Russians, so as to avoid a race which he saw as being catastrophic for both sides. He had in fact been under surveillance by the FBI as early as 1943 on account of his pre-war leftist sympathies. The cloud of suspicion thickened, and in 1953 he was accused of having associated with Communists in the past, of delaying the naming of Soviet agents (one of the Manhattan team had confessed under British interrogation to passing atomic secrets to the Russians) and of opposing the building of the hydrogen bomb. In the McCarthyite atmosphere of the time, a security hearing found him not guilty of treason but ruled that he should no longer have access to military secrets, and he was removed from his post with the Atomic Energy Commission. Oppenheimer became the international symbol of the scientist who is racked by moral doubts about the consequences of his work and becomes the victim of a witch-hunt carried out by lesser and less complex men. But he retained his headship of the Institute for Advanced Study at Princeton, to which he had been appointed in 1947, and in 1963 he was, in effect, 'pardoned' when President Johnson presented him with the Enrico Fermi Award of the Atomic Energy Commission. He retired from Princeton in 1966 and died from throat cancer a year later.

Oppenheimer was a loyal American, and certainly no agent of the Soviet Union. But like many Jews he believed in 'universal values' and the possibility of a better life for all of humankind, in a world in which national boundaries would cease to matter. His misfortune was to occupy a crucial position at the centre of an America that, in only a decade, had moved from pre-war isolationism to being fully engaged in a deadly rivalry with another superpower. Physics – together with many other areas of science – was no longer marked by a free exchange between colleagues, as in his youth, but had become locked behind jealously guarded national boundaries. This was, and is, the world of Edward Teller and not that of Robert Oppenheimer.

6. Leonard Bernstein (1918-1990)

Born Louis (he changed his name to Leonard in his teen years) to entrepreneurial immigrant parents, he was expected to follow them into the family business, but he had different ideas. According to an extensive account in *The Economist*[125] he was a man whose broad achievements are unique in musical history; a conductor whose interpretive gifts over the course of half a century shone light on the classics from Haydn to Mahler, Bartok to Stravinsky; a composer, not just of Broadway masterpieces like *West Side Story*, but ballet, opera and chamber music, comprising orchestral, instrumental, choral and vocal works ('Bernstein's own music is eclectic... ingeniously uniting disparate musical elements and [forging] a path for future musical mixologists that would have been unthinkable without him'); and a fine concert pianist and pioneering broadcaster.

The Bernstein legend was forged on November 14, 1943 when the 25-year-old was woken by a morning phone call requesting that he replace the indisposed maestro Bruno Walter in a major concert that afternoon. It was to be a live, nationwide radio broadcast with the New York Philharmonic (Bernstein was two months into a gig as assistant conductor), featuring a formidable programme that included Schumann, Strauss and Wagner. Ahead of the hundredth anniversary of his birth, the Philadelphia National Museum of American Jewish History celebrated the Jewish musician – he always associated himself with his people.

In November 1948, Bernstein toured Israel during its War of Independence to perform and conduct a series of concerts with the Israel Philharmonic. Even earlier, in 1947, he led the then Palestine Philharmonic in a series of nine concerts. Over the years he conducted the Israel Philharmonic in 25 different seasons, including in the US and Europe. He also brought the New York Philharmonic to Israel. At the fall of the Berlin Wall in 1989, he conducted a concert of Beethoven's Ninth Symphony, replacing the word "joy" with "freedom"; it became known indelibly as the Berlin Freedom Symphony.

7. Saul Bellow (1915-2005)

When Bellow died, *The Economist* obituarist began[126] with an ode to his appearance: 'Bellow's trouser creases were blade sharp, his fingernails sheened, the brim of his fedora tipped just so'. It was a long way from his childhood in an impoverished polyglot suburb of Montreal, to which his parents had emigrated from Russia in 1913. Nine years later they moved on to Chicago, where he lived for most of his life, hugely enjoying the cranks, crooks and wide boys of that city. His childhood was trilingual: English, Yiddish and French. Hebrew was for prayer and Talmudic study (his very pious mother wanted him to be a scholar or a rabbi). He read widely: the Old and New Testaments, Shakespeare, the great 19th-century Russians.

Bellow graduated in anthropology and sociology at North Western University. (On the advice, intended to be friendly, of the chairman of the English Department, he had abandoned his plans to study that language: "no Jew could really grasp the tradition of English literature"). After a stint of teaching and working for the Encyclopaedia Britannica, he served in the US Merchant Marine in the last year of the war, having earlier been rejected for military service on health grounds. While in the Marine he wrote his first novel *Dangling Man* (1944). Edmund Wilson hailed it as 'one of the most honest pieces of testimony on the psychology of a whole generation'; and it was lauded by the *New York Times* 'as an imaginative journal, set against fresh and vivid scenes in Chicago.' Bellow was launched, but combined his writing career over the next 55 years with teaching university literature courses.

Bellow's protagonists live in settings that are much less than noble, but they have inner lives of romantic aspiration – rather like Chandler's hero, Philip Marlowe. Many of the central characters of his 13 novels are Jewish: *The Adventures of Augie March* is a picaresque novel about a Jewish boy from Chicago during the depression of the 1930s; the hero of *Herzog* is an endlessly ruminating Jewish professor struggling comically, but futilely, to relate in a humane way to a dehumanised world; Bellow's own growing aversion to the liberal establishment underpins *Mr Sammler's Planet,* in which an elderly Polish Holocaust survivor surveys, with his one good eye, a world of pickpockets, student revolutionaries and an ill-mannered younger generation.

The interior monologues of Bellow's protagonists range from the sublime to the absurd. But the external, real world, peopled by incorrigibly practical people, is never far away. He combines the refined, cerebral delicacy and intellectual sophistication of Henry James with the exuberance of Damon Runyon, delighting in his imaginary Broadway and its gallery of ticket scalpers, horse players and minor and major criminals. Henry James – the 'great American novelist' of the 19th century, as Bellow was of the 20th – would not have been amused. *The Economist* wrote '10 years before Mr Bellow was born, Henry James returned to New York [after many years in Europe], and heard 'the hard glitter of Israel' in the street chatter of the Lower East Side. He was revolted at having to share the sanctity of his American consciousness, the intimacy of his American patriotism with the inconceivable alien'.

Was Bellow a 'Jewish' novelist? He liked to say he was an American novelist who happened to be a Jew. But he also said that his Jewish heritage was a 'gift, a piece of good fortune with which one does not quarrel'. And he was a fairly early translator from Yiddish into English of work by I.B Singer, who in 1978, two years after Bellow, was awarded the Nobel Prize in Literature. He took issue with Sartre's view of 'the great value conferred on the Jews by their suffering, by their heritage of permanent persecution, which is infinitely precious'. As a result, claimed Sartre, 'the State of Israel must set an example; we have to demand more from the state than from others'. Bellow demolishes Sartre's thesis. In Israel, he visited his 'Riga cousins... who have known arrest, deportation, massacre and war, and are glad to lead ordinary lives'. In all, Bellow, almost a first-generation North American, had the same wry affection for his 'tribe' as Berlin, a first - generation Englishman.

Saul Bellow died in 2005, in his 90th year. He had three sons from his first four marriages and, from his fifth, a daughter, born in 1999.

No fewer than three American Jews have won the Nobel Prize in Literature, most recently, Bob Dylan, (although his prize evoked considerable controversy, surrounding both his merit and the dilatory and churlish manner of his acceptance).
Isaac Bashevis Singer did not move to the United States until he was 35, and wrote only in Yiddish.

Chapter Eleven

Palestine and Israel, 'the hinge of fate': May 8th, 1945 to mid-April 1949

Introduction

The Yishuv had spent the war years largely in spectator mode, looking on with helpless horror at the fate of European Jewry. Until the British 8th Army's victory over the German Afrika Korps at the battle of El Alamein in October 1942, followed by a complete German retreat from Africa, they had faced the prospect, for at least the preceding year, of being overwhelmed by the seemingly invincible German forces (commanded by Rommel), so adding the 550,000 members of the Yishuv to the rest of the Holocaust victims. In sharp contrast, the Egyptian military and royalty, resentful of British suzerainty, were awaiting a German victory with a degree of pleasurable anticipation. 'In Alexandria shopkeepers had their Hitler and Mussolini pictures ready and Axis bunting hanging outside their shops… Anwar Sadat helped draft a treaty between Germany and a group of nationalist officers in the Egyptian army. In return for independence, Sadat's men offered full support in a drive to rid the Middle East of the British forever. The document… was put in an aircraft and flown west by another anti-British nationalist. Sadly, for them, Rommel's men shot it down'.[127]

Many thousands in the Yishuv served in the British forces, acquiring significant skills and experience. The conflict with the British had been largely suspended for the duration of the war; at its end there was a resumption of the struggle both with the British and with the Arabs of Palestine. For the next three years Palestine saw a complex four-sided conflict: the Yishuv against the British; the Yishuv divided against itself; the Yishuv against the Arabs of Palestine; intra-Arab deadly rivalry. The vote on the partition of Palestine in the UN General Assembly on November 29, 1947 was, for the Zionist Movement, the most important political event since the Balfour Declaration of 1917 and had even more far-reaching effects.

This chapter's heading borrows Churchill's term, 'The Hinge of Fate', to denote the period between the Allied victory in Europe and the November 1947 UN vote for partition (and the civil war between the Jews and Arabs of Palestine that immediately followed). The signing of armistice agreements, by mid-April 1949, with the surrounding Arab states that had attacked the new State of Israel (declared on May 15th 1948) as the British left, ended – albeit temporarily – the conflict with those states, with Israel in the ascendant. Conversely, with an Arab victory (forecast not only by the Arab leadership but by outside military experts), the whole Zionist enterprise could (indeed would) have been terminated, or severely set back. An understanding of the nearly four-year period from May 8, 1945 (VE Day) to mid-April 1949, requires a summary of the main events and the leading players, both national and individual.

Britain at the end of the World War
The leading historian of 'Imperial overstretch', Paul Kennedy, asserted: 'In securing a victorious outcome to the war, the British had severely overstrained themselves, running down their gold and dollar reserves, wearing out their domestic machinery, and (despite an extraordinary mobilisation of their resources and population) becoming increasingly dependent upon American munitions, shipping, foodstuffs and other supplies to stay in the fighting.'[128]

Peter Hennessy, historian of post-war Britain, commented: 'We were, in short, morally magnificent but economically bankrupt, as became brutally apparent, eight days after the ceasefire in the Far East, when President Truman severed the economic lifeline of lend lease without warning.[129] Moreover India, the 'jewel in the crown' of the still intact British Empire, was actively seeking independence. It was in that context that Britain, now under a Labour government with an overwhelming majority, and committed to a far-reaching and costly programme of internal British change, contemplated the burden of the Mandate of Palestine.

Britain and the Jews of Palestine

The British Prime Minister, Clement Attlee, was from a conventional upper-middle-class background: public school and Oxbridge. His Foreign Secretary, Ernest Bevin, came from a very different world, the heart of the manual working class. He had left school early, entered trade union politics, and became General Secretary of the Transport and General Workers Union, the incarnation of organised labour. Until he became Minister of Labour in Churchill's wartime government in 1940, in his 60th year, he never held a ministerial post, never sat in Parliament, and had not even been a member of the National Executive of the Labour Party. But from May 1940 until his death in April 1951 he was to remain in office through one of the most eventful periods in British history and to play a part in these events, second only to that of the two prime ministers, Churchill and Attlee. An extraordinary transformation for a man who began his working life carting mineral water around the suburbs of Bristol. He became a quite outstanding wartime Minister of Labour, not a far cry from his trade union background, but his appointment as Foreign Secretary in 1945 catapulted him into a very different world, one in which his predecessor, Anthony Eden (Eton, a Double First from Oxford, an accomplished linguist) was totally at home. Yet Bevin played a major part in constructing the post-war international world and its institutions.

When it came to Palestine and the Jews, however, he shared the view of Prime Minister Attlee and the Foreign Office officials: stick to the White Paper (of 1939) even if it is unworkable, and regard the Jewish survivors of the Holocaust as no different from other Europeans who had been through the war. Attlee and Bevin thought that the Jews were 'pushing to the head of the queue', and indeed, should be prepared to return to their European countries of origin, rather than seeking entry to Palestine. The dominant official view of the Foreign Office was well illustrated by a note written by a senior official, Armine Dew: 'in my opinion a disproportionate amount of the time of this office is wasted in dealing with these wailing Jews' (September 1, 1944). Connor Cruise O' Brien suggested: 'people who disliked the Jews before the Holocaust generally didn't dislike them any the less because of the Holocaust. On the contrary. The Jews were seen as more pushing, strident and demanding than ever – and cashing in cunningly on their new asset of enhanced entitlement to sympathy.'[130]

British officials administering the Palestine Mandate, who were used to a certain deference from the local inhabitants in the many territories they governed, expected it also from the Jews of Palestine. They did not receive it. Nicholas Bethell[131] quotes David Hacohen, a local Zionist leader in Haifa: 'the best doctors in the country were Jews. The best architects were Jews... We paid taxes, but we never went to the government schools. We went to our own schools, paid for with the money we collected from Jewry. The Weizmann Institute and the University [of Jerusalem] belong to us. The place belongs to us. There were more English books in our houses than in their houses. Most of the local British administrators didn't read serious books. They read detective stories.' Bethell also quotes a senior political officer with the Palestinian secretariat, who complained that the people of the Yishuv 'were meant to be subject to British rule. Instead, they behave as if they were an independent nation'. Indeed, the civil servants of the Palestine administration were far from being the first team of the British Civil Service; th4 best were in London, followed by their counterparts in India. Moreover, while the London and Delhi officials were very long-serving, particularly the former; the Palestine officials might well have seen their postings as relatively short-term.

On the whole, the British much preferred the Arabs of Palestine, particularly the upper-class. Isaiah Berlin compared Palestine to a minor English public school: there was the headmaster, the High Commissioner, trying to be firm and impartial; but the assistant masters favoured the sporting stupid boarders [the Arabs] against the clever swot day boys [the Jews] who had the deplorable habit of writing home to their parents on the slightest provocation to complain about the quality of the teaching, the food and so on.[132]

According to Richard Crossman, a member of the Anglo-American Commission of Enquiry into Palestine: 'It's easy to see why the British prefer the Arab upper-class to the Jews. This Arab intelligentsia has French culture, amusing, civilised, tragic and gay. Compared with them, the Jews, seemed tense, bourgeois, central European.[133] And a British officer told Crossman, "All through the Arab Revolt, when our men were being shot in the back protecting the Jews, most of them liked the Arabs ...the old Arab will take a pot shot at you in the night, but he will offer you coffee next day, when you come to investigate. The Jew doesn't offer you coffee, even when you're protecting him".[134] The British military commander in Palestine, General Evelyn 'Bubbles' Barker, had a passionate affair with Katy Antonius (who gave the best parties), widow of George Antonius, a leading anti-Zionist Christian Arab.

The Jewish and Arab key players

1. Jewish figures

On the Jewish side they were Chaim Weizmann, David Ben-Gurion – both familiar names across the years – and a new player, Menachem Begin, whose influence has continued beyond his death, in 1983, to the present day.

By the end of the war, **Chaim Weizmann,** aged 71, was in poor health and with failing eyesight. But a little over two years later he was to play the crucial role, from the Zionist point of view, in the run-up to the UN vote on partition in late November 1947, which opened the door to the establishment of the Jewish State on May 15, 1948. A contribution of equally long-term impact was his emphasis on the importance of pure and applied scientific research; he was the key figure in the establishment of the Hebrew University of Jerusalem in 1926, and of the Research Institute at Rehovoth, which was later named after him. These institutions, together with the Haifa Technion (foundation stone laid in 1926) and the new universities established in the 1960s, underpinned the flowering of Israeli technology from the 1980s on, leading to the appellation 'Start-up Nation'. An opponent of Zionism, Lord Passfield, architect of the negative 1930 White Paper, commented that the whole Arab-Jewish controversy was unfair because the Jews had Dr Weizmann and the Arabs did not.

In contrast to Weizmann, **David Ben-Gurion,** in 1945 aged 59, was still at the height of his powers; he became Israel's first Prime Minister in 1948 and continued in that role over most of the next two decades. The distinguished Israeli novelist, Amos Oz described him as 'a short tubby man with a prophetic shock of silvery hair around his bald patch, the prominent defiant jaw of an ancient mariner and the laser beam willpower of a visionary peasant'.[135] He led the preparations for the war of 1948 'with a Clemenceau-like concentration of purpose.[136] (Clemenceau was the French leader in WWI.)

Throughout his career, Ben-Gurion grappled with what Zionists called 'the Arab question'. As early as 1910, he recognised that a conflict existed between Arab and Jewish aspirations, and spoke openly of the hatred felt by the former for the latter. After 1936 Ben-Gurion admitted that the Arab-Jewish conflict was fundamentally political and as such not susceptible to a peaceful resolution. He himself never learned Arabic (although he taught himself ancient Greek, so as to be able to read Plato in the original, and Spanish, to read Cervantes). But he had able lieutenants who were fluent Arabists, particularly Moshe Shertok (later Sharett), who became Israel's long-serving foreign minister. After his rise to the leadership of the Zionist movement, Ben-Gurion concentrated his energies on the acceleration of Jewish immigration to Palestine. The question of *numbers* is still central to discussions about any possible settlement to the Israeli-Palestinian dispute.

Menachem Begin's formative years were spent in Poland, from his birth in 1913 (he was at least a generation younger than Weizmann, and Ben-Gurion). At Warsaw University, and well before, he experienced severe antisemitism and relative poverty. He rose quickly to head Betar, the youth wing of the Revisionist movement, particularly strong in Poland, and at the right flank of Zionism. When Hitler invaded Poland, Begin was still in Warsaw but made his way to Vilna, which was located in the half of Poland taken over by the Soviet Union after the Nazi- Soviet pact. He was arrested by the secret police and held for nine months in prison, before being sent to a work camp near the Arctic Circle. One of many released in 1942 to join the Polish army in the Middle East, he was stationed in Jerusalem. While still in uniform, he was appointed head of Betar in Palestine. By that point, the Irgun, the military wing of the Herut political movement, was in an advanced state of disintegration. At the end of 1943 Begin was appointed its head. Undaunted by the knowledge that they had barely 600 trained fighters, Begin proclaimed his revolt against British rule on 1 February 1944. In November 1944, two members of the Stern gang (which was even more extreme than the Irgun and known in Hebrew by the acronym LHI) assassinated Lord Moyne in Cairo. The British resident minister of state in the Middle East was a personal friend of Churchill, who was moving towards approving Jewish statehood. The Moyne murder set in train the *saison* – the hunting season – carried out by the Haganah, in effect the military wing of the then politically dominant Mapai, against the Irgun and the LHI. Begin himself managed to evade capture. The *saison* petered out with the end of the European war and the approach of the British general election. Actions against the Mandatory Authority were then conducted jointly by Haganah and Irgun, with the former focusing on bringing as many Jews as possible to Palestine from Europe, and the latter on direct attacks against the British, particularly military personnel.

Like his hero and mentor, Jabotinsky, Begin tended to extreme positions and maintained them to the end. As leader of the opposition in the Israeli parliament in the 1950s and 1960s he bitterly, and sometimes violently, resisted any contact between Israel and the Federal Republic of Germany, even under the anti-Nazi Adenauer.[137]

2. Arab figures

Transjordan ('on the other side of the Jordan') was established by Winston Churchill – 'by the stroke of a pen' – in the early 1920s, in his capacity as colonial secretary; it gave **Abdullah,** the youngest son of Ibn Saud of Saudi Arabia, his own kingdom. British influence was powerful from the beginning and has continued for decades. Abdullah's army, the Arab Legion, was British armed, trained, and largely led. As the Zionists came to recognise that no compromise with the Palestine Arabs could be reached, Transjordan emerged as a central point of reference in Zionist calculations. The key was Abdullah's outstanding political realism and willingness to give it expression in a long-term collusion with, at first, the Jewish Agency, and later the State of Israel. Transjordan was in a pivotal position from both the military and strategic points of view. During the struggle for Palestine in the late 1940s, Abdullah's stance meant that the hostility of the Arab states to Israel was not monolithic. Moreover, the Zionists shared a common enemy with Abdullah, namely the unyielding leader of the Arabs of Palestine, Haj Amin. Abdullah, alone among the Arab leaders, realised the considerable strength of the Jews, and provided that he was able to seize and retain the predominantly Arab part of Palestine, the West Bank of the Jordan, his involvement in the 1948 War, on the Arab side, would be relatively limited.[138]

Throughout the Mandate period, the political life of the Palestine Arabs revolved around the landowning and clerical families, of which two, the Husseinis and the Nashashibis, were dominant. The former gained the upper hand in 1922, with the appointment by the High Commissioner, Sir Herbert Samuel, of **Haj Amin al-Husseini** to the position of Mufti of Jerusalem (the major religious authority) and to the presidency of the Supreme Muslim Council. He also dominated the Palestine Arab Party. Though fragmented as a political community, the Palestine Arabs were united in their refusal to recognise the legality of the authority of the British Mandate, and by their fear of the Zionist intrusion. Haj Amin was the leading figure in the failed 1936 Arab Revolt against the British, and his Arab Higher Committee was outlawed; he fled into exile. But whether in or out of the country, he had a decisive influence on the direction of the Palestine Arab community in its encounter with both the British authorities and the Jews. ... 'his rigid and intransigent posture was in no small part responsible for the disasters that befell the Arabs of Palestine'.[139]

Whatever the moral rights and wrongs of the conflict, the most expedient solution was to partition Palestine into an Arab state and a Jewish state, with a British enclave in Jerusalem. This was accepted by the Jews, but rejected by the Arabs still under Haj Amin's influence – a response that seemed to bear fruit with the British government's White Paper of 1939, which came close to reversing the Balfour Declaration.[140]

The Arab Revolt of 1936-9 against the British Mandate resulted in the deaths of about 4,000 Arabs and damaged their ability to fight effectively when they rejected the partition plan of 1947 and launched a civil war. Haj Amin was exiled by the British and initially made his way to Iraq, where he assisted in a rebellion against Britain that was put down. At the end of 1941 he found refuge in Nazi Germany. Hitler found that he and the Mufti shared the same enemies. As he put it, Germany was engaged in a life-and-death struggle with the citadels of Jewish power – Britain and the Soviet Union – and naturally there would be no Jewish state in Palestine. Hitler admired Husseini's blue eyes and reddish hair, deciding that he definitely had Aryan blood. Haj Amin boasted that he supported the Nazis 'because... if Germany had carried the day, no trace of the Zionists would have remained in Palestine.'[141]

Indeed, Haj Amin consistently rejected any territorial compromise and espoused a solution to the Palestine problem that saw all of Palestine as an Arab state with a Jewish minority, composed only of those who had lived in the country before 1914 (sometimes, more generously, 1917). His influence lived on over the years in the Palestine National Charter of the Palestine Liberation Organisation (PLO), clause 6 of which states: 'the Jews who had normally resided in Palestine before the beginning of the Zionist invasion (defined as 1917) will be considered Palestinians'.

In the wake of the 1948 Arab-Israel War, Abdullah took over the West Bank of Jordan and the Old City of Jerusalem, incorporating both into his state, which became Jordan (rather than Transjordan). But on 20 July 1951 he met his nemesis: while at prayer on the Temple Mount in Jerusalem, he was shot dead by an Arab agent of Haj Amin.[142]

The main events as the Mandate moved towards its end

The Jews attack the British
The Irgun mounted a series of direct attacks against British soldiers, including a tit-for-tat series of hangings and whippings. Much the most serious, and certainly most dramatic event was the blowing up of one wing of the King David Hotel in Jerusalem, by the Irgun under Begin's command. The hotel had been requisitioned by the administration and intelligence agencies of the Mandate. On 22nd July 1946, Irgun operatives disguised as Arab hotel staff stowed in the basement milk churns filled with 350 pounds of explosives. The Irgun made anonymous calls to the hotel to warn of the imminent attack so that it could be evacuated. But the calls were either ignored or were too late. Bombs shattered

the entire wing of the King David, killing 91, including Britons, Jews and Arabs. While the King David bombing intensified the severity of the British counter-attack, it arguably succeeded in accelerating London's retreat from the Mandate. In October 1946 the Irgun blew up the British Embassy in Rome – at night, so almost empty.[143] Operatives of the LHI sent letter bombs to British officials in London, but they were all intercepted.

While the Haganah and its strike force, the Palmach, attacked British installations and infrastructure in Palestine, particularly bridges and railway lines, their main effort in the two-pronged attack on the Mandate was to bring as many 'illegal' immigrants as possible from Europe to Palestine. The detention camps in Cyprus held 12,000 prisoners, taken from intercepted ships, and were full. Whitehall resolved to send captured illegal immigrants back to Europe. On 12th July 1947, a converted American ferry, renamed the Exodus, left for Palestine from southern France with 4,500 DPs aboard. The ship was shadowed across the Mediterranean by the Royal Navy, was intercepted, and seized. Haganah had decided, in advance, to resist, with an eye to highlighting Jewish weakness and suffering, and British brutality. The boarding was strongly opposed but finally succeeded. The British towed the stricken vessel to Haifa and transferred almost all the passengers to three ships, which then departed for France. But the French refused to cooperate. Next, the British ships set sail for Hamburg, where the army forcibly disembarked the passengers and sent them to hastily prepared camps. The ordeal of the Exodus seemed to symbolise contemporary Jewish history and British insensitivity to it; in the end it served to promote the Zionist cause.[144]

Even before this, Churchill (now leader of the opposition) had pressed his advice: "If we cannot fulfil our promises to the Zionists we should, without delay, place our mandate for Palestine at the feet of the United Nations, and give due notice of our impending evacuation from that country". His argument carried great weight. On February 18, 1947 came the announcement: 'His Majesty's government have of themselves no power under the terms of the mandate to award the country to the Arabs or the Jews, or even to partition it between them... We have therefore reached the conclusion that the only course open to us is to submit the problem to the judgement of the United Nations.'[145] In turn, the

UN set up a Special Committee on Palestine to report at a later stage to the UN General Assembly. When it did so, recommending partition between Jews and Arabs, the stage was set for Britain's departure from Palestine after three decades.

The UN vote on partition

The British government and its advisers disliked the recommendation, and the Arab League (of the many Arab nations, created by Britain a few years earlier) publicly condemned it. There was still a hope, albeit fast fading, that a 'blocking third' might be mustered against it in the General Assembly (in order to be accepted, the recommendation required a two-thirds majority). The alternatives now available to Britain were effectively the same whether the resolution carried or fell just short of a two-thirds majority even with both superpowers voting in support. (To Britain's surprise, the Soviet position was in favour; less surprisingly, the US State Department seemed to be in two minds. In either case, the Mandate and the White Paper were both untenable.) Those alternatives were: to remain long enough to ensure a transition to partition that was as smooth as possible, or simply to withdraw and leave Jews and Arabs to fight it out. On October 17, the British government stated: 'It would not accept responsibility for the enforcement, either alone or in concert with other nations, of any settlement antagonistic to either Jews or Arabs, or both, which was likely to necessitate the use of force'. In the background, Bevin was negotiating, with both Egypt and Iraq, for the protection of the Suez Canal and for British oil concessions, and to integrate the two countries into the Western alliance. All this would have been ruined if Britain had played a part in creating the State of Israel. That is, it is likely they believed (or perhaps hoped) that without heavy British reinforcements the Yishuv would be overrun and a Palestinian state come into being.[146]

The Zionists welcomed the recommendation, but they realised that without intensive lobbying it was by no means a foregone conclusion that the General Assembly would pass it by the necessary two-thirds majority. 'And so began one of the most intricate and dramatic lobbying exercises in modern diplomatic history.'[147] Weizmann, although frequently ill and able to read only with the greatest difficulty, carried out this exercise for which his entire history had prepared him. He appealed to Leon Blum, an influential figure in French politics, hoping that he would also influence the stands of Holland, Belgium and Luxembourg. He turned to Samuel Zemurray (the 'banana king') head of the United Fruit Corporation, to use his influence with the smaller republics of Central America. Most notably, he did everything he could to sway President Truman in favour of partition and to bring the wavering State Department into line.

When the roll call was taken on 29th November, 1947, the issue was still in doubt. But the proposal passed by 33 to 13 votes, with 10 abstentions, just attaining the required majority. The support of the Soviet Union, together with its compliant Eastern European satellites, was crucial. It had not suddenly become Zionist; rather, it took a pragmatic view: firstly, a Jewish state, largely socialist, would be open to Soviet influence; secondly, its existence would enable the Soviet Union to supplant Britain as the major great power in the Middle East.

Civil War: winner takes all

In rough demographic and geopolitical terms, the Arabs were far stronger than the Yishuv. The Palestinian Arabs themselves outnumbered Palestine's Jews by a factor of two to one. The surrounding Arab states mustered a total population of 40 million, with additional millions from a vast demographic hinterland. But the Yishuv had organised for war and the Arabs hadn't. The compact Jewish community in Palestine was economically and politically vibrant, and a potential powerhouse if adequately organised and directed. It also enjoyed a unity of purpose and a collective fear – of a new Holocaust – that afforded high levels of motivation. The fact that the Yishuv was the victim of aggression and that each Jewish soldier was almost literally defending his own home, added to the motivational edge.

The Palestinian Arabs failed to mobilise their resources or to prepare. Like the surrounding Arab states they had a socio-economic elite with no tradition of public service or ethos of contribution and sacrifice (typical was the almost complete absence of sons of that elite among the fighters of 1936-1939, and 1947-48).

When war came – at their instigation – the Palestinians were unprepared: most members of the Arab Higher Committee were outside the country for most of the civil war. They were also short of arms and ammunition. The 800 Arab villages and dozen or so Arab towns of Palestine, in December 1947, did possess more light arms than the Yishuv. But they were dispersed and under local, rather than coordinated control, and most of them had probably never seen a battlefield. The Palestinians lacked the economic or organisational wherewithal to import arms and ammunition in significant quantities. The Arab states were niggardly with material support – and despite talk of 'jihad' on behalf of the Arabs of Palestine were looking to their own future gains from what they hoped would be the dismemberment of Mandatory Palestine.[148] Abdullah wanted Palestine within his kingdom; Damascus coveted a greater Syria; King Farouk of Egypt's regarded himself as the rightful leader of the Arab world and hated the Hashemites of both Jordan and Iraq, who in turn loathed King ibn Saud who had ejected them from Arabia. They all awaited their opportunity, when the British had finally left Palestine, to pursue their own ends.[149]

The Palestinian militias performed moderately well when they were on the offensive, between late November 1947 and the end of March 1948, though they and the external-origin reinforcements of the Arab Liberation Army did not conquer a single Jewish settlement. But once the Yishuv went over to the offensive, it was all over. From early April, the Haganah was able to concentrate its forces and pick off Arab towns and villages. Almost no villages came to the aid of townspeople and vice versa. Very few young men from the areas of Palestine assigned to an Arab state by the UN actually participated in the battles and few of them died in the fighting in Jewish-assigned Palestine. In effect, each Arab community was on its own.

Between early April and mid-May, Palestine Arab society fell apart and was crushed by a lightly armed and, in many ways, rag-tag Jewish militia.[150]

Kastel
The Arab village, perched high over the only road to Jewish Jerusalem from the coastal strip of securely Yishuv-held territory, shelled crucial civilian and military supplies, both running short. An alternative road was under construction but would take time to become usable. It was vital that Haganah could take and hold Kastel, which changed hands several times. Largely by chance, the advantage shifted decisively and permanently in favour of the exhausted Haganah fighters. The commander of the Arab forces, Abd al-Qader al-Husseini, hugely popular among his men and the Palestinian Arab public, was shot dead. His death stunned his men, who streamed down to the Temple Mount for the funeral, leaving Kastel to the Haganah. It was never lost thereafter; the main road to Jerusalem remained open.

This was one of the decisive turning points of the civil war. Another was the capture by the Haganah of the Arab part of Haifa, the Jewish inhabitants of which had been warned by local Arab friends that they would be massacred if they remained. They were saved, most of the Haifa Arabs left, not all, there is still a substantial (largely Christian) Arab population.

The above is a brief overview of a very confused situation which justified the term 'the fog of war', in which civilians and soldiers, some of them local militias, were intertwined. Possibly the main difference between the Arabs and Jews of Palestine was that the latter had a reasonably functioning command and control system, headed by officers who had either served in the British Army during the war, or had been trained by years in the Haganah, and who knew that for the most part their orders would be carried out.

The Palestinian Arab exodus: Deir Yassin and Arab propaganda
The attack on Deir Yassin, an Arab village on the outskirts of Jerusalem, was one of the pivotal events of the civil war. The Irgun and the LHI, 120 fighters in all, jointly attacked it and, both during and after the battle, committed a notorious atrocity. Much assisted by several Palmach squads who helped capture key points, they overcame strong resistance. Despite clear instructions from their local commander not to kill women and children, or

POWs, the view now accepted by historians is that once they were in Yassin, the Jewish fighters tossed grenades into houses and killed men, women and children. The number of victims was long debated but is now agreed as being at 100, including entire families. The Irgun were undoubtedly aware that a massacre would terrify many Arab civilians and encourage flight. (Their overall commander, Begin, managed to deny that the atrocity had taken place while boasting of its utility: "The legend of Deir Yassin was worth half a dozen battalions to the forces of Israel". Panic overwhelmed the Arabs of Palestine. Ben-Gurion apologised to King Abdullah, who rejected the apology.

Arab vengeance was swift. On 13th April, a convoy of ambulances and food trucks set off for the isolated Hadassah Hospital on Mount Scopus in the north of Jerusalem. It was attacked by Arab militia. Seventy-seven Jews, mainly doctors and nurses, were killed and 20 wounded before the British intervened. Deir Yassin was one of the pivotal events of the civil war: it became the centrepiece of an Arab media campaign that amplified Jewish atrocities; designed to fortify resistance, instead it encouraged deep foreboding in a population already at war. By March 1948, before Deir Yassin, 75,000 Palestine Arabs had left their homes. Two months later, 390,000 had gone.[151] Perhaps they believed that they would return once the Jews had been defeated by neighbouring Arab nations. This was, in the event, a vain hope.

Independence declared

On May 12, 1948, the Jewish People's Council (a sort of provisional government) held a decisive meeting. The heads of the Haganah thought the Yishuv's chances of withstanding the Arab nations' attacks were 50-50 as the Jewish soldiers were exhausted from months of continuous fighting. Weizmann advised from New York: 'Proclaim the state, no matter what ensues'. In the end, the decision was 6 to 4 to declare statehood, Ben-Gurion putting all his weight behind it. The council members were taking a tremendous gamble on the future of the Yishuv.[152]

On May 14, Ben-Gurion proclaimed the Declaration of Independence. "We hereby declare the establishment of a Jewish state in Eretz Israel, to be known as the State of Israel". Ben-Gurion wrote in his diary: "In the country there is celebration and profound joy – and once again I am a mourner among the celebrants, as I was on November 29." That evening he began a new diary notebook, which opened with the dry, understated comment... "at 4 o'clock in the afternoon, the state was established. Its fate is in the hands of the security forces."[153]

On Passover Eve, April 23, 1948, Weizmann had received a message through one of Truman's advisers: 'I have Dr Weizmann on my conscience'. The President ignored the advice of his Secretary of State, Marshall, and of the State Department, who urged caution. On the day after the proclamation of Israel, the British mandate expired; only eleven minutes later Truman announced United States' *de facto* recognition of Israel: The old Doctor will believe me now", he said.

Ben-Gurion sent Weizmann a message on behalf of his government: 'On the occasion of the establishment of the Jewish state, we send our greetings to you who have done more than any other living man towards its creation.... We look forward to the day when we shall see you at the head of the state established in peace.'[154]

Weizmann did indeed become the first President of the State of Israel, but was less than happy to find that his duties were largely ceremonial. He said: "The only thing I'm allowed to stick my nose into is my handkerchief."

The War of Independence

In February, 1948, Ernest Bevin was notified of King Abdullah's intention to take over, after British withdrawal, the areas allotted to the Arabs under the General Assembly resolution on partition. He indicated his approval, but added: "Don't go and invade the area allotted to the Jews." This advice carried weight. Transjordan had become formally independent in 1946, but it still remained, in substance, a British protectorate.

According to O'Brien, Bevin's advice helped to precipitate the conflict, for two reasons. First, it freed the Arab Legion to take over the areas assigned to the (Palestinian) Arabs under the UN resolution. This aroused the desperate antagonism of the Mufti – whose sway it would end – and the competition of the other Arab leaders. Neither Egypt nor Syria, let alone the Mufti, was prepared to let Abdullah inherit Palestine. By confining his advice to 'the area allotted to the Jews', Bevin left it open to Abdullah and his military leaders to move into Jerusalem. That was inherently attractive, because of the prestige that would be acquired by the King, as protector of the mosques.

The mood of the Arab leaders generally was triumphalist. The Director General of the Arab League, Azzam Pasha, compared the coming fate of the Jews to the carnage inflicted by the Mongol Hordes. This mood was infectious. According to Attlee's biographer, Kenneth Harris, the Foreign Office and the British Chiefs of Staff reported categorically that if war broke out between Jews and Arabs, 'the Arabs would throw the Jews into the sea'.[155] Indeed, on paper, the regular armies of seven Arab states were overwhelmingly strong. General Barker, who had now left Palestine, gleefully predicted to Katy Antonius 'as a soldier' that 'the Jews will be eradicated'.[156]

The Course of the War: 1948-1949

For Israel, the month of fighting between the Arab invasion, immediately after the declaration of the state, and the first UN-imposed ceasefire, was the most difficult and dangerous part of the entire war. During that month some 1,600 Jews were killed, about one quarter of all the war's fatalities. The Syrians swept from the Golan Heights down to the Jordan Valley and invaded the heartland of Jewish settlements there – an incursion that was deadly for the Jews. The Syrians were halted through the sacrifices made by the inhabitants, and their own weakness, since they ran out of steam and were forced onto the defensive after encountering resistance. The Iraqi force (a long way from home) penetrated south of the Syrian one into the Jordan Valley after failing to take a key kibbutz, Gesher – an important setback, It next moved into Samaria, (part of the West Bank of the Jordan) together with the Liberation Army, which had penetrated central Galilee. Next it attempted to take another important kibbutz, Sejera, the key to Lower Galilee, with the aim of linking up with central Galilee and threatening Haifa. This attempt, too, ended in failure, and from that point on the Iraqis confined their action to Samaria, which had been assigned to the Arab state by the UN.

The Arab Legion's goal had been to take control of areas designated as part of the Arab state, and to avoid clashing with the

Jews as far as possible. In the event, the Legion went for Jerusalem, which Ben-Gurion saw as the heart of the Zionist enterprise, as well as a population centre and the country's strategic hub. The Jews in Jerusalem were supplied by an alternative route (built with great effort) to the one which was under heavy Arab shelling, and most of the Jewish areas survived the Jordanian assault. Only the Jewish Quarter of the Old City and a number of isolated settlements were lost.

Another front that seemed extremely dangerous was in the south, in the area assigned to the Jews under the UN plan where the Jewish population was very sparse. The Egyptian army invaded, but was finally halted with great difficulty, well short of the main Jewish population centres.

Months of incessant fighting in the civil war had left the newly designated Israeli army depleted, and it had to learn, on the run, larger-scale warfare in active combat situations: mobilising an army, deploying large forces, air-ground coordination (the Israelis had a few planes), field intelligence, supply transport, and so forth. The soldiers were exhausted and short of equipment, but they had weathered this first critical test and were satisfied that they had halted the Arab armies.

A four-week truce was agreed on, and a UN mediator was appointed – the Swedish Count Bernadotte. However his mission was a total failure. The Arabs would not accept any proposal whatsoever that meant de facto recognition of the State of Israel. The Israelis rejected any proposal that offered less territory and sovereignty than the UN resolution had given them. Both sides violated the ceasefire. The Israelis brought military equipment into the country, greatly assisted by funding from American Jewry that procured arms shipments from Czechoslovakia, with the blessing of the Soviet Union.

The fighting resumed on July 9, 1948, and continued for 10 days. The main thrust of the Israeli offensive was against the Arab Legion forces on the central front. (The Israelis were unaware that the Legion, short of ammunition, had been forced on to the defensive; the British maintained a policy of not supplying arms to either side.)

A second truce was declared on July 19, 1948. The Arab governments, and especially the Arab Legion command, were in favour of it. But since the press in the Arab states portrayed the fighting as crowned with Arab victories, their public was angered by the ceasefire which they saw as surrendering to the dictates of the Western powers, thus enabling the Zionists to regroup and strengthen their forces.

The largest, and strongest, invading army belonged to the Egyptians. Bernadotte proposed a territorial exchange: Israel would relinquish the Negev – which was assigned to it by the partition plan, but which it did not hold – in exchange for Western Galilee, which it had conquered but which was originally assigned to the Arab state. This was an option the Israelis would not accept – the Negev comprised some 50 percent of the Jewish state's area. Yet attacking the Egyptian army and driving it out of Israeli territory would mean breaching the truce and provoking the UN, which Israel was not eager to do. Eventually, Ben-Gurion decided in favour of the attack.

On October 15, an operation was launched to break through the Egyptian lines and open the way to the Negev. It was aimed at routing the Egyptian army, but before this could happen the UN declared a ceasefire, so the Egyptians remained sitting in Gaza and Beersheba. The latter was taken after a last-minute decision by the Israelis. This operation marked a watershed in the history of the war, for despite several previous failures, particularly against the Jordanians, the IDF had proved itself capable of overcoming a regular army in a breakthrough battle. However, the Egyptians were still control of Gaza, and this remained the case until the Six Day War in 1967.

At the end of October, Israel had control of central and northern Galilee, as well as territory along the northern border with Lebanon and Syria. By the end of December 1948, a tremendous change was evident in the balance of forces, and in Israel's operational capability, since the UN resolution on partition. The IDF fought straight through the Negev, overcame the lines of the Egyptian strongholds, and destroyed the southern arm of the Egyptian army. They even began to operate inside the Sinai Peninsula, but withdrew to the international border under British and American pressure.

In the wake of this operation, Israel and Egypt negotiated an armistice on the island of Rhodes, with the aid of a particularly capable American mediator, Ralph Bunche. On February 24, 1949, an agreement was signed, making Egypt the first Arab state to withdraw from the war. Ben-Gurion wrote in his diary: 'After the establishment of the state and our victories on the battlefield, this is the greatest event in this year of epic events'.

Just as the Arab states had invaded separately and did not collaborate in the fighting, so the war was concluded separately with each state. Following the agreement with Egypt, the other Arab states sought a dignified exit from the war. Israel made a secret agreement with Jordan, which involved dividing Jerusalem between them, and King Abdullah, encouraged by the British, retained control of what came to be known as the West Bank of the Jordan. As part of that agreement, Iraqi forces withdrew and handed over the area of the West Bank, which they had held, to the Arab Legion. An agreement with the Lebanon then followed, involving recognition of the existing international border. The last agreement to be signed was with Syria, on July 20, 1949.

Rejecting the advice of some of his younger military leaders, Ben-Gurion decided against occupying the entire country, but instead concentrated the depleted resources of the new state on bringing in masses of new immigrants and absorbing them. The State of Israel emerged from what came to be called the War of Independence, with high casualties and the destruction of a number of settlements and towns. But Israel had been established as a reality and had successfully overcome its attackers. It had become the strongest army in the region, a position which it maintained up to and including the Six Day War of 1967, after which Israel was seriously threatened by the Yom Kippur War of 1973.

An Arab historian, Aref al-Aref, estimated the number of Palestinian dead in the war at 15,000, amounting to more or less the same percentage loss of the population as the Jews had suffered. The bulk of the Palestinian population of Israel was no longer in the country, but were refugees in the surrounding states.[157]

My own appraisal of both the civil war and the War of Independence is that, in both, *Israel was fortunate in its adversaries.* Had the forces of the Arabs of Palestine or the armies of the surrounding Arab states, or both, been of the calibre of Transjordan's Arab Legion, Israel might indeed have been "thrown into the sea".

In 1948 there were two incidents that consolidated state power and a single professional army under the Prime Minister and Minister of Defence, David Ben-Gurion. The first was what was known as the Altalena (the pen name of Jabotinsky) affair. Although an agreement had been made that essentially ended the independent existence of the Irgun (IZL) forces, the cargo ship Altalena, loaded with several hundred immigrants, IZL members and a large shipment of arms, sought to land so that the IZL could distribute the weapons 'their' IDF battalions. The government refused, whereupon, without obtaining government permission, the IZL took control of a beach and began to unload both immigrants and arms. On 21st June, having been surrounded by IDF troops, the IZL men surrendered, but the ship set sail for Tel Aviv, to the south. There, on Ben-Gurion's orders, IDF artillery fired on the ship, which soon sank. Most of the arms were lost. At the same time, IDF troops took over IZL headquarters in Tel Aviv and arrested and disarmed the dissidents. Altogether, 18 men died in the clashes, most of them IZL. The IZL and LHI units were dispersed into different IDF units by mid-September, the disbandment being completed in the wake of the assassination of Count Bernadotte.[158]

On September 17, 1948, UN mediator Count Bernadotte was killed by former members of LHI. The government took decisive action, arresting activists from the two dissident organisations and eliminating their last vestiges of independence. In addition, in September 1948, Ben-Gurion ordered the Palmach disbanded. It did not breach IDF discipline, but its headquarters were linked politically with a party to the left of Ben-Gurion's Mapai. He wanted an army whose primary loyalty was to the state, so as to guarantee the army's non-involvement in politics and other key areas of national life.

Jews of the Muslim World

These communities, long separated from the main centres of Jewish life in Europe, were to have a decisive influence on the demographic composition and political tenor of Israeli life.

Apart from the Iranian/Persian community centred in Tehran, all were minorities in an intermittently hostile Arab world. In contrast, the Jewish community of non-Arab Turkey, at the heart of the Ottoman Empire, which dates from the expulsions from Spain and Portugal at the end of the 15th century, was and remains relatively stable and secure. Some of the communities of the Arab world dated back to biblical times, others were much more recent. Those of North Africa and the Levant (Syria and Lebanon) were under heavy French influence, as France participated in the "Scramble for Africa" in the late 19th century and the apportioning of the collapsed Ottoman Empire after World War I. Egypt, though nominally part of the Ottoman Empire and supposedly independent, was strongly under British influence, even control, from the latter part of the 19th century up to the early 1950s. For the latter part of the 19th century there was a struggle between Britain and Russia for influence in Iran, part of the 'Great Game' for control of central Asia and the passage to India. An important complicating factor was the discovery of major oil deposits in Iraq and Iran near the end of the 19th century, and their commercial exploitation by British and American companies.

In these and other European conflicts, the Jews of the Muslim world had an essentially passive role, prospering when they could, merely surviving when times were more difficult. World War I affected only the Jewish community of Iraq, where the armies of Britain and Germany/Turkey fought hard battles. World War II was much more comprehensive; it involved almost the whole of North Africa, the conflict between Germany and Italy, on the one hand, and Britain and the United States, on the other, reaching as far east as 50 miles from Cairo, so threatening the Jewish community of Palestine.

In 1881 **Tunisia** became a French protectorate; under this Western influence the condition of the Jews of Tunisia improved somewhat, but, in August 1917, the Jewish quarters of a number of towns were looted by Tunisian troops during a rebellion against French rule. With Tunisian independence won in 1956, the treatment of the Jews rapidly worsened. In 1948, the year of Israel's founding, the Jewish population of Tunisia was approximately 110,000, declining to 2,000 in 1974.

The start of French rule in **Morocco** in 1912 was marked by riots by local Muslims in the major town of Fez, in which 60 Jews were killed and the Jewish quarter of the city sacked. Some years earlier, in the town of Casablanca, Muslim rioters killed 30 Jews and 200 women, girls and boys were abducted, raped and then ransomed. Successive kings of Morocco tried to reduce the extent of anti-Jewish violence and it was notable that the mass departure of Jews from Morocco to Israel did not begin until 1956. Moreover, there remains today a small Jewish community in Morocco, directly protected by King Hassan II. Nevertheless, some 265,000 Moroccan Jews did leave, the majority moving to Israel while the better educated went to France and Canada, where they prospered.

Algeria also came under French rule during the 19th century. There were periodic attacks on Jews and their property over the subsequent years. After a violent uprising against French rule, between 1956 and 1962, Algeria became independent. Most Jews had left for Israel after 1948; almost all the remainder left for France after Algerian independence, when the Jews were deprived of their principal economic rights.

The thriving life of the mediaeval Jewish community of **Egypt** was dramatically revealed by the discovery, in 1896, of the Cairo Genizah, an extraordinary trove of Jewish religious and commercial documents, lost for centuries in the attics of a Cairo synagogue. They demonstrated the network of contacts between Cairo Jewish merchants and Arab and other traders across Asia. In more recent times the Jews of Egypt, together with Greek and Armenian communities, formed a cosmopolitan sector of Egyptian life under the British protectorate, the vital core of which were the Suez Canal and the Canal Zone.

During the 19th century and the first half of the 20th, there were sporadic attacks on Egyptian Jews, sometimes centering on blood libels, at other times sparked by resentment of Jewish immigration into Palestine. In 1948 the Egyptian Jewish community numbered 75,000. Many left at that point, others did so in 1956, the year that saw the Suez War between the newly assertive Egyptian government under Colonel Nasser, and a strange military partnership between Britain, France and Israel. By 1974, the Egyptian Jewish community had shrunk to 350.

Throughout the 19th century, the Jewish community of **Iran** suffered intermittent persecution and discrimination. There was considerable emigration to Palestine and a Zionist movement developed. Under the Pahlevi dynasty, established in 1925, Iran was secularised and oriented towards the West, heavily influenced by Britain and the United States. This greatly benefited the Jews, who played an important role in the economy and in cultural life. After the CIA and MI6 orchestrated the deposition of the Iranian Prime Minister, Mossadegh, in order to secure Persian oil wealth for the West, the Shah was restored to power and there began a prosperous era for the Jews of Iran. In the 1970s, only 1 percent were classified as lower class; 80 percent were middle-class and 10 percent wealthy. Between then and the revolution against the Shah, led by the Ayatollah Khomenei, there was a close commercial relationship between Iran and Israel. When this came to an abrupt end in 1979, some 80,000 Jews were living in Iran. In the following years there was a gradual departure for Israel and the United States.

The Jewish community of **Iraq** goes back to ancient times. In 1534, the capital city Baghdad became part of the Ottoman Empire, which held control, with only a brief pause, until 1917, when Ottoman rule was ended by military defeat and replaced, in 1921, by a British Mandate. For a while Jews were successful. The well-educated were prized by the Iraqi government for their proficiency in foreign languages and for their ties outside the country. Iraq's first Minister of Finance, Yehezkel Sasson was a Jew. Iraqi Jews also played an important role in the development of judicial and postal systems.

After Iraq became an independent state in 1932, Jews suffered intermittent persecution, especially in reaction to events in Palestine. In June 1941, when it looked as though the Germans were about to defeat the British, as part of the Iraqi expectation of that outcome, an Iraqi mob murdered 180 Jews and wounded almost 1,000. The tide of battle turned, the British army re-entered Baghdad and the success of the Jewish community resumed. They had built a broad network of medical facilities, schools and cultural activities. Nearly all the members of the Baghdad Symphony Orchestra were Jewish. A considerable number of Jewish writers and poets emerged, whose works in Arabic became well known and well regarded. Jewish journalists founded a number of newspapers and magazines in Arabic. From the 1920s Jews were prominent in Iraqi music and theatre.

This flourishing environment ended abruptly in 1947, with the UN vote for the partition of Palestine and the fight for Israel's independence. From 1950 Iraqi Jews, who wanted to leave the country had to forfeit their citizenship; a year later the property of Jews who had emigrated was frozen, and economic restrictions were placed on Jews who chose to remain in the country. From 1949 to 1951, Israel evacuated 104,000 Iraqi Jews directly to Israel; another 20,000 were smuggled out through Iran. In 1963, additional restrictions were placed on the remaining Iraqi Jews. The sale of property was forbidden and all Jews were forced to carry yellow identity cards. After the Six Day War of 1967, further repressive measures were imposed: Jewish property was expropriated; Jewish bank accounts were frozen; Jews were dismissed from public posts; businesses were shuttered; trading permits were cancelled; Jews were placed under house arrest for long periods of time. By 2004, only a tiny handful of Jews remained in Iraq.

While there had been Jews in **Turkey** since the 5th century BC, the major influx came after 1492, with the expulsion of Jews from Spain and Portugal. They were seen as useful on account of their international trading connections. Thus, Turkish Jewry, over the centuries, was largely Sephardi. A small number entered from Germany in the 1930s, including academics welcomed by the universities. The Jewish community was largely secure and prosperous over the centuries. About 15,000 have emigrated to Israel since 1948, though there was no pressure to do so from the Turkish authorities.

Chapter Twelve

Israel: The Main Events, Civilian and Military, 1948 to 2020

A. Constructing the infrastructure of the state – building on the pre-state Yishuv

1. De-politicisation, across-the-board

This took all of the first decade of the state. De-politicisation of the army was followed by the same process in the civil service (Even doing so for the legal system was not straightforward; continuing from the mandatory pattern, while many judges had no clear political affiliation, others were close to the Mapai party. But within about five years the courts came to be seen as ideologically neutral and did not hesitate to criticise government institutions.) The civil service took much longer; each minister had swiftly staffed his ministry with his cronies. The idea of professional civil servants, who could serve as a counter weight to a minister, was barely accepted. However, by 1959 a number of civil service laws had been enacted. These established universal, meritocratic criteria for appointments (an approach influenced by the British pattern; Edwin Samuel, the son of Herbert, who had 'stayed on' after his father's departure played a considerable part here). A National Insurance Institute was set up, over time providing a network of social support and welfare mechanisms.

Before 1948, the Socialist section of society had its own school network, emphasising collective principles. That network then took on a more neutral character as the main, de-politicised state system; alongside it was a moderately religious stream, providing both religious and secular education, and an ultra-Orthodox stream, which eschewed the latter. The tripartite pattern largely continues to the present day.

In the early years of the state a tension developed between collective norms supporting dedication to society – for the good of the state – and people's, particularly parents', aspirations to improve their standard of living, secure an education for their children, and climb the social ladder. This tension has persisted over the decades, particularly in the first two decades of the 21st century, with the explosion of thousands of start-ups – essentially an individualistic achievement, although with encouragement from the state. At the same time, volunteerism, in a myriad of directions, was a feature of the early years of the state and has remained, in the form of a large number of non-governmental organisations, across the political spectrum. The public expected their political leaders to lead modest personal lives and for the most part that was the case; it was true on the Mapai side, particularly of Ben-Gurion, and on the Herut side, both Begin and his successor, Shamir, lived modestly. This has not been true, to say the least, of more recent leaders of that party, now termed Likud.

2. Higher education

In 1949, there were only three institutions of higher education and basic and applied research: the Hebrew University, the Haifa Technion, and what would become the Weizmann Institute. Ben-Gurion and his colleagues, following in Weizmann's footsteps, recognised the importance of science as a national resource. Given the tremendous demographic superiority of the Arab states, they always believed that the one factor that would guarantee Israel's existence was its ability to harness the population's intellectual, technological and scientific abilities to benefit society. There was a keen awareness of Jewish academic achievements in the Diaspora, and a desire to replicate it in the new state. Hence, the establishment of new universities in the 1960s: Tel Aviv, Haifa, Beersheba and Bar Ilan (in a suburb of Tel Aviv). The stream of university graduates eventually underpinned the development of high tech and in the immediate term provided well-educated people to fill the large number of posts in the civil service. But as far as science was concerned, high calibre people were not enough; considerable funding was needed to establish long-term research programmes. Other countries, America in particular, had lavish resources. The result, for several decades, was that Israel lost many of its PhD level graduates to the United States, where they had much better facilities, as well as tenured positions in the expanding universities. Some of the shortfall in government funding was made up by financial contributions from Diaspora Jews.

3. The kibbutz and the moshav

By the end of the 1950s, 400 agricultural settlements had been established, of which 270 were set up in the first three years of the state (100 were for new immigrants, many of whom had little or no agricultural background). But the availability of means of production – land, water and workers – made agriculture the quickest and most effective solution to the problem of immigrant employment and housing, while also meeting the state's security needs along the borders and providing food for the growing population. Whereas the kibbutz was a collectivist enterprise, based on an education from early years in socialist values, and hence unsuited to the vast majority of the new immigrants, the moshav was cooperative and organised around the family unit. Agriculture was one major form of employment; construction, to provide housing for the masses of new immigrants, was another. In the 1950s, governmental efforts were focused on these two areas.

4. The Knesset (Parliament)

From 1949 to 1977, Mapai, for most of the first two decades dominated by Ben-Gurion, formed the core of government. The National Religious Party was a permanent partner; it was moderate before 1967, but after Israel's apparently miraculous victory in the Six Day War, and conquest of the West Bank, took on a markedly messianic aspect. Maki (the Israel Communist Party) and Begin's Herut (Freedom) party were excluded, apart from a brief period associated with the Six Day War, when Begin served as minister without portfolio. Herut had two main themes and objectives: opposition to socialist control of the economy and the 'liberation of the entire "Land of Israel"', not only the West Bank of the Jordan (held by Transjordan after the 1948 War, and soon formally annexed by King Abdullah), but also his original kingdom. Heruts' long-standing aim to conquer 'both sides of the Jordan' is embodied in the title of its anthem.

5. A free press

Each party owned its own newspaper, and there were also several independent papers (perhaps the most important being the unswervingly leftist Zionist, *Haaretz*, edited from 1939 to 1990 by the redoubtable Gershon Shocken, a German immigrant early in the Nazi period, and since headed by his son, Amos).

6. Mass immigration: numbers and composition

In the first three years of the state, everything was subordinated to two principal objectives: victory in the war to ensure Israel's existence, and immigrant absorption. By the time the war ended in the spring of 1949, more than 100,000 people had been mobilised and consequently had not contributed to the economy. On the other hand, 100,000 new immigrants had arrived during the war, more than in any previous year. In the first 42 months of the state's existence, the average monthly number of new immigrants reached some 16,000; all in all, 690,000 immigrants arrived in Israel, and within three years the Jewish population doubled. The vast scope of this immigration relative to the size of the host population – unheard of in any immigrant country – created tremendous pressures on the economy. Shortage of funds, both for the manifold needs of the state, and for individual recipients, was partly alleviated by German reparations agreed in the early 1950s. Over the long term, all the problems associated with daily life were laid at the door of the Mapai party; although it had steered the state through enormous economic and military difficulties, it was seen as responsible for the travails along the way. Persistent difficulties in everyday life were blamed, particularly by the mass of new immigrants, on the labour movement. This simmering anger eventually found its outlet at the ballot box, with great force, late in the 1970s.

The degree of difficulty in absorbing the different segments of the mass immigration was related to the composition of each particular group, and the extent to which they had common features with the long-established Yishuv.

The first to arrive were from the DP camps in Germany – the survivors of European Jewry. Although the education of the young had been greatly truncated, the adults had in common with veteran Israelis various Western occupational skills and, above all, a common language, Yiddish. Those who came from Arab countries had been either forcibly expelled, or driven to leave by conditions imposed by the authorities which made life no longer viable. The Jews of Yemen were the first, conveyed by a massive airlift; next were immigrants from the Jewish community of Iraq, often well-educated. The Jews from North Africa came mostly from Morocco, particularly between the mid-1950s and the mid-1960s; most of the community's educated, professional sector preferred to go to France or to Canada. A much smaller number immigrated from Egypt.

Irrespective of their country of origin, many hundreds of thousands of new immigrants found themselves in the early years of the state in very temporary and essentially unpleasant housing, which took years to be replaced by permanent accommodation in established communities, or in new 'development towns' on the periphery of the country. The economic structure of the moshav, with its emphasis on family ties, played a bigger part in absorption than did the kibbutz, which remained a largely elite set of communities, contributing disproportionately to the leadership of the state in all key areas. However the communal ways of the kibbutz were alien to the vast majority of new immigrants, particularly those from the Arab world with their emphasis on the family as the core institution, respect for the elderly and adherence to traditional religious practices. They became known as Mizrachim – literally 'Easterners' – or Sephardim (the latter a misnomer since it denotes Jews from the Iberian Peninsula, but the appellation stuck). Those of European origin were called 'Ashkenazim'. The terms are still used, though marriages between the two broad groups have increased considerably. Political loyalties are still largely in place: the Mizrachim continue to support right-wing and religious parties; secular Ashkenazim, in the main, the parties of the centre and left.

7. The Arab population

After the War of Independence, the Arab population of Israel numbered 156,000, about 20 percent of the total population, mostly living in the Galilee. Stung by the defeat, and the flight and expulsion of their communities, they had no acknowledged leadership. Israel seized abandoned property and expropriated Arab land for Jewish settlement. According to some estimates, between 40 percent and 60 percent of land that was Arab-owned in 1948 was now transferred to Jewish ownership. Ben-Gurion was persuaded that the Arabs could not be trusted and that 'military government' should be imposed. This meant, among others, that they were excluded from the right to defend themselves in the Israeli judicial system. In Israel's second decade military rule was reduced and restrictions on movement abolished. The military government was finally ended in 1966, during the prime ministership of Levi Eshkol, Ben-Gurion's successor in 1963. Independent Arab parties finally appeared in 1981.

By 2020, the Arab population of Israel had reached nearly 1.8 million, still around 20 percent of the total population, in large part due to a higher average birthrate than in the Jewish population, and access to good neonatal services. Not all are Sunni Moslem: about 140,000 are Christian, a slowly growing section of the population despite departures, mainly for the United States. About the same proportion are Druze, a sect that broke away from Sunni Islam several centuries ago, and which adheres to the key theme of being loyal to the country in which they live; the Druze have served in the IDF for many years, some attaining high ranks. The Bedouin, formerly nomadic herdsmen but reluctantly moving into more urban accommodation, are a fast-growing sector – now about one-sixth of the Arab population – and, like the Druze, they serve in the IDF.[159]

Approximately 20 percent of the current Arab population attend Israeli universities, a proportional share that is increasing, although it has not yet reached the Jewish share of undergraduates. Most Israeli Arabs vote for Arab political parties. To date, no Israeli governing coalition has included an Arab party, as such, but most political parties, particularly of the left, include one or two Arab MKs. With a small number of exceptions, the school system is separate between Arabs and Jews. Socially, there is not a great deal of mixing, even in the universities, though it is fair to say that this is largely by the choice of the two communities, and there is little intermarriage.

B. The Wars of the First 30 Years

There were three wars in all: the first, in 1956, involved a long-denied collusion between Israel, Britain and France, and an attack on Egypt known in the West as the Suez Affair, and in Israel as the Sinai campaign; the second, generally termed the Six Day

War, was a dramatic Israeli victory over Egypt, Syria and Jordan; the third, in 1973, the Yom Kippur War, involved initial Egyptian and Syrian successes, but final defeats for those two countries, albeit at a high cost to Israel.

1. The strange case of the Suez (Sinai) campaign

Winston Churchill had returned to power in 1951, and had hung on for four years, despite a series of strokes, before finally handing over to his long-serving understudy, Anthony Eden. Unfortunately, Eden was, by then, subject to chronic ill-health, a problem that impaired his judgement of foreign affairs, despite his long experience in that area.

His opponent in the Suez War was Col. Nasser, born in obscurity, now the beau ideal of the Arab world – a young officer wounded in the Israeli encirclement of 1948, and determined to restore Arab pride. He became the most popular Arab leader for centuries, yet he also ruled as a dictator, supported by the secret police. Known across the Arab world as El Rais, the Boss, Nasser promulgated a socialist pan-Arabism that inspired his people to deny Western domination and the Zionist victory, and raised soaring hopes that Egyptian defeat could be avenged.

Nasser supported Palestinian cross-border raids into Israel, which responded with increasing violence. His leadership of the most powerful Arab nation alarmed Israel. In 1956, he challenged the vestiges of the English and French empires by nationalising the Suez Canal. London and Paris determined to destroy him, and made a secret alliance with Ben-Gurion whereby Israel would attack the Egyptian army in the Sinai desert; Britain and France would then intervene, while the battle was still on, 'to secure the safety of the canal'. The Israeli attack was successful, and provided the Anglo-French pretext to invade Egypt, ostensibly to separate the two combatants. Unfortunately, the Israelis wrapped up their part of the agreement before the British and French were fully on the scene. Israel lacked the power to sustain this last imperial adventure, and the United States forced it to withdraw, thus notably humiliating Britain; Anthony Eden, broken in health, and deeply depressed, resigned. As one consequence, King Hussein, Abdullah's grandson, dismissed General Glubb, the long-serving British commander of his army. Nineteen-fifty-six was the twilight of British Middle Eastern imperium and the dawn of American ascendancy.

Although defeated militarily Nasser went on to target the two Hashemite kingdoms, Jordan and Iraq, where his pan-Arabist radicalism was increasingly popular. Nasser officially merged Egypt with Syria in the United Arab Republic, encircling Israel, and dominating Jordan.[160]

2. The Six Day War

In 1959 Yasser Arafat, a Palestinian-raised veteran of the 1948 war, founded a militant liberation movement called Fatah (Conquest). Its beginnings were slow but Arafat's image – packing a pistol, wearing an Arab headdress, khaki-clad – gradually placed the Palestinian cause at the centre of the world stage. He inspired a generation of young men – and some women – to carry out a succession of terrorist acts in the 1970s: hijacking and blowing up airliners. These activities followed the Arab debacle in the Six Day War.

Ben-Gurion had retired in 1963, to be replaced by Levi Eshkol, a dogged plodder in his late 60s. Following Syrian attacks on northern Israel, there was a dogfight in which the Syrian air force was decimated over Damascus – a precursor of Israel's crucial air superiority in the coming war. In response, Syria backed more Palestinian raids into Israel.

Nasser, himself humiliated by Israeli reprisal raids on the ground, sought to show that as a pan-Arab leader he would not tolerate an attack on Syria. Moving his troops into the Sinai Peninsula, he then asked the UN to remove its peacekeepers from Sinai. A crisis of foreboding and fear swept over Israel, which seemed to have lost the initiative to Nasser.

Next, on 23 May, Nasser closed the seaway to Israel's Red Sea port of Eilat. The Israeli Chief of Staff, Rabin, advised Eshkol to launch a pre-emptive strike against Egypt or face annihilation. Eshkol refused until all political options had been exhausted. In Amman, King Hussein felt he had little choice but to join Nasser if Egypt attacked Israel – otherwise he would be regarded as a traitor. He placed his 56,000-strong army under an Egyptian general and declared "all of the Arab armies now surround Israel". Thus, Israel faced war on three fronts simultaneously. With the

Holocaust only a little over 20 years in the past, Israelis feared a repetition. At that point, Eshkol appointed as defence minister, Moshe Dayan, Israel's most respected soldier and a cool-headed, charismatic national figure. The brilliant, British-educated Abba Eban reported from Washington that while America did not approve military action, it would not move to prevent it.

The surrounding Arab nations could, in theory, field half a million men, 5,000 tanks and 900 planes. The Israelis had 275,000 men, 1,100 tanks and 200 planes. A factor concerning the last-named asset, little noticed at the time but logistically crucial, was the turnaround time (to refuel and rearm, etc.): the Israeli air force, after years of assiduous practice, had a time of 20 minutes; the Egyptian equivalent was 12 hours. This meant that the Israeli planes could spend far more time in the air than their Egyptian equivalents.

Moreover, Israel attacked early in the morning of June 5th and from an unexpected direction, wiping out the Egyptian air force on the ground. An hour later, Dayan, ordered the IDF into Sinai.

Israel assured Hussein, through three different foreign intermediaries, that Israel would not attack Jordan, if Jordan maintained the quiet. The converse would also be true. Hussein was informed by the Egyptian commander, Amer, that Israeli forces had been smashed – an Egyptian victory both on the ground and in the air was confirmed by Nasser himself. Hussein was not to know until too late that this claim was a complete fiction. He told his people: "The hour of revenge has come". Jordanian artillery launched a heavy bombardment on Jewish Jerusalem. Dayan then ordered a strike against the Jordanian air force; watching with his eldest son, the future King Abdullah II, Hussein saw his planes destroyed.

More misinformation from Nasser who told Hussein, now embroiled in a ground war in and around Jerusalem: they should claim that the US and Britain had defeated the Arabs, not just Israel on its own – again pure fiction. Israeli troops stormed the Old City of Jerusalem, capturing it and the Temple Mount. The Chief Rabbi of the Army, Shlomo Goren, wanted to accelerate the messianic era by dynamiting the mosques on the Mount. The Israeli general in charge, Uzi Narkiss, vetoed this. Dayan himself – always the Israeli who most respected and was most respected by the Arabs – proclaimed: "To our Arab neighbours, Israel extends the hand of peace and to all peoples of all faiths, we guarantee full freedom of worship". Ten days later, he went to the Al Aqsa mosque on the Mount and, sitting with the Sheikh of Al Aqsa, Dayan explained that while Jerusalem now belonged to Israel, the Waqf (the Moslem religious authority) would control the Temple Mount and he ruled that Jews were forbidden to pray there.

President Nasser offered his resignation, but his people demanded that he remain. He never recovered from the overwhelming defeat he had suffered and died of a heart attack. Three years later King Hussein admitted that 5 to 10 June, "were the worst days of my life". By a massive miscalculation he had lost half his territory – and particularly the prize of Jerusalem. For Israel the victory over Jordan was pyrrhic: the government had to decide what to do about the Arab population of East Jerusalem and the West Bank – for 18 years, they had been under Jordanian rule, using Jordanian currency and to all intents and purposes as much a part of Jordanian life as those living on the East Bank of the Jordan. The West Bank population, constantly increasing, is a factor that has challenged Israeli politics, both internal and external, for the more than 50 years that have passed since that conflict – which was not sought by Israel though its outcome was welcomed by most Israelis at the time.

Most Israelis did not think about the problems posed by the conquest of the West Bank: for religious Jews it was a sign of deliverance and redemption; for the secular nationalists, the heirs of Jabotinsky, the military victory was political and strategic – a chance to secure a Greater Israel with safe borders. Internationally, Israel's victory against the Soviet-armed regimes of the Arab states convinced the United States that Israel was its ally in the struggle against Soviet Russia in the dangerous Middle East. But in the Arab world, things were different. Yasser Arafat and his Fatah movement took over the Palestine Liberation Organisation in 1969 and intensified guerrilla attacks on Israel. They built up their base in Jordan, forcing Hussein in 'Black September', 1972, to confront, defeat and expel Arafat and the PLO, after his control of Jordan had been challenged. Arafat moved his headquarters to Lebanon and Fatah embarked on a campaign of hijacking and killing of civilians to bring the Palestinian cause to the attention of the world, most memorably in the murder of 11 Israeli athletes at the Munich Olympics of 1972.

3. The Yom Kippur War of October 1973

This began with a major Israeli intelligence debacle. Both the political and the military establishments failed to interpret correctly large Egyptian 'manoeuvres' on the other side of the Suez Canal (the Sinai Desert in-between was still held by Israel). Together with a simultaneous Syrian attack – also not anticipated by Israeli intelligence – the combined forces of the two Arab countries scored early successes. But the Israelis, assisted by an initially withheld American airlift of vital military materiel, were able to turn the tide and restore the pre-war status quo. However, Israel paid a very high price in casualties, including 2,600 dead soldiers, and the pre-war hubris was severely punctured. There were two beneficiaries: Gen. Ariel Sharon, who played a major part in the final Israeli victory and subsequently moved into a political career; and the PLO, which was recognized by King Hussein as 'the sole representative of the Palestinians' after the Arab League persuaded Hussein to thus acknowledge his former deadly enemy. In the longer term, Israeli policy makers began to understand that they could not depend on foreign countries to supply major armaments, and that they should instead aim to be self-reliant.

In 1977, at his eighth attempt, Menachem Begin won an Israeli election. Unlike the formerly dominant Labour Party, he had learned how to appeal to the masses of Mizrachi Jews. Sharon, whom he appointed his defence minister, promptly urged the eager religious nationalists to 'seize every hilltop' (in the West Bank). They did so, setting up a large number of scattered settlements. At the same time, with support across the political spectrum, Israel developed a series of what are now called 'large settlement blocs', adjacent to Israel's pre-1967 borders, which – as compared with the more remote settlements – have attracted large numbers of Israelis, both secular and religious. Moreover, these blocs, actually towns of increasing size, tend to be regarded by the international community as part of Israel in any future agreement with the

Palestinians; this is emphatically not the case with the scattered small settlements.

In a dizzying series of events in 1978 the Egyptian leader, Anwar Sadat, flew to Jerusalem and offered peace in a Knesset speech. Steered by Moshe Dayan, whom Begin had appointed Foreign Minister, despite his Labour roots, and much encouraged by President Jimmy Carter, Israel and Egypt signed a peace treaty in which Israel restored the Sinai to Egypt, which the Egyptians agreed to demilitarise. Begin made it very clear that withdrawal from Sinai would not be followed by withdrawal from the West Bank. For his courageous efforts, Sadat was assassinated by fundamentalists – the punishment that had been meted out to Abdullah 30 years earlier, also for compromise with Israel.

4. A 'war of choice'

Pressured his defence minister, Ariel Sharon, Begin decided to deal a final blow to the PLO, increasingly entrenched in southern Lebanon. In 1982 he authorised an incursion by the IDF into Lebanon so as to control the 25-mile strip north of the Israel-Lebanon border. But Sharon ordered the army to press on northward to the Lebanese capital, Beirut, with the highly ambitious aim of expelling the PLO from Lebanon, and installing in power a puppet, Christian-led regime. The plan went badly wrong. Although the PLO leadership and fighters did move to Tunis, the intended Lebanese leader was assassinated by the Syrians, and the Israel army allowed Christian militias to murder several hundred Palestinian inhabitants of the Sabra and Shatilla refugee camps. A high-level Israeli judicial enquiry ruled that Sharon should leave his post as defence minister, and should never again serve in that capacity.

The IDF withdrew to the Litani river 25 miles north of the international border and retained control of southern Lebanon for close to 20 years, before finally withdrawing during the reign of a Labour government, led by Ehud Barak. In 1983, ill and depressed, Begin resigned as Prime Minister, saying, "I cannot continue". He was replaced as Likud leader by Yitzhak Shamir who, in the subsequent general election, won the same number of Knesset seats as Labour, led by Shimon Peres. For the next four years they rotated the premiership. During that period, their attention was largely occupied by an exceptionally high level of inflation, and economic matters had a higher place than before on the political agenda.

Two intifadas, two peace talks and an assassination

The first Intifada (Arabic for 'uprising') broke out in Gaza, which had been occupied by Israel since 1967, and soon spread to Jerusalem. For the most part it involved spontaneous stone-throwing by youths against soldiers and settlers. In 1987, Islamist radicals founded Hamas, a branch of the Egyptian Muslim Brotherhood, which was dedicated to a war of destruction against Israel. The first intifada arose indirectly from the secret Oslo peace talks which continued over some years, with Israel represented by Shimon Peres, the foreign minister, and his deputy, Yossi Beilin. On 13 September 1993, Rabin, now prime minister, signed a treaty with Arafat at the White House, supervised by President Clinton. The West Bank and Gaza were partly handed over to the newly designated Palestinian Authority.

On 4 November, 1995, just four days after Beilin and Arafat's deputy, Abbas, had come to an informal understanding about Jerusalem, Rabin was assassinated by a Jewish religious fanatic. His killing was preceded by an intense campaign of vilification and incitement, at least passively approved by the Likud leader, then a new name on the national and international scene, Benjamin Netanyahu. He was elected prime minister six months later, following a campaign of Hamas-orchestrated bus bombings, which nullified an initial post-assassination lead for Peres.

With Netanyahu replaced as prime minister by Ehud Barak (Labour), a decorated war hero and former chief of staff and defence minister, a further attempt at peace took place in July 2000 at the presidential retreat, Camp David, again overseen by Clinton. In hindsight, Barak appears to have made a generous offer: 91 percent of the West Bank, all the Arab suburbs of East Jerusalem, where the Palestinian capital would be based, as well as three-quarters of the Old City. Nevertheless, despite Saudi pressure to accept, Arafat felt he could neither negotiate a final settlement of the Palestinian 'right of return', nor approve any form of Israeli sovereignty over the Temple Mount. In talks later that year, in the last weeks of Clinton's presidency, Israel offered full sovereignty on the Temple Mount, keeping only a symbolic link beneath, but Arafat rejected this.

On 18 September 2000, Ariel Sharon, now opposition leader, toured the Temple Mount. His visit was coordinated with the Palestinians and he did not enter the mosque area, but during its course he asserted Jewish rights to pray anywhere on the Temple Mount, in contravention of the status quo. The next day, thousands of Muslim worshippers on the Temple Mount erupted into violent rioting. Sharon's tour had provided Arafat with an opportunity to bolster his position by embracing force. For the next several years, there was a wave of suicide bombings throughout Israel and the West Bank – approximately 150 in all – with several hundred Israelis killed and many more wounded. There was also much loss of life among the Palestinians, in addition to the suicide bombers themselves. The second intifada was crushed with great force by Sharon, now prime minister; the Palestinian Authority was severely damaged and Arafat humiliated. He died in 2004; his successor, Mahmoud Abbas, and the Fatah organisation have continued to control the Palestinian areas of the West Bank, in uneasy coexistence with the Israeli authorities. The West Bank was divided from Israel by a security barrier, intended to thwart suicide attacks. These were indeed greatly reduced, not least on account of Fatah's security cooperation with Israel. The security barrier, and its route which diverges from the Green Line into Palestinian-owned land, has severely affected the lives of the local Palestinians.

In Gaza, Hamas was stronger than Fatah. It existed alongside Israeli settlements that had a population of about 8,000, and an IDF presence. In a surprise move, Sharon, saying "the view from here [the Prime Minister's office] is not the same as the view from there", ordered the Israeli settlements in Gaza to be evacuated, if necessary by force. The settlers resisted the young Israeli soldiers charged with the task, but the evacuation of 2005 was carried out. Several relatively remote Israeli settlements in the northern West Bank were also removed.

Small wars, north and south

With what was now effectively a free hand in Gaza, Hamas consolidated its control by forcibly expelling Fatah officials, and began launching rockets on adjacent settlements in Israel proper. Despite his rapidly increasing corpulence, Sharon conveyed an image of great energy and decisiveness. His premiership came to an abrupt end when he suffered a massive stroke and he spent several years in a coma before his final demise.

Following a general election, the centrist Kadima party, led by Ehud Olmert, attained power, but before very long, Olmert had to resign office on account of well-supported allegations of corruption during a previous spell as mayor of Jerusalem, resulting in a period of imprisonment. Before he left office, to be replaced by Netanyahu, Israel became embroiled in a war in southern Lebanon with the Shiite Hezbollah organisation, who were much encouraged by Iran. In addition to the loss of soldiers on both sides, Israeli civilians in the north of the country, as far south as Haifa, were subjected to some weeks of rocket bombardment, against which American-supplied defences were essentially ineffective. This gave a further spur to Israel's own attempts at anti-rocket missiles; the resulting 'Iron Dome' system was largely effective in subsequent Hamas rocket attacks from Gaza on southern Israel, in the course of two relatively limited conflicts between Hamas and the IDF in 2012 and 2014. Israel's shift from more traditional forms of warfare – such as close-combat infantry encounters – to military action that applies high tech developments to the battlefield and to the protection of the civilian population, has since continued through Israeli advances in technology.

Civilian Life

1. Immigration in the last half century

(a) From Russia

There were two large-scale immigrations from Russia: in the 1970s, with numbers approaching 200,000, and in the 1990s and beyond, with a total of about 1 million. Since the German immigration of the 1930s, Israel had not known immigrants with a comparable level of education to these two Russian waves. This was particularly true of the latter group, which had a higher level of education than that of the host society (60 percent of the immigrants held undergraduate degrees, compared with 30 percent of Israelis). But there was a difference between the two Russian groups: the 1970s immigrants had come mainly from peripheral states that had been under Soviet rule for only 30 years, or from central Asia. In these regions an active Jewish memory and a Zionist tradition still prevailed. This was not true of the 1990s immigrants, who came from the Slavic heartland and the major cities, where Jews had been exposed to the Soviet ethos ever since the Revolution. They were lacking in Jewish culture, either religious or secular. In a further contrast, the 1970s Russian immigrants had fought for the right to emigrate from the USSR and came to Israel out of choice. Most of the 1990s immigrants simply wanted to leave Russia because of its political instability and the economic crisis in which it was mired. Many might have preferred to go to the United States, but Washington had imposed strict quotas on immigration from Eastern Europe. A further difference between the two immigrations was that many of the 1990s wave already had relatives in Israel who had arrived in the 1970s. Moreover, their high qualifications (ranging from nuclear physics to membership of international-level classical orchestras) made them very welcome to the Israeli government.

The Israeli society that received the 1990s newcomers was very different from that of the 1970s, which had been socialist and centralised. It was now a country that supported a free market, private enterprise, privatisation of services and a reduced role for the state. In the 1970s, the Russian immigrants were kept in absorption centres for months in order to learn Hebrew and find their way round the complexities of the new country. In contrast, the 1990s Russians were absorbed in a much more informal way, being largely left to themselves. What the two large groups of Russian immigrants had in common was a rejection of Soviet top-down socialism and its rigid opposition to private enterprise in any form.

The larger Russian immigration doubled the numbers of engineers and doctors in Israel. They brought with them massive technological and scientific knowledge. Without this, Israel's rapid development of high tech in the 1990s and beyond would have been immeasurably more difficult. At the same time, the 1990s immigrants, who were steeped in Russian culture but had little knowledge of Israeli and Hebrew activities in the arts, retained the former, while slowly acculturating to the latter. Indeed, they tended to look down on what they found in Israel, particularly science education, and the relatively informal educational atmosphere of Israeli schools. So they established their own educational system, particularly focusing on mathematics and science. These schools taught in Hebrew but included lessons in Russian language and culture. A high degree of internal cohesion fostered the development of specifically Russian political parties. These have existed for many years, but at the present time, the sole remaining party is in slow numerical decline, as the younger generation, born or raised in Israel, feels increasingly at home in the general run of Israeli political parties, particularly on the right, an enduring feature of their parents' hostility to socialism.

In contrast to the 1970s immigrants, many of whom were religiously observant, the much larger 1990s group was overwhelmingly secular. This boosted the secular section of Israeli society, which had become a diminishing minority in comparison to those who were self-described as traditional, Orthodox or ultra-Orthodox. A final feature of the two Russian immigrations is that they tended to perceive Israel's relations with its Arab citizens and neighbouring Arab countries in the same way that, in the USSR, they had learned to perceive the rest of the world: as immutably threatening. But it may be that, in time, the "Russians", particularly those born or raised in Israel, will become more like the majority of educated and secular veteran Israelis in their attitudes to the Arabs of Israel and to the neighbouring Arab countries, that is, patriotic but largely prepared to compromise, rather than nationalist and expansionist.

A complicating factor among the "Russians" is the approximately 350,000 who entered Israel under the Law of Return – having one Jewish grandparent – rather than being Jewish according to the rabbinate; by law the rabbinate determines who is eligible for Jewish marriage. Since a large proportion of current immigration from the former Soviet Union enters Israel under the Law of Return, their numbers are increasing annually by around 10,000. As far as their own self-perception is concerned, the overwhelming majority 'feel Israel is their home', and almost 100 percent say they will remain in Israel.[161]

(b) Ethiopian immigration

This has reached nearly 100,000 and is not expected to increase beyond a few thousand over the next decade. While there were initial doubts about the 'Jewishness' of the Ethiopians – and hence their eligibility to enter under the Law of Return – these were eventually resolved by rabbinical decree and a series of airlifts brought them to Israel beginning in the 1980s. Their socialisation and adaptation to life in Israel has been relatively difficult and protracted. The cost of absorbing an Ethiopian immigrant was estimated at twice that of a Russian immigrant. While many of the Ethiopians came from the largest city, Addis Ababa, rather than remote villages, few had education beyond high school. However after two generations in Israel, the community is now approaching the Israeli average for educational level, their integration much assisted by military service, which has been compulsory for most Jews since 1949.

Social mobility

Social mobility is high for two groups in particular: Israelis of Ethiopian origin and Israeli Arabs. As far as the former are concerned, a study by the Israel Finance Ministry[162] found that while the parental generation were on average at the 22nd percentile for income, their children were in the 42nd percentile. Overall, Israeli intergenerational mobility compared favourably with other developed nations, the study found. Among 23 countries, Israel had the fifth highest level after Norway, Denmark, Canada and Finland and was well ahead of other countries usually considered to enjoy both mobility and equality, including Australia, Sweden, Germany, Japan and France.

The Arab population of Israel

'The Jewish majority of Israel takes for granted that it is the Jewish state, in which a home has been built for the Jewish people in its ancient homeland. The Law of Return, which grants preferential citizenship rights to Jews and their offspring over other immigrants, seems to the Jews to express the nature of the state as the ingathering of the Jewish exiles [...] From the Jews' point of view, this is self-evidently the State of Israel. It therefore opposes the 'right of return' of Arab refugees and also tries to block Arab emigration to Israel from the occupied territories'.[163]

Israel's Arab minority has remained at about 20 percent of the total population for the past 70 years despite obstacles to Arab immigration, largely due to a high Arab birth rate over most of that period and access to reasonably good perinatal services. This large Arab minority, about 70 percent of which is Moslem, diverges somewhat in attitude to the Jewish state between Moslems, Christians, Druze, and Bedouin. The last three subgroups, each comprising about 10 percent of the non-Moslem minority, tend in varying degrees to be more positive towards the Jewish majority. Israeli Arabs, in general, are well versed in state law and active in protecting their rights. There is an increasing tendency for qualified Arabs to work in the Jewish sector of employment, including high-tech (where security concerns are sometimes cited as obstacles to entry). For example, the Hadassah Medical Organisation, a Jewish-American founded, and still largely funded, entity, includes many Arab doctors, Moslem and other, up to the highest level of seniority. Pragmatism is increasingly found on both sides. Among Israeli Arabs, social mobility was indicated by an improvement from the 31st percentile of average income for the older generation, to the 41st percentile for the younger one.

Recent data on the number of Israeli Arabs in higher education suggests a rising trend. A survey by the Council for Higher Education[164] found that the number pursuing bachelor degrees at Israeli universities and colleges jumped 60 percent over seven years to 47,000 in 2017. In Masters programmes the percentage more than doubled, from 6.2 percent to 13 percent, while in doctoral programmes the figure climbed 60 percent, from 3.9 percent to 6.3 percent. If this trend continues over the next decade the current inequality in income is likely to be further reduced. It also is important that the share of Israeli Arab graduates in the high-earning areas of employment, for example, in high-tech, continues to increase. This is the case at the Haifa Technion, where in the academic year 2016-17, 22.2 percent of students were from Israel's Arab population – an increase over the years paralleling the general increase in first degree students.

Nevertheless, at the representative political level, there is a clear view, expressed by the High Follow-Up Committee for Arab citizens of Israel, an extra-parliamentary umbrella organization that includes Arab members of the Knesset, as follows: We are in favour of the two-state solution: a Palestinian state [in the West Bank], alongside a bi-national state [the current State of Israel]. The idea of a bi-national state was espoused by a very small but influential group, including Martin Buber, before 1948, and is currently supported by a limited section of Jewish Israelis.

At the end of 2017, 60 percent of Israel's Arab population lived in the north of the country, where they comprise 52 percent of the total population. In north-east Israel, in an area known as the Triangle which abuts the West Bank, some 97 percent of the population is Arab. Several right-wing Israeli politicians have proposed that in any final settlement the borders of Israel/ Palestine should be redrawn so that the Triangle, with its inhabitants, would become part of Palestine. Surveys over the years have found that no more than a third of the Arab inhabitants of the Triangle would favour such an outcome. Pragmatism appears to determine the view of the remaining two-thirds – it is likely that education, health and social services would all be less adequate on the other side of the border, certainly for some time to come. The remainder of Israel's Arab population may also take a pragmatic view, namely to remain as a minority in the Jewish state while continuing to press for a more equal share of resources, rather than seeking a bi-national state encompassing the entire Jewish and Arab populations of Israel and the West Bank.

An extensive survey, the 2017 Index of Arab-Jewish relations in Israel, found that nearly 60 percent of Israeli Arabs recognise Israel's right to exist, down from 66 percent in 2015. Similarly, the percentage of Arabs recognising the state as Jewish and democratic dropped from 54 percent to 50 percent, while the share of those seeing it as a Zionist state went down from 42 percent in 2015 to 36 percent in 2017. There was a dramatic decrease in the percentage of Israeli Arabs acknowledging that Israel is a Jewish-majority state, from 60 percent in 2015 to 44 percent in 2017. In that year 50 percent acknowledged that Hebrew was the dominant language in the country, compared to 63 percent two years earlier.

A parallel survey among the Jewish population found that in 2017 only 61 percent viewed the country's Arabs as full members of Israeli society, down from 70 percent two years earlier. The percentage of Israeli Jews agreeing that Arabs have the right to live as a minority enjoying full civil rights was down from 80 percent in 2015 to 74 percent in 2017. Just 52 percent of Israel's Jewish population were willing to have Arab children in their kids' school class, down from 58 percent in 2015. A similar decline was found in the percentage of Jews willing to have Arab neighbours. There was also a slight increase in the percentage of Jews refraining from entering Israeli Arab towns, from 59 percent to 64 percent.

This survey has been conducted since 1976 by Prof. Sami Smooha of Haifa University. It concludes that while Israeli Arabs increasingly question the state's legitimacy, they still wouldn't leave the country. In 2017, 77 percent said they weren't willing to live in a future Palestinian state, up from 72 percent in 2015. Some 60 percent said they preferred living in Israel over any other country in the world, very slightly up from 59 percent two years earlier.

The most recent survey was conducted, face-to-face, with 700 Arabs and 700 Jews across the country between May and August 2017.[165]

A study by the Taub Centre found that the percentage of Israeli Arab women succeeding in the *bagrut* examination now surpasses that of Israeli Arab men (the same disparity is found between Israeli Jewish men and women throughout the West; women first catch up and then surpass men). The next stage is that Israeli Arab women will overtake their male counterparts at the first-degree level, too. In Israel's Arab population there is a considerable disparity between the minority Christian group and, at the other extreme, the Bedouin population, which is largely impoverished and greatly disadvantaged in terms of educational and other facilities. The educational performance of the former, both of men and women, is at the level of Jewish Israelis; that of the latter, far below. Another problem for the Arab sector is that the field of education attracts much the highest number of undergraduates; the

STEM subjects are seriously under-represented. The Taub Centre report concludes: 'alongside improving trends, there are problematic areas and barriers facing Arab Israeli women, who could be a significant source of growth in the Israeli economy in the coming years.'[166]

Jewish religious affiliation – or lack of it

Broadly speaking, at the present time Israeli Jews report themselves as falling into one of four groups: 45 percent secular (little or no religious observance, except for major life events, such as circumcision and barmitzvah); 23 percent traditional (eating kosher at home, but not always outside, perhaps attending synagogue on Sabbath morning, and a football match in the afternoon); 12 percent traditional with religious leanings; 10 percent Orthodox (varying in degree, but always involving weekly synagogue attendance, also sometimes on weekdays, eating kosher everywhere); 10 percent Haredi i.e. ultra-Orthodox (ideally this means, for men, studying Talmud daily for many years, to the exclusion of work in the outside world, and the full range of religious observance; wives are frequently trained for some kind of work, so as to support the family).[167]

The rise and rise of the Haredi community, and where next for them?
In the early years of the state, Ben-Gurion was persuaded by one of the Haredi leaders to exempt their young men from compulsory military service, and the young women from the social service incumbent on non-Haredi religious women. The objective was to allow the ultra- Orthodox community to recover from the Holocaust. Ben-Gurion was asked to exempt from military service only 400 young men; in fact, the numbers were much greater, and the privilege applied to them too.

One of those exempted was Rabbi Shteinman, the only member of his family to survive the Holocaust. He then devoted his life to building the Haredi Jewish community in Israel. Rabbi Shteinman remained exceedingly modest, sleeping on the same mattress for six decades. He died in December 2017; contrary to his wishes, his funeral was attended by several hundred thousand – testimony to the extraordinary rate of natural increase of the Haredim. This had been augmented, particularly in the early days after 1967 and the apparently miraculous victory, by converts from outside the ultra-Orthodox community. In Eastern Europe, the stronghold of ultra-Orthodoxy, it was normal for members of the community to work, though not to engage in secular educational studies. Only those particularly gifted in religious studies spent a number of years full-time in a yeshiva (religious seminary), most of them afterwards working. The situation in Israel has been very different; about half of Israel's adult ultra- Orthodox male population do not work – a considerable increase from the situation (one-third working) even a decade ago.

Rabbi Shteinman acknowledged that a lifelong devotion to the study of the Torah, eschewing secular learning, was not for everyone; on the contrary, he gave his blessing to thousands of Haredi men who sought to leave the yeshiva to enlist in the Army and/or to pursue a secular education and get a job. Over the past decade, the situation has been changing and will likely continue to do so. The number of children per Haredi family is falling, though it is still far above that of the rest of the Jewish population (5.9 versus 2.4, according to a report by Prof. Dan Ben David).[168] Hence, the Haredi population continues to increase as a proportion of the total Jewish population – 12 percent in 2017 – exceeding one million for the first time. Projecting forward, the proportion is expected to increase to at least 16 percent by 2030.

Enrolment in Haredi schools is falling, relative to the past, as parents are increasingly likely to send their children to non-Haredi religious schools that offer a core curriculum, so that their children will have better employment opportunities as adults than their parents had. As this cohort comes through they will join older ultra-Orthodox young people who have been enrolling at an increasing rate in Israeli institutions of higher education – universities and colleges – an eight-fold increase from 1,000 to 8,000 over the decade from 2005 to 2015. Nevertheless, according to a report by the Israel Democracy Institute, of the ultra-Orthodox students in higher education, 70 percent are women and only 30 percent men. The breakdown of first degree subjects taken by ultra-Orthodox students differs greatly from that among the general population: 34 percent study education, compared with 18 percent of the general population; 11percent study paramedical subjects (6 percent of the general population); and only 8 percent study engineering (18 percent of the general population).

Two other alternative routes from traditional lifelong Torah studies are military service and high-tech training and work. In the former case, there are now four Haredi battalions in the IDF, typically in combat roles. (Each battalion is about 500 in number.) High tech is one of the areas where Haredim have thrived most. Their intense, methodical study of religious texts has proved remarkably applicable to computer programming. There are now about 220 Haredi start-ups – about 3 percent of the Israeli total

Overall, then, there is change: after well over half a century of a monolithic, ultra-Orthodox community, with generation after generation of families following the pattern of living in near-poverty (reliant on the wives for family income, together with stipends from the government handed out by the heads of *kollels*, yeshivas for married men). Through the sheer pressure of economic necessity, and with new access to information via technology, there has been a shift. However, Haredi patterns of study (kollel versus higher education) and military service (delayed and briefer, or, more rarely, regular) respond to government policy; this, in turn, depends on the extent to which ultra-Orthodox parties participate in the governing coalition of the day.

There is a growing group of young Israelis who choose to abandon the Orthodox Judaism in which they were raised in favour of a non-observant – or at least less religious – lifestyle. In Israel they are known as 'formerly religious', a term that refers specifically to Israelis who grew up in the religious Zionist community (Modern Orthodox).

A study by the Taub Centre for Social Policy Studies in Israel found that the number of Orthodox Israeli Jews leaving the fold, particularly among the religious Zionist community, is much larger than was previously assumed. According to the study, 20 percent of children who start first grade in state-run religious schools have left by eighth grade, and 30 percent by 12th grade. The majority of those who leave – about two-thirds – enroll in secular state schools. Their departure, probably supported by their parents, is in reaction to increasing gender segregation in religious schools and stricter dress codes. An earlier study by the Pew Research Centre found that only half of Israeli Jews (54 percent) who had been raised Modern Orthodox still identified as such as adults. The Israel Democracy Institute estimates that anywhere between one-quarter and one-third of Israeli Jews raised in Modern Orthodox families eventually leave, attracted by the freedom of the secular world.[169]

Demography

The predicted annual increase in the population of Israel (problematically high, at 2 percent) will be mainly due to a continued preponderance of births over deaths, with (Jewish) immigration making a relatively small contribution, though still strongly encouraged by every Israeli government. In 2017, 75 percent of the total Jewish population was 'sabra' (Israeli-born), compared with 35 percent native-born at Israel's independence in 1948. Over half of the Jewish population is Israeli-born to at least one parent who was also Israeli-born. Israel's population can be considered young relative to the population of other Western countries. Twenty-eight percent of the population was aged 0-14, while only 10.3 percent were older than 65; within the Jewish population, the Haredi component tilted even more towards the under 14's and away from the over 65's.

A study by the World Health Organisation (WHO) published in the British medical journal *The Lancet* in September 2015,[170] ranked Israel 6th out of 188 countries in global 'healthy life expectancy'. (This term takes into account years of life without a terminal disease.) In 2014, average life expectancy was 80.2 years for Jewish men and 84 years for women; for the Arab population the number of 'healthy life' years is slightly lower. For life expectancy, Israel ranks above the United States, Canada, France and other developed countries. The data on life expectancy underpin the projected population rise – to over 10 million by 2030, from the current 9.0 million, and also, of course, the projected increased share of the over 65's in the total population.

Overall, then, in numerical terms Israel's current population is likely to maintain a significant, in fact *excessive*, rate of increase. Of at least equal importance is the *quality* of the population in terms of its ability to cope with the accelerating pace of change in the contemporary world. The key areas for international comparison are the universities, educational performance in the schools and, above all, the calibre of the high tech sector, which is increasingly of paramount economic importance for every developed country, especially a relatively small country like Israel.

Chapter Thirteen

Israel among the Nations: International Comparisons

1. The universities

There are seven Israeli universities. The longest-established of these is the Hebrew University of Jerusalem. At its inauguration on July 24, 1918, Chaim Weizmann, a distinguished scientist as well as a statesman, commented: "It seems, at first sight, paradoxical that in a land with so sparse a population... In a land crying out for such simple things as ploughs, roads, and harbours, we should begin by creating a centre of spiritual and intellectual development."[171] The Hebrew University's first board of governors included Weizmann, Albert Einstein, Sigmund Freud and Martin Buber. The Haifa Technion followed in 1926 and the Weizmann Institute, as it would later be called, in 1934. The other universities were established much later: Bar Ilan in 1955, Tel Aviv in 1956, Haifa in 1963 and the Ben-Gurion University of the Negev at Beersheba – named for Ben-Gurion after his death – in 1969. Over the years some 30 colleges have been set up, all teaching only at the BA/BSC/Masters level; until very recently none were counted as research universities for international comparisons and rankings. The Inter-Disciplinary Centre (IDC) secured approval in 2018 to offer PhD degrees.

The ARWU rankings
Produced annually by a Shanghai university, these are based on a meticulous analysis of 10,000 worldwide universities to produce a top 500 and a top 200 across-the-board for 21 disciplines combined, as well as a top 20 for each of the 21. The ARWU ranking is the only one of its kind based solely on research criteria – other rankingss are a mix of research, undergraduate appraisal and employer appraisal. The ARWU research criteria combine Nobel and Fields medal awards, publication in the leading science journals and citations in the leading science journals and indices

University rankings do not just feed humanity's competitive urges. They are also an important source of consumer intelligence about a good on which people spend huge amounts of time and money and about which precious little other information is available. When the Shanghai rankings were first published, the 'knowledge economy' was emerging into the global consciousness, with educational institutions as the engines of future prosperity – generators of human capital, of ideas and innovative companies. As the originator of the modern research university, Germany's relatively poor performance was particularly galling and in 2005 the government announced an initiative to channel money to institutions that might become world-class universities; by 2017 it had spent over €4.6 billion on it – to some effect: in 2020 Germany had 10 universities in the top 200 and the trend was improving. Indeed, 31 rich and middle-income countries have announced an excellence initiative of some sort. According to *The Economist*[172] the most unrealistic targets were Nigeria's (to get at least two universities in the world top 200) and Russia's (to get five in the world's top 200), both by 2020, a prediction that proved correct. While the highest rankings are still dominated by America and Britain, China is rising, having 45 universities in the Shanghai top 500, but still has a long way to go to compete with Harvard, MIT, Cambridge and Oxford. Japan, despite being one of the world's leading economies, is still doing relatively poorly in the Shanghai rankings. *The Economist* attributes this to Japan's insularity – it does not seek to attract academics from other countries – in contrast to Western universities.

In 2020 four Israeli universities (Jerusalem, Tel Aviv, Haifa Technion, and the Weizmann) were in the top 200 of the world's universities. No fewer than 58 of the top 200 were from the United States; 20 from the United Kingdom (respectively 65 and 20 in 2017). Equally striking, China now supplied 20 but Russia still had only one. Perhaps the most spectacular achievement is that of France, which in 2020 had one university, Paris-Saclay (an amalgamation of several Paris universities, driven by President Macron) at 14th overall (and 1st for Mathematics). Saclay will now be a magnet for top research scientists from other countries, as well as retaining its own stars.

A full appraisal of the top 200 results by country requires relating the number per country to both population and wealth (measured by GDP per head). When this is done, Israel performs rather well: Switzerland is first of the top six smaller countries of the 200 by population per university (seven universities for a population of under 8.4 million i.e. 1.2 million per university), followed by the Netherlands (seven universities, population 17 million), and Israel (four universities, population 9 million). Australia, Sweden and Belgium are close behind. The next stage is to compare GDP per head of population. When this is done, for the above six countries, Israel (GDP per head, $37,000) moves to the head of the six, in terms of top 200 achievement enabled by GDP (Switzerland's GDP per head is $80,000; Sweden's $51,000 and the Netherlands, $45,0000).

There are other factors which militate against Israel's potential ranking in the top 200: the Haredi population has eschewed university entrance to the present time (with occasional exceptions); 25 percent of Israeli government expenditure is devoted to the military – several times higher than the other five countries in this top 200 group of six – potentially allowing less resource for universities; finally, compared to the remaining five countries, Israel's universities are relatively young. All countries outside the US lose many of their most promising university researchers to the US; Israel is no exception. According to a leading Israeli economist, Dan Ben David[173], 25 of the top thousand economists in the world, as measured by citations of their work between 1990 and 2000, were Israelis, only 13 of whom were actually based in Israel. A decade later, only four remained in Israel, full-time. (Ben David is one of the four). His estimate is that 3,000 tenured Israeli professors, one in four of the total number, have relocated to universities abroad, where 'abroad' means the USA.

Two of Israel's other three research universities, Bar Ilan and Ben-Gurion, rank between 401 and 500 in the world top 500. The remaining university, Haifa, falls just outside the 500 cut- off, at least partially because it is largely concerned with the humanities and the social sciences, which play relatively little part in the ARWU rankings, rather than with the basic and applied sciences and technology.

Turning to the top 20 universities, ranked by ARWU by subject, two Israeli computer science departments, those of the Technion and Tel Aviv, figured in the top 20 in 2017 for that discipline. (By way of comparison, two world-class British universities, Cambridge and Imperial College, fell just outside the top 20). The United States supplied 16 out of the 20 top- ranked computer science departments, Canada one and Switzerland one; Israel's two was thus a creditable achievement which helps to underpin high tech developments in Israel. (In 2020 ARWU rankings did not appear separately for Computer Science, which was combined with Engineering). The Turing award, considered the Nobel of computing, was won in 2013 by Prof. Shai Goldwasser, the second Israeli in a row to win it. Her award was particularly noteworthy given the relative lack of women at all levels of the computer science field.

From time to time, a member of the Haredi community attains the upper levels of science achievement. One example, which came to light in 2004, is Dr Aviva Joseph, a microbiology specialist at the Hebrew University, who for 10 years, from the age of 18, had led a 'double life', pretending to be a secretary at the University, a profession acceptable to the Haredi world.[174] Having obtained her Hebrew University PhD, Dr Joseph moved on to an active and productive career in the field of molecular biology, both in the University and the private sector. No doubt there are others in Israel's research universities who continue to hide their secular activity from their ultra-Orthodox communities.

2. Other international comparisons

The economy
1. The Grant Thornton Global Dynamism Index. In 2015 Israel was ranked 2/60. Economies are scored for overall dynamism and also for five key areas: business operating environment; economic success and growth, science and technology, labour and human capital, financing environment. Dynamism is defined as changes in the economy which will enable recovery from the 2008-09 economic recession and are likely to lead to a fast rate of future growth. The model was developed by The Economist Intelligence Unit. In 2020 Israel was ranked 8th out of over 150 economies.
2. The Global Competitiveness Index of World Economic Forum analyses the ability of countries to provide high levels of prosperity to its citizens. This in turn depends on how productively a country uses available resources. It measures

institutions, policies and factors that set the sustainable current and medium-term levels of economic prosperity. The report notes that as a nation develops, wages tend to increase, and that in order to sustain this higher income, labour productivity must improve for the nation to be competitive.

Israel is ranked 16/137 countries and is out-ranked by Switzerland, USA, Germany, Sweden, and the United Kingdom, among others, though it is ranked ahead of Austria, Belgium, Australia and France.

Military

Global Firepower Index. This relies on over 50 factors to determine a given nation's score, but crucially: weapon-diversity, geographical factors, natural resources and local industry. Available manpower is a key consideration; nations with large populations tend to rank higher. NATO allies receive a slight bonus. In 2020 Israel was ranked 18th out of 133. It is out-ranked only by considerably larger-population countries, at a minimum, seven times larger. Israel out-ranks many countries with larger populations, including Brazil, Poland, Iran, Australia, Canada, and Spain. The next highest ranked countries with relatively similar populations to Israel are Greece (28) and Sweden (29).

Politics and Governance

1. Transparency International: 2020 Corruption Perceptions Index. The CPI annually ranks countries by their perceived levels of corruption as determined by expert assessment and opinion surveys. It generally defines corruption as the 'misuse of public power for private benefit' and currently ranks 176 countries on a scale from 100 (very clean) to 0 (highly corrupt). Israel was ranked 28/176 countries, below Denmark (1), the United Kingdom (10), Japan (20), and France (23), though above Poland (29), Spain (41), and South Korea (52).

2. The Economist Democracy Index, 2020. The index is compiled by The Economist Intelligence Unit in order to measure the state of democracy in 167 countries, of which 166 are sovereign states and 165 UN member states. It was first produced in 2006, with updates for 2008, 2010 and for each year since then,

and is based on 60 indicators grouped in five different categories, measuring pluralism, civil liberties and political culture. In addition to a numeric score and ranking, the index categorises countries as one of four regime types: full democracies, flawed democracies, hybrid regimes and authoritarian regimes.

Ranked 29/167 Israel is categorised as a flawed democracy, as are the United States, Japan, Italy, France, South Korea, Portugal, [Israel], Czech Republic, India, Belgium, South Africa, Greece, Argentina. The 19 full democracies are headed by Norway, with the United Kingdom at 16. Both Russia (134) and China (136) are categorised as authoritarian.

The 2018 report in which Israel was placed 30th was given a detailed analysis by Anshel Pfeffer.[175] Essentially, Israel scores amongst the world's leaders for most sections of the index and *particularly* so for electoral process, and for pluralism and political participation, both of which score near to the maximum possible. But it is dragged down by the civil liberties category, in which Israel scores only 5.88 – on account of the poor performance on equality, human rights, religious tolerance, racial discrimination, and personal freedom. Pfeffer concludes that if it weren't for the rabbinical hegemony over personal status, such as marriage, and the way Israel treats its non-Jewish minorities, especially the West Bank Palestinians, it would be a model democracy! But based on civil liberties alone, Israel has no right to call itself a democracy, even a flawed one. This brings us back to the argument which has raged in Israel since the Six Day War of 1967: should it withdraw from all the occupied territories to the pre- 67 borders, or live with the many consequences of continuing to rule over the West Bank, and controlling all aspects of life in Gaza, albeit without an internal presence? The extent to which there is full equality for the Arab population of Israel is another crucial question.

3. Standard financial indicators
These have improved dramatically since the middle 1980s, when inflation soared to 400 percent and supermarket prices posted in the morning had risen by the end of the day, thanks to the strength of the underlying economy and the sound professional expertise of the governors of the Bank of Israel. The Economic and Financial

pages of *The Economist* tell the story: for GDP, industrial production, consumer prices, unemployment, current account balance, and budget balance, Israel ranks with the countries of northern Europe, rather than with those of the typically unstable and economically less successful southern part of the continent.

Turning to various areas of debt: the EU target figure is 60 percent of GDP for government debt (a figure achieved in practice only by a small number of EU members). At the end of 2020 Israel's stood at just over 68 percent – a marked worsening, due to the pandemic, over the previous year when it was under 60 percent, the best figure on record for the country. The figure for public and household (private) debt (132 percent of GDP in 2017) is reasonable by EU standards.

Spending on research and development (R and D) is again satisfactory for Israel by international comparisons: the Israeli percentage of GDP is second only to South Korea – but a significant proportion is military R and D, although this does have a civilian spin-off.

However, as already noted, the pandemic has upended economies everywhere and Israel is no exception. After years of steady growth, GDP declined in 2020 by over 4 percent. As elsewhere, Israel will not return for some time to its past upward trend.

High Tech

Origins
The economic changes of the 1990s were marked by a shift from traditional industries such as textiles, machinery, construction, mining, and fertilisers, to knowledge-based high tech industries. The traditional industries were labour-intensive, did not require a high level of specialisation, and in most cases paid relatively low wages. Above all, productivity levels were low. In these sectors of the Israeli economy, this is still the case by international standards.

The high tech industries that began to flourish in the 1990s, and have burgeoned ever since, required higher education, particularly in the STEM subjects. Israel's high tech sector was active in internet-related fields, such as life sciences and medical projects. Their success was the combined result of many years of investment in research and development, as well as steps taken by institutions of higher education to lay the scientific foundations for knowledge-intensive industries, and the influence of defence industries that invested in R&D projects in which a large number of first-generation high tech entrepreneurs acquired the relevant business skills and ideas.[176]

The lessons of the Yom Kippur War were well learned, among them, the need for a locally-based armaments industry, rather than a dependence on the goodwill of a foreign country – which might shift as the interests of that country shifted. The required capital investment has been both local and international as the success of Israeli high-tech has become clear. The relevant statistics are: high tech employs only 10 percent of the Israeli workforce, but is responsible for 50 percent of industrial exports by value. For more than a decade, Israel's GDP growth has been in the region of 4 percent per year, for which the tech sector deserves much of the credit. Relative to the size of the population there are more researchers working in R and D in Israel than in any other country (outstripping Finland, Singapore and South Korea, amongst others); Israel has more companies quoted on NASDAQ (the New York stock exchange, specialising in tech stocks) than any other country except for the United States and China.

Some key reasons for the success of Israel's high tech sector:

1. The traditional Jewish emphasis on innovation, the pursuit of the new, rather than simply repeating what had been done before.

2. Close links between the research universities and commercially viable applications of initially basic research: several of the universities have established facilities which enable both the university and staff members, in the course of developing new inventions, to benefit from their commercial success.

3. Close links between universities and the future digital workplace. Here the Technion is pre-eminent – it was the world number one, in rankings published by the *Times Higher Education Journal*, in teaching digital skills to its graduates and preparing them for the digital workplace.[177] Israel has had largely universal military service since its inception and can thus draw on the full range of young talent, a fact of particular importance in the intelligence and related sectors, most recently in the areas of

cyberattack and cyber defence (Unit 8200, which specialises in such matters, is one of the largest in the IDF).

4. The massive Russian immigration of the 1990s, which, as noted, has been a major source of technical manpower. Significantly, the number of entrepreneurs among immigrants is three times that of entrepreneurs in the veteran Israeli society

5. Easy contacts between school, army, and university friends facilitate the formation of new high tech enterprises.

It is worth noting some well-established individual projects that demonstrate the diverse nature of Israeli high tech:

1. Re Walk Robotics. This is an exo-skeletal system that enables a paralysed person to walk. A Chinese investment company has joined the funding with the intention of opening up the massive Chinese market in this field.[178]

2. Waze. A GPS navigation software that works on smartphones and tablets to provide navigation information, travel times and route details. It won the best overall app award at the 2013 Mobile World Congress. In 2018 it was acquired by Google for one billion dollars, but will remain in Israel.

3. Opgal/Lumus. A night-vision system for security purposes, enabling the user to see in the dark as they would in the daytime

4. Stratasys, a joint Israel-US company, is the top producer of advanced 3-D printing equipment, whose uses range from car manufacturing to dentures and surgical implants.

Major sectors that consistently produce new high-tech products

1. Agritech

This goes back to 1950s Israel when water use was greatly reduced by drip irrigation – applying it directly to the roots of plants. The resulting company, Netafim, is now the world's leader in the field. Newer enterprises are exploiting advances in plant biology and artificial intelligence. Very recent start-ups include one that is developing edible coatings to extend the shelf life of fruits and vegetables; another uses AI to automate beehive maintenance. The kibbutzim have played a major role in Israeli agriculture from the beginning of the Zionist enterprise and continue to do so; today 54 percent of Israel's agri-tech ventures are led by someone who grew up on a kibbutz.

2. Cyber security

By the end of 2017, Israel's cyber-security industry (in which the earliest company was Check Point, now with a market cap of over $15 billion) came second only to the United States and accounted for some 16 percent of overall cyber security investments worldwide. It continued to be attractive to multinational companies, 30 of which have cyber-security related R and D centres in Israel in a variety of areas including automotive systems, financial security and internet. In the last year several new major international companies entered the local industry, opening R and D and innovation centres, including Renault, Daimler, AG and TD Bank. According to data compiled by Start-Up Nation Central, which tracks the Israeli tech ecosystem, by the end of 2020 there were 436 active cyber-security companies in Israel.

Cyber threats include threats to the Internet of things (IoT), because more and more devices are being connected to one another, posing new and significant problems to enterprises, individuals and nations. An official of Start-Up Nation Central stated that 2017 will be remembered as the year when the cyber security sector, both worldwide and Israeli, began to invest a highly significant effort in defending IoT and connected devices, including medical devices, automotive systems, and industrial control systems.[179]

3. Biotech

In 2020 there were about 1,400 life sciences companies active in Israel, and about $800 million was invested in the industry, accounting for 20 percent of all investments in Israeli high-tech. Companies were developing a range of innovations, from a universal flu vaccine, to cell and immune therapy technologies, and drugs that target blood vessels to stop the spread of cancer. All were moving towards the commercialisation of their products.

Many biotech developments involve complex science and have very specific applications. One recently developed device, which has potential applications to tens of millions of patients worldwide, is intended to replace finger-pricking for sugar levels in diabetes patients. At present the need to track and record levels of glucose requires multiple finger pricks each day, a painful and tedious process. An Israeli start-up, Cnoga Medical Ltd, has developed a meter that uses a camera to provide a reading of such levels by observing the changing colours of the user's finger.

Another Israeli start-up, Now Nuclear, is developing an AI system to help pathologists process and analyse biopsies for cancer, more accurately and quickly. The current method, using slides and a microscope, has remained largely unchanged over the past century and requires years of training. There is a growing need for pathologists' diagnostic skills as the prevalence of malignant diseases increases, but the number of pathologists in the world is declining – in Israel, there are only 100. The new technology is now being deployed in hospitals and research centres in Israel and the US. According to Frost and Sullivan, a research and consulting firm, the artificial intelligence market for healthcare applications is expected to expand rapidly, globally, with revenues reaching nearly $7 billion by 2021. The same report stated that AI has the potential to 'improve outcomes by 30 to 40 percent, while reducing the costs of treatment, by as much as 50 percent. AI systems are poised to transform how we think about diagnosis and treatment.'[180]

Another medically oriented Israeli high-tech start-up, Voice Sense, is undertaking a clinical trial of its speech-based 'predictive analytics technology' for detecting depression, to see if there is a correlation between speech patterns and depression and other mental illnesses, such as schizophrenia, which affect millions worldwide. The trial will also see if it is possible to track changes in speech patterns in order to understand changes in a person's state of mental health. According to Prof. Y. Levkovits, chairman of the Department of Psychiatry at Tel Aviv University, "the preliminary results are significant and show the efficacy of the system", whereby typical speech patterns that characterise the depressive population are compared to those of others', and show changes in speech patterns when a person is depressed. Importantly, the software is designed so as to be usable in a large range of languages, from English to Polish and French, as well as Far East languages, such as Mandarin and Punjabi, that are tonal (i.e. saying words in different tones changes the meaning of the word, even if the pronunciation is the same). Given that more than 300 million people of all ages suffer from depression globally, and that the illness is the leading cause of disability worldwide, according to the World Health Organisation, if successful this technology could bring enormous worldwide benefits.[181]

4. Water

This is a universal concern, particularly in the 80 percent of the world affected by drought, or uncertain water safety. Israel is located in a geographical area with an overall water shortage, a problem exacerbated by its rapidly rising population. A National Water Carrier to bring water from the more plentifully supplied north to the south of the country was built in the 1950s. But the problem of dependency on rainwater to replenish Lake Kinneret in the Galilee – in effect a massive natural reservoir – has been largely solved by a series of desalination plants which take sea water from the Mediterranean and then distribute it throughout the country. Israel has also developed expertise in recycling used water, and a generally efficient management of a limited resource.

What of the potential for exporting that experience? According to the Israeli company Water Gen, it has developed technology to make water available everywhere, at a reasonable price. While the process by which air is turned into water is not new, Water Gen has succeeded in making it efficient enough to allow widespread low-cost use and is working with some large consumer product companies, as well as with several armies and in a number of disaster areas.[182] In January 2018, a large number of Israeli companies set out their stalls in India as part of a concerted commercial effort. One of them was Water Gen, which reported that significant-sized demonstration contracts had been signed.

Another universal problem is the safety of water. A Jerusalem-based company, Lishtot (Hebrew for to drink), has developed a simple-to-use device that the company says detects contaminants in water such as bacteria, harmful minerals, and chlorine, in just two seconds. According to the company, the next stage will be to advise customers on how to purify water in which impurities have been detected, with similar speed.[183]

(Of course, some scepticism is in order. A solution to water security problems, which affect literally billions, would be of immeasurable global importance, but while the proven success of Israeli high tech across-the-board is considerable, this area is so crucial that judgement must be suspended until rigorous data on effectiveness are in.)

Meanwhile, a partnership has been forged between Israel's Start-up Nation Central and the US State of Wisconsin's Water Council to address problems of water supply.[184]

Way Care, an Israeli system that monitors traffic and accidents, warning of risks and cutting response times, has been installed in Las Vegas.[185] The UK's National Health Service has launched the UK Israel National Health Initiative to 'streamline Israeli innovation in digital health into the NHS'.[186]

5. Helping the ageing population

A 2015 report by the UN estimates that between 2015 and 2030 the number of people in the world aged 60 years or more will grow by 56 percent. Globally, the number of people aged 80 years or over, defined as the 'oldest of the old', is growing even faster. The UN projects that in 2050, this group will number 434 million, more than triple the number in 2015. Hence it is essential to prepare for the economic and social shifts associated with an ageing population. This UN report lies behind an initiative to show entrepreneurs that the needs of senior citizens are part of a nexus involving family, friends, changing medical circumstances, the need to keep the brain busy, and welfare requirements. A lab has been set up in Beersheba with joint funding by Israel's National Insurance Institute and the Centre for Digital Innovation. It seems likely that the digital health sector for the elderly will expand very rapidly and will involve the use of robots, such as the AI-based robot companion developed by Intuition Robotics, which it says will keep older adults active and engaged with family members by helping to make technology use easier.

6. The construction sector

This is an area that is highly regulated, conservative and traditional. The technologies used are sometimes hundreds of years old; hammers were first used in the Stone Age. The aim of the Israel Builders Association is to build a construction tech sector. Clearly, this is a development of potentially huge dimensions. It is still at an early stage, but some interesting local technologies have already appeared. For example, Datumate, founded by Arab-Israeli entrepreneur Jad Jarroush, is using computer vision, big data analytics, machine learning, and drone and camera technologies to digitally transform the civil engineering processes used in construction, surveying, and infrastructure inspection.[187] Another development is the partnership formed between Solel Boneh, a large Israeli construction company, and Int Site, a start-up founded in 2017, to develop autonomous cranes for construction sites using Internet of Things devices, machine learning, computer vision and natural language-processing technologies. The aim is to increase the productivity of cranes – a major cost item in construction – as well as improving safety and cutting costs.[188]

Productivity per work hour in Israel is lower than that of other industrialised nations. By spreading high-tech innovations to traditional Israeli industries, the reckoning of Google's local branch is that Israel has the ability to generate 6 percent growth in sales in such industries and could contribute some $14 billion annually to the economy over the years. Google Israel has initiated a partnership with Israel's Finance Ministry, and the Manufacturers Association, to achieve that objective.

7. The autonomous car and auto tech industry
Early in 2017, Intel Corp acquired the Jerusalem-based Mobileye firm for more than $15 billion. This company has been at the cutting edge of the highly competitive autonomous car and auto-tech industry. Intel has been involved in Israel for many years, producing very large numbers of computer chips. In 2018 Intel used Mobileye's scientists and technologists to test a large number of autonomous cars in and around Jerusalem. Tests are planned to extend to the United States, particularly Arizona. Clearly Intel, like the major auto companies, believes in the worldwide, long-run future of autonomous vehicles. Their widespread use will cut road traffic accidents by several tens percent, hence reshaping the insurance industry, increasing premiums on drivers continuing to

use traditional vehicles, and reducing them on users of autonomous vehicles

In an intriguing partnership, relevant to the automobile industry, Israel's gene mapping start- up NR Gene has significant orders from abroad, including Australia and Latin America, and has partnered with Bridgestone, a leading tyre company, to develop a novel rubber-producing plant.

Looking across the entire hi tech field, *Time* selected the 100 best inventions for 2019 that made the world 'better and smarter'. Israeli technologies claimed 9 places out of the 100. Inventions included talking glasses (which tell blind people what they are looking at); a device for the treatment of acute migraine; a home appliance to create drinkable water from ambient air for domestic use; a hand-held device for remote medical exams; an 'on demand robot butler'; an artificial product to replace concrete; a robot social companion for the elderly; and an all-electric small aircraft, a prototype for large commercial models.[189]

Military developments
1. Armaments
By 2017, Israel was one of the top six arms-exporting countries in the world.
Plasan
The IDF's military vehicles are protected by a dense, composite material designed and produced by an Israeli company, Plasan, located in a small kibbutz in the Galilee. Its innovative armour can protect vehicles from rocket propelled grenades (RPGs) and improvised explosive devices (IEDs), and does so without adding significant weight. (The latter device was a major cause of casualties in Afghanistan, for both American and British forces). Orders at Plasan have risen from an initial $23 million to over $500 million a year. Among other military products, Plasan is described in *The Weapon Wizards: How Israel became A High-Tech Military Superpower*, by Yaacov Katz and Amir Bohbot.[190]
2. Drones
These vary from the lightweight Skylark which is launched like a football thrown by a quarterback, and which provides key over-the-hill intelligence, critical for infantry operations, to models that are much larger. An example of the latter is a vertical-take-off

drone developed by the APG company, among the first systems of its kind in the world, with four engines enabling it to transition from horizontal to vertical flight, and from horizontal flight to vertical landing. Such unmanned aerial vehicles provide solutions for a variety of military missions, as well as civilian applications and commercial uses, such as ship-based take-off and landing, offshore drilling rig access, package delivery, and precision farming. The current model, termed the Peres 2, has a wing span of more than 2 meters, a maximum take-off weight of 42 kg, and an endurance of up to 8 hours. The near-term plan is to design and build Peres 3 and 4 models, which will weigh more than 200 kg and have a flight endurance of 12 hours. According to the CEO of APG, "the family of UAVs that we are unveiling will 'break the market' because the aircraft in it will allow regular flights, combined with the option of moving between vertical and horizontal flights while using the same engines". At present, Israel is a world leader in drones, with about 60 percent of the export market by value.[191]

3. The IDF: Unit 8200

The unit is the equivalent of America's National Security Agency (NSA), and Britain's Government Communications Headquarters (GCHQ). According to an article in the *Financial Times*[192] it is the largest single military unit in the Israel Defence Forces. An important feeder system is a three-year after-school program for 16 to 18-year-old students with exceptional computer code and hacking skills. The program is funded by the Israeli government and the Rashi Foundation, a private organisation devoted to helping underprivileged youth, which targets gifted children in Israel's poorer south and north. In 2014, Israel's export of cyber security products topped $6 billion, exceeding exports of military hardware for the first time. Israel has captured about 10 percent of the global cyber security market (which is growing rapidly, as noted). Reed quotes Peter Roberts, senior research fellow at Britain's Royal United Services Institute "Unit 8200 is probably the foremost technical intelligence agency in the world and stands on a par with the NSA in everything except scale... They are highly focused on what they look at – certainly more focused than the NSA – and they conduct their operations with a degree of tenacity and passion that you don't experience elsewhere."

4. Women
Young women, both Orthodox and secular, are becoming more involved in the IDF. The former are increasingly serving in the military, rather than solely civilian social service: the numbers have risen from 935 in 2010 to 2700 in 2017.[193] Young, secular women see themselves as able to serve in the full range of combat units (including special forces). For example, the number training and serving as pilots is now in the teens, including one as a squadron commander.

The continuing PISA evidence

Israel's research universities tell a reasonable story of success by international standards; the high-tech sector, both civilian and military, can boast a remarkable level of achievement.

Both concern exceptionally able people, with innate high talent, which is then sought out and nurtured, firstly by special programs for gifted pupils, and then by careful development, both in the universities and in the army, particularly in units like 8200.

The picture is very different if one looks at the level of achievement across the full spectrum of school pupils, as measured by the Programme for International Student Assessment (PISA) carried out every few years in the more advanced countries of the world, including Israel.

Overall, Asian nations led the most recent rankings of 76 countries published by the OECD, with Singapore taking first place; European nations came next, with Finland in sixth place, followed by Estonia, Switzerland and the Netherlands. It is striking that Sweden has declined over the years, now placing at 35th, just four slots ahead of Israel (39th). The US ranked 28th, Britain 20th. Taken together with TIMSS (Trends in International Mathematics and Science Study) the OECD education directorate claims this is the first time that a truly global scale of the quality of education is available. The report notes that 'high quality schooling and oil don't mix easily', referring to the finding that the high-income Arab world trailed far behind on the list.[194]

Both PISA and TIMSS found that Israel had the largest gap of any country between the students who are outstanding in mathematics and sciences, and those who struggle. In short, the Israeli educational system is producing an elite – but also a much larger number who lag far behind. (It should be noted that the results exclude ultra-Orthodox students, both boys and girls – 23 percent of the total of Israeli Jewish school students – as they receive very little or, more often, no secular education).[195]

An analysis by Prof. Ben-David concludes that, according to data collected by OECD in 2013, Israel ranked at the bottom for expenditure per pupil, relative to GDP per capita, in the public education sector, but the highest for private, secondary education. It seems that better-off parents are supplementing their children's public education to improve results in the *bagrut* examinations (taken between 16 and 18 years), which determine access to universities; entrance is also partially dependent on the psychometric test, which includes verbal, non-verbal, and mathematical reasoning (as opposed to knowledge). Ben-David recommends a curriculum that is uniform and mandatory for all students, improvements in the way teachers are chosen, trained and remunerated, and a reorganization of the Education Ministry.[196]

The Donors' Wall

Foreign philanthropy has always been important to Israel – from the earliest days of Jewish settlement in the 1880s to the present. Money from abroad was used for purposes like purchasing land, establishing communities and building public institutions, as well as providing continuing support for universities, hospitals, museums and school education. The sums of money involved are still very considerable – in the billions of dollars per year, from throughout the Diaspora – and are still increasing. A selective overview follows.

The British branch of the Rothschild family is behind the largest philanthropic foundation in Israel, Yad Hanadiv, which donates millions of dollars to Israeli projects every year. The money comes from the interest generated by the fund, which is estimated to total $50 billion-$100 billion.

Yad Hanadiv is identified with large national projects, such as the Knesset and the Supreme Court buildings in Jerusalem, the establishment of Israel Educational Television and other education initiatives. It is now involved in the construction of the new National Library in Jerusalem.

The French branch of the family has established the Caesarea Foundation, which draws its funding from its ownership of more than 120,000 acres of land in Israel. After 1948, the family donated almost all that land to the state, including some 7,400 acres in the area of today's Caesarea. The Rothschilds reached an agreement with the state whereby real estate income on that tract of land would be vested as the Rothschild Caesarea Foundation and would be tax-exempt; the income would be used to fund education projects in Israel.

Edmund Safra, who died in 1999, was descended from a famous banking family from Aleppo, Syria. Along the way, he invested in Harvard University, amongst other institutions. After his death, his widow, Lily, became chairwoman of the Safra Foundation which, in Israel, mainly invests in education, culture and health. The foundation has supported the Israel Museum for many years, as well as the Tel Aviv Museum of Art, Haifa Museum and the Hebrew University. In 2010, it donated $50 million toward the establishment of the Edmond de Rothschild Centre for Brain Sciences at the Hebrew University.

The late Gustav Leven was the founder of the Rashi Foundation. His fortune came from the mineral water company Perrier, which he founded several decades ago. In 1984, Leven set up the Sacta-Rashi Foundation, one of Israel's three largest philanthropic foundations, which primarily provides funding for education initiatives. The foundation was one of the first to ask the state to match the funds it donates – an eminently sensible requirement. It has given over $700 million to various causes, primarily education projects in outlying areas, as noted.

The Russell Berrie Foundation has donated $26 million towards the Russell Berrie Nanotechnology Institute. The Israeli government matched this contribution, enabling the Technion to establish the biggest academic project in its history. The Berrie Foundation was also one of the main donors to Bar Ilan University's Faculty of Medicine in Safed – training medical students to fill a serious shortage of doctors and health professionals in the north of Israel.

The Mandel Leadership Institute (funded by Morton Mandel) grants fellowships every year to 15 Israelis of about 40 years of age who are deemed to have leadership potential. They receive a scholarship to the Institute's varied programmes of study, in exchange for their commitment to join the public sector on completion of the programme. Over 500 people have completed the programme so far.

In 2011 the brothers Eddie and Jules Trump (no relation to the other Trump), who were born in South Africa but have long been domiciled in the US, established the Trump Foundation to improve teacher quality in Israel in mathematics and the sciences, allocating $150 million over 10 years for this purpose, and identifying a serious shortage of maths teachers as the main obstacle to the improvement of maths studies in Israel. Over 350 new teachers (mainly aged 35 to 45), often former technology professionals, have been recruited and trained to teach high school maths every year. There has been some improvement, according to the chief executive of the project, but there's still a long road ahead. Only 5 percent of students who started studying five units of maths in the 10th grade continued with the programme until the 12th grade, indicating a massive drop-out rate – which puts into perspective the sharp increase in the numbers taking five-point maths.

In addition, the Trump Foundation funds long-distance schooling, using computers as part of a virtual high school program. A thousand students study high levels of maths and physics remotely, notably in the Arab and ultra-Orthodox sectors.

Another American billionaire, Bernard Marcus, has funded the establishment of the Israel Democracy Institute. Every year the IDI holds the Herzliya Conference, which is attended by almost every high-ranking person in the government, public and financial sectors. In addition, it is responsible for the publication of many studies and position papers. The Institute is generally regarded as responsible for strengthening the status of the High Court of Justice, the Basic Laws that were passed in the 1990s, and various attempts to improve the system of government in Israel.

Finally, a $400 million bequest to Ben-Gurion University, the largest ever bequest in Israel, was earmarked in large part for water research. The gift was made by the estate of Dr Howard and Lottie Marcus. Mrs Marcus died in December 2013 at age 99, and Howard the following year, aged 104. The gift will establish a permanent endowment which is expected to yield assets that more than double the size of the current University endowment. A substantial portion is set aside for BGU water research, which studies sustainable uses of water resources, desalination technologies, water quality and microbiology. Both Howard and Lottie Marcus lost nearly all the members of their German Jewish families in the Holocaust.[197]

Of course, the above prominent donors are among many thousands of Diaspora Jews – mainly but not exclusively American – whose names appear on the donors walls of many Israeli institutions. They should be borne in mind when considering disparaging remarks by Prime Minister Netanyahu, regarding the continuing relevance of American Jews to Israel. (This was in the context of a heated controversy concerning the assignation of a particular section of the Western Wall in Jerusalem, to enable Conservative and Reform Jews to pray at the Wall.)

Man does not live by algorithms alone: Israel's arts scene

1. The Bezalel Academy of Arts and Design
Israel's national school of art was set up in 1906 by a Jewish painter and sculptor, Boris Schatz, at the time court painter to the King of Bulgaria. It is Israel's oldest institution of higher education, initially established in a Jerusalem property, purchased for Schatz by the Jewish National Fund. Bezalel was named for the biblical figure of that name, appointed by Moses to oversee the design and construction of the Tabernacle. The art created by Bezalel students and professors in the early 1900s is considered the springboard for Israeli visual arts in the 20th century and beyond. In the 1930s, it attracted many teachers and students from Germany, many of them from the Bauhaus school shut down by the Nazis.

2. Sam Spiegel Film and Television School

The school was founded in Jerusalem in 1989. It was renamed in honour of the noted producer Sam Spiegel in 1996, with considerable support from the Spiegel estate. By 2017, the school's films had won 420 international and local prizes, including a twice-won first prize at the Cannes film Festival; 76 percent of the school's graduates work in the industry. The former director of the New York Film Festival, Richard Pena, said at the tribute to the school at Columbia University in 2011: "Israeli cinema can be divided into two periods – before and after the establishment of the Sam Spiegel Film and Television School". In 1999, the school began a two-year track for screenwriters, with the aim of creating a model for co-operation between screenwriters and directors, and in 2004 a specialisation in writing for television. The school was the first to offer a four-year track for entrepreneur producers in Israel. The Sam Spiegel International film lab was launched in December 2011, with the goal of fostering the development and production of full-length feature films by some of the world's most promising young talents. The lab became the third of its kind in the world, along with the Sundance Institute and the Torino film lab in Italy.

3. The Israel Philharmonic Orchestra

Founded as the Palestine Symphony Orchestra in 1936, at a time when many Jewish musicians were being dismissed from European orchestras, its inaugural concert took place in Tel Aviv on December 26 that year, under the baton of Arturo Toscanini, who did so as a public protest against the rise of fascism in his native Italy and of Nazism in Germany. During the Second World War, the orchestra performed 140 times before Allied soldiers, including a 1942 performance for soldiers of the Jewish Brigade at El Alamein. With the declaration of the state in 1948, the orchestra was renamed the Israel Philharmonic Orchestra. Notable conductors in the history of the orchestra have included Leonard Bernstein and the long-serving musical director, Zubin Mehta. Israeli-born Lahav Shani has appeared as a guest conductor with the orchestra each year since 2013, and has been appointed as its next musical director, effective with the 2020–2021 season.

4. Habima Theatre

Habima ('the stage') is the National Theatre of Israel, and one of the first Hebrew-language theatres. Its foundations go back to Russia in 1912. From 1918 it operated under the auspices of the Moscow Arts Theatre, but encountered difficulties under the Soviet government after the Russian Revolution. The secret police attempted to cut off state funds to Habima, branding it counter-revolutionary. In 1926, the theatre left the Soviet Union to tour abroad, beginning in New York, and in 1928 members of the theatre took the company to Mandatory Palestine. Habima gained a reputation with a permanent repertoire and stage in Tel Aviv, and has been officially considered the national theatre of Israel since 1958, the year in which it received the Israel Prize for theatre. In January 2012, the theatre reopened after several years of renovations. The premises now have four auditoria. At the present time Habima employs 80 actors, and another 120 staff members work at the complex.

5. Bat Sheva Dance Company

Israel's leading dance company is based in Tel Aviv and was founded by the famous American choreographer, Martha Graham, and Baroness Batsheva de Rothschild, in 1964. Over the years, the company began to include in its repertoire the works of emerging Israeli choreographers. Ohad Naharin, appointed artistic director in 1990, founded a youth company for dancers aged between 18 and 24. Its graduates include a number of Israeli choreographers. The ensemble toured the United Kingdom and performed at the Edinburgh International Festival in 2012. Naharin has developed a movement language known as Gaga. This has been so influential in the modern dance world that, in 2015, a documentary entitled Mr Gaga was created by Tomer Heymann.

Each of the above areas of the arts now has a number of Israeli companies, from orchestras to ballet, including the New Israel National Opera. The Israeli arts scene is vibrant, and, once more, owes much to Diaspora Jewry, particularly American, for the funding of permanent auditoria.

5. Literature

Well over a dozen Israeli writers in Hebrew have achieved major international reputations. Perhaps the best-known are Amos Oz, David Grossman, A. B. Yehoshua and Etgar Keret, all of whom have been translated into at least 20 foreign languages and have achieved significant sales in translation (very important for writers from a small country like Israel with an inevitably limited home market). In 2017, Oz and Grossman were shortlisted for the Man Booker International Literary Prize, which was awarded to Grossman for his novel, *A Horse Walks into a Bar*. Amos Oz, who died in 2018, was the recipient of a number of literary awards, including the prestigious Goethe Prize.

Chapter Fourteen

Explaining Exceptional Jewish Achievement: The Inheritance of Potential

Introduction

From Moscow to Los Angeles, Jewish achievements have far exceeded Jewish shares of the general population, both at a level wholly exceptional (Nobel Prizes, Fields Medals etc., and virtuoso musicians) and at a less exceptional level across the professions, from doctors and lawyers to scientists and businessmen (initially small shopkeepers, and later department store owners). This was all too often in spite of considerable obstacles to achievement being placed in the way of Jews, particularly in Europe but also in the United States up to the mid-20th century. Murray's summary for Russian Jews, in both the Tsarist and in the Soviet periods, will stand for many countries of Europe, particularly in the east of that continent, and for much of the modern period in Germany:

'Russia drove out a large portion of its Jewish population. It persecuted the ones who remained, through legal restrictions and virulent antisemitism. After the revolution, Stalin killed substantial numbers of the most able elements of the remaining Jewish population. Socially, antisemitism remained a fact of Soviet life as it had been a fact of Czarist life. And despite all that, Jews are disproportionately represented among Russian significant figures from 1870-1950 by a ratio of 4 to 1'.

Once obstacles were removed, great advances were made for a century up to the Holocaust and even in the years since 1945, despite the loss of 6 million European Jews, including about one and a half million children. This chapter and the next explore the reasons for this, in Europe and the US, where Jews were and remain overwhelmingly Ashkenazi. There were also Sephardim in several countries of southern Europe, but their numbers were far fewer than the Ashkenazim of the rest of Europe and the US, so that the record of Diaspora Jewish high achievement is essentially Ashkenazi. In Israel, the high-achieving section of the population is again largely Ashkenazi (veteran Israelis plus the massive Russian influx of the 1970s and 1990s.)

Explanations of exceptional Jewish achievement

1. There is nothing to explain

Before dealing with the two broad classes of explanation of exceptional Jewish achievement – put simply, nature (in this chapter) and nurture (in the next) – we need to consider an iconoclastic argument which asserts, in two different versions, that there is, in effect, nothing to explain that is peculiar to Jews: according to the first, the Jews were lucky in becoming urbanised earlier in Tsarist Russia and, especially, in the Soviet Union; according to the second, Jews were simply one of a number of able immigrant groups to the United States, with a record of subsequent success.

The first of these arguments is set out in *The Jewish Century*[198] by Yuri Sletzkine. According to the author, there are two classes of ethnic tribe – the 'Mercurians' (after the god Mercury) and the 'Apollonians' (after Apollo). The former, which includes, amongst others, the Jews, have assumed certain occupations and dispatched them in a certain way, by serving as craftsmen, merchants, or healers. In contrast, the latter have tilled the soil, herded animals, or lived by the sword. Sletzkine considers that the past century has been the Mercurian century and that Jews have long been the most visible, and successful Mercurians in the West, hence 'the Jewish century'. During that time, success has demanded precisely the sort of skills that Jews have honed for many generations. Essentially, Jews were the first into the modern urban milieu.

He then goes on to describe the highly successful integration of Jews in Soviet bureaucracy and government, and their influence in the fields of energy, science, academia, arts, etc. To some extent, Russian non-Jews have caught up with Jewish achievements in these fields, assisted by the massive persecution of leading Soviet Jews in the late 1930s, and in the last years of Stalin's further decline into paranoia and murderous antisemitism. Nevertheless, the fact remains that Jewish pre-eminence in the sciences remained even after Stalin's death, to the extent that, in the last years of the 20th century, Putin bemoaned the large-scale Jewish emigration from Russia in the immediate post-Soviet period, because it entailed a huge loss of intellectual talent. Moreover, the great mass of Polish and Hungarian Jewry had become impoverished through deliberate state policy in the pre-war period, considerably reducing the opportunity for achievement. It does seem that outstanding Jewish performance in Eastern Europe required – in addition to the genuine potential for achievement, as compared to the general population average – the opportunity to succeed. This is one of the general themes of this book: the Jewish intellectual potential was always there, but all too often the obstacles for that potential to achieve success in the Diaspora have been too great to overcome.

On the other hand, *The Triple Package: What Really Determines Success*[199] argues, in effect, that there is nothing peculiar to Jewish success that requires specific explanation. The authors are a husband and wife team, Amy Chua and Jed Rubenfeld, who themselves represent two particularly successful American groups, Chinese and Jewish. They consider Jews to be only one of several immigrant groups that have succeeded in American society, including Cubans, Nigerians, South Asian Indians, and Iranians. However, all of these groups arrived with the advantage of good education, often with a command of English, and were screened by the immigration authorities for their potential to contribute to the American economy by virtue of their qualifications, often for work in high tech jobs in California. By contrast, the Jews arriving from Eastern European in the late 19th century and the early 20th were usually poverty stricken, had little or no secular education, and certainly did not speak English. It was their children and grandchildren who seized the opportunity of American schooling to achieve the heights of success. On the whole, it was the better-educated European Jews, those with a more secure economic position in society, who did not leave until forced to do so in the 1930s by the sheer weight of persecution in Germany and Austria. The 'triple package' of the book's title refers to the three factors that determine success: insecurity (being outsiders), a sense of superiority, and good impulse control; these once formed the puritan mindset, long ago abandoned by white Protestant America – the sector of the US population that now has below-average wealth. The authors assert that immigrants from certain parts of the world tend to possess such a mindset, and that it represents an advantage. Unfortunately, they offer no quantitative data for the triple package, including how to measure its components, and no evidence that all three are found more frequently in first-generation immigrant groups than in indigenous white Protestant Americans.

Finally, both of the above 'explanations' apply only to specific geographical areas, the first to Russia, the second to the US. But since the phenomenon of disproportionate Jewish achievement is found throughout the modern world from 1800 onward, such explanations can be put aside.

We now turn to well replicated research, in this chapter biological (that is genetic) and in the next social; some interaction of the two is to be preferred to a sole emphasis on one, to the exclusion of the other.

2. Intelligence and genetics

The concept of intelligence, conceived as a critical dispositional variable – that is, to assign people, particularly children, to different educational destinations – has been criticised on two grounds. One is that psychologists do not agree on the meaning of the term; the other, that IQ (Intelligence Quotient) tests measure only a person's ability to do IQ tests. There is no support for either assertion. As regards the first, over 600 experts in the field were questioned on this (and many other) points. Over 99 percent agreed that intelligence was concerned with abstract thinking or reasoning, nearly 98 percent agreed that it was concerned with problem-solving, 96 percent agreed that it was concerned with the capacity to acquire knowledge.[200]

The notion that IQ tests do not measure vitally important ingredients of worldly success is equally mistaken. They predict extremely well to scholastic success, both at school and university, they predict occupational success, both for blue-collar and white-collar jobs; they predict success in the Armed Forces, and the police, and government jobs generally. It is difficult to think of any area, allowing for free competition, where IQ tests failed to be predictive, and more so than alternative measures. Furthermore, and this is an equally strong argument, as we shall see, *IQ has a strong biological basis.*[201]

Genetic inheritance influences both average intelligence and exceptional intelligence, but it is not the only influence; environmental factors also play a part in both,

The key method, which has been used for many years, is to study pairs of twins, both identical (that is, born from a single egg), as opposed to non-identical twins (born at the same time but from two eggs). The former are universally found to be more concordant, that is, more similar to each other, than are the latter. In turn, non-identical twins are more concordant than are siblings born in the same family, even if they share the same rearing environment. (This is even more likely if they are of the same gender.) School environment is also important, particularly in the case of boarding schools with a strong ethos of conformity; for example, Eton and Harrow, in Britain, and the American equivalent private schools

The discovery of DNA, and the human genome project and its aftermath, have turned genes from abstract concepts to actual pieces of DNA. Today, the important role of genes in politically sensitive areas such as intelligence is acknowledged by all but a few diehards. Not only do identical, as opposed to fraternal, twins provide a natural experiment; identical twins reared apart from birth, but later available for comparison, also do so. Twin studies carried out in many countries over many years demonstrate the importance of genetic inheritance, from intelligence to human perception, particularly the senses of smell and taste, and those that result from stimulation of the skin. (To complicate matters, a person's genes might shape the environment they act on as much as the environment shapes the actions of the genes.)

A very broad conclusion is that genetic inheritance accounts for well over half of measured intelligence. The proportion for personality characteristics, which can make all the difference in realising that potential, is about 50 percent.

There are few differences between the sexes in IQ scores: males tend to exceed females at the lower end of the distribution, males score a little higher on visuo-spatial tests, females a little higher on verbal tests – but, overall, the story is one of overlap rather than of marked gender differences.[202]

A general intellectual ability, 'g', accounts for a large portion of any particular individual's IQ score, but there are also a number of specific abilities, such as verbal, numerical, visuo-spatial, and so on. Genius (or even high achievement) in any field is likely to be linked not only to ' g', but also to special ability in a given field. Indeed, in the case of music, geometry and the visual arts, the specific abilities may play a particularly important role, perhaps even overshadowing 'g'. IQ is the best single behavioural predictor of future success, but the prediction is far from perfect; other factors are also involved. According to Asbury and Plomin, these include self-confidence and motivation. The former has a significant impact, even when 'g' is controlled for. Indeed, it is almost as important as 'g'. The authors put it this way: 'g' is a gift, the ability to use it is a talent. Writing in the 1940s, a Canadian psychologist, Donald Hebb, made an important distinction between intelligences A and B: the former is *potential*, essentially genetic, the latter is what is actually achieved and involves a number of environmental factors, such as child rearing experiences and social opportunity.

To return to Asbury and Plomin: they conclude that continuity is genetic and change is environmental. Further, they assert that genes are generalists and that environments are specialists. They also point out that people (parents in a child's earlier years) select environments on the basis of their own genetically influenced behavioural traits. That is, there is a constant and complex interaction between genes, which set the scene, and environmental possibilities and opportunities.

The political dimension of intelligence testing is well exemplified by the decades-long controversy in Britain over the 11 Plus examination. This was introduced in 1944 so as to select children, irrespective of their social class background and their access to good or poor primary education, but rather on their native level of intellectual ability, and hence their potential to benefit from a high level of secondary education. It was not a test of attainment. The 11 Plus transformed the lives of hundreds of thousands of British working-class children, by setting them on to a different educational and hence occupational track from that followed by their parents and grandparents – doctors rather than dockers, lawyers rather than labourers. But it evoked very strong criticism, particularly from the Left side of British politics, on the grounds that it was socially divisive. In addition to the grammar school stream, the 1944 Act was intended to establish technical, rather than academic, training for children who were more suited to skilled manual work in a range of technical skills that were in great demand in industry and commerce. This had been the situation in Germany for decades, and laid the foundations, together with excellent university science departments, for Germany's industrial pre-eminence leading up to 1933 (which resumed after the Second World War).

Instead, the technical stream was never established in Britain, so that while about a quarter of the school population had access to a good grammar school education, the rest did not and left school at 15, without qualifications. Clearly there were problems with the 11+. In the late 1960s these were resolved – at the expense of working-class beneficiaries with a high potential (middle-class parents could afford fee paying schools) – by the Labour Party Secretary of State for Education, Anthony Crosland, himself from an upper middle-class background and a fee- paying boarding school. He declared: If it's the last thing I do, I'm going to destroy every 11 Plus grammar school in England. And Wales. And Northern Ireland. A leading contemporary historian, Ben Pimlott, described this as 'a sentence which deserved to be chiselled in stone over the entrance to British education's hall of infamy.[203]

IQ scores among Ashkenazi Jews and the non-Jewish population

Several academic reviews of such comparisons have come to the same conclusion. For example, Gregory Cochrane and colleagues stated: 'Ashkenazi Jews have the highest average IQ of any ethnic group for which there are reliable data'. They score well above the general European average of 100, with an average IQ of 112-115. While the mean IQ difference between Ashkenazim and other northern Europeans may not seem large, such a small difference predicts to a larger difference in the proportion of the population with very high IQs. For example, if the mean Ashkenazi IQ is 110, then the number of northern Europeans (mean IQ 100) with an IQ greater than 140 should be 4 per thousand, while 23 per thousand Ashkenazim should exceed 140, a nearly six-fold difference. This is exactly what has been found in many studies and provides a partial basis for explaining the over-representation of Ashkenazi Jews in occupations with the highest cognitive demands.'[204]

The high Ashkenazi IQ and corresponding high academic performance, given the opportunity, have been long known. In 1900 London, Jewish children, although mostly from recently-arrived parents, took a disproportionate number of academic prizes and scholarships in spite of their poverty.[205] A 1920s survey of IQ scores in three London schools[206] with mixed Jewish and non-Jewish student bodies showed that Jewish students had higher IQs than their schoolmates in each of three schools, one prosperous, one poor, and one very poor. The average IQ differences between Jews and non-Jews were all around 12 points. The students at the poorest Jewish school in London had IQ scores equal to the overall city mean of non-Jewish children.

Ashkenazi Jews have an unusual ability profile as well as a higher than average IQ. They have high verbal and mathematical scores, while their visuo-spatial abilities are typically somewhat lower, by about 6 points, than the European average. Eysenck noted:[207] 'The correlation between verbal and performance tests is about 0.77 in the general population, but only 0.31 among Jewish children. Verbal performance differences of 10 to 20 points have been found in samples of Jewish children; there is no other group which shows anything like this size difference'. The Ashkenazi pattern of success, according to Cochrane and colleagues, is what one would expect from this ability distribution – great success in mathematics and literature, more typical results in representational painting, sculpture, and architecture.[208]

Miles Storfer reviewed two large Israeli IQ studies of schoolchildren.[209] The first[210] found a 14-point differential between the scores of 11,000 children of Ashkenazi heritage and those of 7,000 children of Middle Eastern and North African (Mizrachi) heritage. The second[211] reported a study of 1,200 children aged 6 to 14 from a large number of Israeli kibbutzim; the IQ scores of the offspring of Ashkenazi fathers with more than an elementary school education (who comprised the large majority of Ashkenazi fathers living on kibbutzim) averaged 117.

David and Lynn[212] reviewed more recent studies comparing Mizrachim and Ashkenazim in Israel. They found that the former had an average IQ 14 points lower than the latter and suggest that this supports the theory that in their countries of origin the Mizrachim were permitted to engage in a much wider range of occupations and hence did not come under the selection pressure to develop the high verbal and mathematical intelligence that was present for Ashkenazim. (However, there was a strong tendency for the better-educated North African Jews to move to France and Canada, rather than to Israel, during their mass exodus in the 1950s and early 60s. Hence, the studies reviewed by David and Lynn may not be strictly comparing like with like. A considerable degree of success was enjoyed in France, relatively soon after their arrival, by Jews from Algeria; although domiciled in North Africa for close to a century, their ancestors were originally from France, and they continued to be exposed to French, rather than Arab culture, as were the rest of the French 'settlers'.

3. Personality factors and high achievement.

The term personality refers to the non-intellective areas of individual differences which might contribute to high achievement. Over the past hundred years there has been a great deal of research into this question. But as compared to work on intelligence there is still a long way to go. Psychologists are in broad agreement on the major dimensions of personality, as measured by self-administered questionnaires, and while there is some evidence of a partially genetic basis for these, many questions remain, including systematic personality differences between Jews and non-Jews, and the extent to which, if these are found, they contribute to differences in achievement.

1. The General Factor of Personality (GFP)
Dunkel and colleagues[213] reported a continuing series of large-scale studies to compare sizeable samples of American Jews and non-Jews on the GFP as well as on a measure of intelligence. Broadly speaking, the GFP can be considered as a measure of social effectiveness. When controlling for intelligence, Jewish groups were found to be significantly more socially effective,

which in turn might relate to social skill and emotional intelligence. The question as to whether high Jewish GFP is manifested in behavioural (especially) and social outcomes, including high achievement, is a topic for further research, but this group's work has made a useful, quantitative, beginning.

2. Ego strength

Eysenck[214] efines this as 'the inner strength to function autonomously, to resist popular pressure, and persist in endeavour in spite of negative reinforcement'. He expands on this by quoting from Cox[215] who, having studied the boyhood characteristics of 'young geniuses' concluded that 'forcefulness or strength of character, as a whole, and persistence of motive... rate high.... as high as the intellective factor'.[216] Writing of Albert Einstein, C.P. Snow,[217] a British scientist and novelist, considered his most important characteristic to be that he was 'unbudgeable'. When he was 26 years old, and an unknown patent examiner, Einstein published five papers on physics. Three of them, Snow writes, 'were among the greatest in the history of physics'. He consulted no mentor, but simply sent them to the leading physics journal of the day.

3. 'Intensity'

This is a personality variable which has considerable intuitive appeal, but seems not to have been studied quantitatively. According to Raphael Patai,[218] a Hebrew University scholar in the mid-20th century, 'the Jewish personality' is characterised by 'greater intensity, greater sensitivity, and greater impatience'. He writes, referring to many non-Jewish criticisms of 'Jewish loudness, vulgarity and pushiness' – 'all of these are but more specific manifestations of Jewish intensity'. Patai even sees intensity as the basis of the relationship of Jewish parents to their children, the motive force behind the attitude and behaviour of the Jewish mother so often satirized by modern Jewish writers (think of Philip Roth's *Portnoy's Complaint*).[219]

4. Creativity

High general intelligence has to be supplemented by creativity, a key component of which is the ability to form 'divergent' associations – that is, the less obvious ones when presented with a range of choices. These are seen as creative when the task requires it. This ability probably underlies the thinking of both the creative scientist and the creative artist. But there is a risk – that divergent thinking might slide into actual psychopathology. The performance tests for divergent thinking have usually been carried out on children and are a long way from the creativity of the mature scientist and artist. In broad terms, the key elements of the Creative Personality Scale[220] are: being resourceful, insightful, individualistic, reflective, intelligent, and having wide interests. At the opposite end of the scale, the elements are: being submissive, honest, suspicious, conservative, cautious and, most of all, being 'commonplace'.

Thus far, positive aspects of personality and achievement. But the opposite is also possible: personality features which might be detrimental to high achievement. To study this, Felix Post, a retired eminent geriatric psychiatrist, carried out a monumental study entitled: 'Creativity and Psychopathology. A Study of 291 World Famous Men'.[221] Selection for the six series – scientists and inventors, thinkers and scholars, statesmen and national leaders, painters and sculptors, composers, novelists and playwrights – was determined by the availability of sufficiently adequate biographies. He then transformed the data into diagnoses in accordance with standard criteria, when appropriate. He concluded that they excelled not only by virtue of their abilities and originality, but also by their drive, perseverance, industry, and meticulousness. These men (no women!) were emotionally warm, with a gift for friendship and sociability. Most had unusual personality characteristics and, in addition, minor neurotic abnormalities that were probably more common than in the general population. Severe personality deviations were unduly frequent only in the case of visual artists and writers. Not surprisingly 'functional psychoses were probably less frequent than psychiatric epidemiology would suggest and were entirely restricted to the affective varieties; only depressive conditions, alcoholism, and, less reliably, psychosexual problems were more prevalent than expected in some professional categories, but strikingly so in writers'.

Post pointed out that 'similar findings have been reported for living artists and writers, and this suggests that certain pathological personality characteristics, as well as tendencies towards depression and alcoholism, are causally related to some kinds of valuable creativity'.

Analysing these results further, Eysenck[222] found that the percentages of severe psychopathology were 17 percent for the politicians 18 percent for the scientists, 26 percent for the thinkers, 38 percent for the artists, and 46 percent for the writers. (Sixty years earlier, Dr Post, who did not analyse his data separately for Jews and non-Jews, had come to Britain from Germany as a Jewish refugee; his promising medical career was interrupted in 1942 by a brief internment as an 'enemy alien'.)

Summarising a large number of studies on Jews and psychopathology: depressive problems, including the bipolar variety, are more frequent than in the general population; alcoholism is less frequent, possibly due to the presence, in about 20 percent of American Jews, of a protective gene.

Epigenetics

Essentially, epigenetics is additional information layered on top of the sequence of letters (strings of molecules) that make up DNA. According to the hype, epigenetics is one of the hottest fields in life sciences. It is a phenomenon with wide-ranging powerful effects on many aspects of biology and enormous potential in human medicine. Its ability to fill in some of the gaps in scientific knowledge is mentioned everywhere, from academic journals to the mainstream media. Potentially, it could help explain why identical twins aren't completely identical. It could contribute to parental outcomes that don't seem to be genetic.

Any outside stimulus, if it can be detected by the body, has the potential to cause epigenetic modifications to the person's DNA. For example, studies of humans whose ancestors survived through periods of starvation in Sweden and the Netherlands, suggest that the effects of famine on epigenetics and health can pass through at least three generations. Nutrient deprivation in a recent ancestor seems to prime the body for diabetes and cardiovascular problems, responses that may have evolved to mitigate the effects of any future famines in the same geographical area. (Cass Ennis in The *Guardian*, 25.4.14).

If this is the case, the massive trauma associated with experiencing the Holocaust might well be inheritable, affecting, in Israel's case, many scores of thousands of offspring to whom the effects of the trauma might have been passed down from Holocaust survivor parents. The numbers are very high. On the eve of Israel's independence, its Jewish population had numbered some 670,000, but by the end of 1952 it had absorbed a further 717,923, among them 173,852 Holocaust survivors. (The term 'Holocaust survivor' refers to all those Jews who were in occupied Europe, and who suffered directly from Nazism, including those who lived in countries allied to or collaborating with the Nazis, such as Romania and Hungary.) In the early years of the State, and in the three preceding years of illegal immigration, Holocaust survivors may have comprised close to half of all immigrants. If their children suffered indirectly from the trauma of the Holocaust, this would have meant an extra burden on the new state, complicating the employment potential for both the survivors and their Israeli-born children.

A study at New York's Mount Sinai Hospital, led by Rachel Yehuda, involved 32 Jewish men and women who had been interned in a Nazi concentration camp, or had witnessed or experienced torture or violence, or had had to hide during the Second World War, constantly in fear of exposure. She concluded that not only were the survivors themselves traumatised, but that their experiences were capable of being passed on to their children, an apparently clear sign that one person's life experience can affect subsequent generations. By comparison, a control group of families and children who were living outside of Europe during the war found no such increased likelihood of stress disorders in their children. According to Yehuda, 'the gene changes in the children could only be attributed to Holocaust exposure in the parents. Through further genetic analysis, the team ruled out the possibility that the epigenetic changes found in the parental genes were a result of the trauma that the children had experienced themselves.[223]

So far, so clear: the Holocaust victimised not only those who experienced it directly, but also their children, with a consequent reduction in the ability of both generations, not only to experience as full a life as would have been the case without the parental experience, but also the ability of both generations to contribute to society – in this case, the developing State of Israel with its considerable initial problems. However, an article in *Haaretz* by Josie Glausiusz[224] concludes that it is impossible to tease out the influence of epigenetic modification on the genes of the parents from that of horrific stories told by survivors to their children. She also points to further, more technical problems in the interpretation of Yehuda's data, including DNA methylation patterns. It might have been possible in the early days of the state to carry out a study based on twin methodology, in which the offspring of some survivors were reared apart from their parents. But in those days, scientists had more pressing demands on their time. (A further complicating factor is that many Holocaust survivors simply did not talk about their wartime experiences to their children, who might have known only in general terms what had happened to their parents.)

All told, we are left with the tantalising but so far unproven possibility that not only was the survivor generation traumatized, but also their children. For the time being, from the point of view of explaining exceptional Jewish achievement, even against the odds, it seems that epigenetics will have to take a back seat to conventional genetics and ordinary environmental experiences, group and individual, over both the short and the long term. However, this is a 'hot area' which will bear watching as research moves from animals to humans. It was found, for example, that female mice that had experienced environmental enrichment learned to negotiate a water maze faster than control mice, and that the offspring of the mice also learned faster, even though they had never experienced environmental enrichment themselves.[225] This study demonstrated the possibility of the epigenetic transmission of *positive* environmental experiences; human studies are the obvious next step.

Chapter Fifteen

Explaining Jewish Achievement: The Amplification of Potential

Jewish experiences through history

According to Cochrane and colleagues,[226] the key factor explaining elevated Jewish intelligence is occupational selection. From the time Jews became established north of the Pyrenees-Balkans line around 800 AD, they were – in most places and at most times – restricted to occupations involving sales, finance and trade. Economic success, in all of these occupations, is far more highly selected for intelligence than success in the chief occupation of non-Jews, namely farming. Economic success is, in turn, related to reproductive success, because higher income means lower infant mortality, better nutrition and, more generally, reproductive 'fitness'. Over time, increased fitness among the successful leads to strong selection for the cognitive and psychological traits producing that fitness, intensified when there is a low inward gene flow from other populations (few mixed marriages), as was the case with Ashkenazim.

Sephardi and Mizrachi Jews – those from the Iberian Peninsula, the Mediterranean littoral, and the Islamic East – were also engaged in urban occupations during the same centuries. But the authors cite evidence that, as a rule, they were less concentrated in occupations that selected for IQ and, instead, more commonly worked in craft trades Thus, elevated intelligence did not develop among Sephardi and Mizrachi Jews – as manifested by contemporary test results in Israel that show the IQs of non-European Jews to be roughly similar to the IQs of non-Jews living outside Israel.

The authors conclude this part of their argument with an elegant corollary that matches the known test profiles of today's Ashkenazim, with the historical experience of their ancestors. The suggested selective process explains the pattern of mental abilities in Ashkenazi Jews: high verbal and mathematical ability, but relatively low spatial and visual ability. Verbal and mathematical talent helped medieval businessmen succeed, while spatial and visual abilities were irrelevant.[227]

In the same article, Murray himself then presents what he calls an alternative to the Cochrane and colleagues' theory ('which suspects that Jewish intelligence was (a) not confined to Ashkenazim and (b) antedates the Middle Ages'). He begins with evidence that Jews who remained in the Islamic world exhibited unusually high levels of accomplishment as of the beginning of the second millennium – for example, Sarton's enumeration of scientists, noted earlier. These were not Ashkenazim in northern Europe, where Jews were still largely excluded from the world of scientific scholarship, but Sephardim in the Iberian Peninsula, in Baghdad, and other Islamic centres of learning. In Spain, under both Moslem and Christian rule, Jews attained eminent positions in the professions, commerce and government, as well as in elite literary and intellectual circles.

After being expelled from Spain at the end of the 15th century, Sephardi Jews rose to distinction in many of the countries where they settled, for example, the Netherlands.[228] Murray points out that some centuries later, in England, there were such notable Sephardim as Benjamin Disraeli and the economist, David Ricardo.

Hence, Murray proposes that a strong case could be assembled that Jews everywhere had unusually high intellectual resources, which manifested themselves outside of Ashkenaz and well before the period when non-rabbinic Ashkenazi accomplishment manifested itself. He argues that some of the elevation in Jewish intelligence occurred even before Jews moved into occupations selected for intelligence, because of the shift in ancient Judaism from a rite-based to a learning-based religion.

'...Scholars agree that about 80-90 percent of all Jews were farmers at the beginning of the Common Era but that only 10-20 percent of Jews were farmers by the end of the first millennium. No other ethnic group underwent this ... occupational shift'. Murray then draws on a paper by Botticini and Eckstein,[229] which rejects the argument that Jews became merchants because they were barred from farming, and point to cases in which Jews who were free to own land and engage in agriculture made the same shift to other, skilled occupations, as happened where restrictions were in force. Instead, they focus on an event that occurred in 64 CE, when the Palestinian sage, Joshua Ben Gamla, issued an ordinance mandating universal schooling for all Jewish males, starting at the age of six. This was not only issued, it was implemented. Within about a century, the Jews, uniquely among the peoples of the world, had effectively established universal male literacy and numeracy.

These authors' explanation for the subsequent shift from farming to urban occupations is: if you were educated, you possessed an asset that had economic value in occupations that required literacy and numeracy, such as those involving sales and transactions. If you remained a farmer, your education had little or no value. Over the centuries, this basic reality led Jews to leave farming and engage in urban occupations. Selection pressure in this form was probably not the only force at work. Between the first and sixth centuries CE, the number of Jews in the world plummeted from about 4.5 million to 1.5 million or fewer. About 1 million Jews were killed in the failed revolts against the Romans in Judaea and Egypt. (And there were forced conversions from Judaism to Christianity, which rapidly became ascendant in the Roman Empire in the 4th century.) Finally, there was a general drop in population that accompanied the decline and fall of the Roman Empire. But that still leaves a huge number of Jews who just disappeared.

What happened to them? Botticini and Eckstein argue that an economic force was at work: for Jews who remained farmers, universal education involved a cost that had little economic benefit. However, in Murray's view, a more direct explanation could involve the increased intellectual demands of Judaism. The ordinance that mandated literacy occurred at about the same time as the destruction of the Second Temple – 64 CE and 70 CE, respectively. This was the moment when Judaism began actively to transform itself from a religion centred on rites and sacrifices at the Temple in Jerusalem, to a religion centred on prayer and study of the Torah at decentralised synagogues and study houses. 'Since worship of God involved not only prayer, but study, all Jewish males had to read if they were to practice their faith – and not only to read in private, but to be able to read aloud in the presence of others.... The Torah and the Hebrew prayer book are not simple texts, even to be able to read them mechanically requires fairly advanced literacy. To study the Talmud and its commentaries, with any understanding, requires considerable intellectual capacity. In short, during the centuries after the Roman destruction of the Temple, Judaism evolved in such a way that 'to be a good Jew meant that a man had to be smart'. Murray suggests that those who could not learn to read well enough to be good Jews – meaning those from the lower half of the intelligence distribution – were those who fell away from Judaism. He argues: 'the remaining self-identified Jews about 800 CE already had elevated intelligence'. (Moreover, Judaism was now portable; the scrolls of the law and the prayer books could be carried wherever Jews went.)

Murray then asks a crucial question: 'Is it the case that, before the first century CE, Jews were intellectually ordinary? Are we to believe that the Bible, a work compiled over centuries and incorporating everything from brilliant poetry to profound ethics, was produced by an intellectually run-of-the-mill Levantine tribe?' In *The Evolution of Man*,[230] Cyril Darlington presented the thesis that Jews and Judaism were decisively shaped much earlier than the first century CE, namely by the Babylonian captivity that began with the fall of Jerusalem in 586 BCE. The biblical account clearly states that only a select group of Jews were taken to Babylon. 'Nebuchadnezzar carried into exile, all Jerusalem; all the officers and fighting men, and all the craftsmen and artisans... Only the poorest people of the land were left' (2 Kings 24:10).

In effect, the Babylonians took away the Jewish elites, selected in part for high intelligence, and left behind the poor and unskilled, selected in part for low intelligence. The returned exiles, who formed the bulk of the reconstituted Jewish community, comprised mainly the descendants of the Jewish elites – a far more able population, on average, than the pre-captivity population. Murray concludes: 'there is a reason to think that selection for intelligence antedates the first century CE'.

Moving forward, Murray[231] suggests that any effects of cultural traits, tending to select for high IQ, would have been intensified in the case of the Ashkenazim, about 500 years ago, when as many as 1,500 Ashkenazi families may have lived in Europe. 'But geneticists at the Hebrew University examining the DNA from large samples of Ashkenazi Jews conclude that many of these family lines subsequently died out and far fewer families, probably about 500, account for all of today's Ashkenazi Jews. They further believe that this subset was selected for better nutrition and lower infant mortality rates – which in turn suggests both greater wealth and greater ability than among the families who disappeared'.[232]

Are Cochrane's and Murray's theories, as to the origin of high intelligence, in at least some Jews, anything more than entertaining speculations? They are certainly entertaining and, together with the traditional Jewish emphasis on the desirability of high intelligence in prospective husbands and wives, and the respect paid by Jews throughout the centuries to learning – initially of religious texts and, in the last 200 years or so, in secular subjects – they provide a useful historical framework for explaining disproportionately high Jewish achievement when opportunity arose.

General social requirements for outstanding human achievement

Murray[233] concluded, after a careful statistical analysis, that the following are necessary conditions for the formation of the 'Significant Figures' referred to in Chapter One.

1. Economic wealth and growth
Accomplishment in the sciences is facilitated by the growth of national wealth through the additional money for the arts and sciences, and economic vitality has a spillover effect on cultural vitality, making funds available for the construction of universities and the purchase of paintings. Murray and Eysenck agree that for all historical eras of which we have some knowledge, creative people have come from the so-called 'middle of the middle classes' – from professional-class homes. One exception to this general principle is that 75 percent of Jewish Nobel laureates, pre-1975, came from lower socio- economic backgrounds,[234] suggesting that it was the motivational properties of their families, and their own native abilities, rather than their financial status, that produced the drive to eminence of the Jewish Nobelists.

2. Living in elite cities

Significant Figures are associated with a particular kind of city, which Murray calls 'elite', where a critical mass of talent can form. Once that critical mass has been achieved, more talent is attracted and so on, in a virtuous circle. Examples are London, New York and Paris; the development of Berlin and Vienna as elite cities before the Nazi period, owed a great deal to Jewish talent.

3. Attending elite universities

This again is a virtuous circle: the most eminent research universities, most of which are in the United States, including Harvard and the Massachusetts Institute of Technology, but also Oxford and Cambridge in Britain, have had that status for many decades and have continually strengthened their standing in the very top tier. They attract the most able students, the most promising researchers and the most distinguished professors who have already achieved eminence, as well as the major share, in each country, of both private and government research funding. As far as Israel is concerned, the four universities in the world's leading 200 have struggled to retain their most talented products, particularly in economics.

As hi-tech start-ups have developed, these have tended to cluster around elite universities, adding to their power of attraction and drawing in talent from around the world; examples are the tech hubs around Stanford University, and Harvard and MIT. The most successful British example is the collaboration between Cambridge University, long pre-eminent in mathematics and physics, and a large array of start-ups; this is often called Silicon Fen. In Israel too, the highly successful start-ups are often clustered between Tel Aviv University and the Haifa Technion, known as Silicon Wadi (valley); in contrast to Israel's universities, its start-ups have managed, in the main, to retain talented individuals and to attract leading foreign high-tech companies.

4. Freedom of action

This is Murray's final requirement for the fostering of high talent: he asserts that political regimes which give de facto freedom of action to their potential artists and scholars produce 'streams of accomplishment'. It is certainly the case that Russia, despite having more than twice the population of Britain, has only one university in the top 200, as compared to Britain's 14, and that China with four times the population of the United States (58 in the top 200) has only nine. His general conclusion is that totalitarian regimes, such as Russia and China, tend to squash talent, particularly in the arts.

Educating gifted children: enhancing achievement

New research shows that countries which do not get the most from their best and brightest face big economic costs. Moreover, the nature-or-nurture debate is a false dichotomy. Intelligence is indeed highly heritable and perhaps the best predictor of success. But it is far from the only characteristic that matters for future exceptional achievement.

One key component, which predicts to a successful future, is the long-established IQ test. It measures general intelligence – not book learning, but the ability to reason, plan, solve problems, think abstractly and so on. The importance of these tests is well demonstrated by the study of mathematically precocious youth (SMPY), which goes back to 1971. Over the space of 25 years, Julian Stanley of Johns Hopkins University recruited 5,000 precocious children, each of whom had intelligence test scores in early adolescence high enough to gain entry to university. These children were followed up into adulthood. Of the SMPY participants who scored among the top 0.5 percent for their age-group in maths and verbal tests, 30 percent went on to earn a doctorate, versus 1 percent of Americans as a whole. These children were also more likely to have high incomes and to file patents.[235]

Unfortunately, the potential of bright, but poor, children is often wasted. A Stanford University study headed by Raj Chetty,[236] published in December 2017, found that children who score in the top 5 percent of standardised tests in the third year of primary school, are many times more likely than the other 95 percent to file patents in later life. But the likelihood is still much greater among smart kids from rich families. Unfortunately, when applications to special schemes for gifted children are voluntary, they come mostly from rich or pushy parents. According to *The Economist* article from which this review is taken:[237] 'In New York City... tutoring companies often charge $200 per hour to help four-year-olds prepare for admission tests for gifted education programs starting in kindergarten. Hence, it helps when schools test every child, rather than rely on parents to put children forward. A paper by economists David Card and Laura Giuliano found that when a school district in Florida introduced universal screening for its gifted education scheme, admissions increased by 180 percent among poor children, 130 percent among Hispanics and 80 percent for black pupils. (Admissions among white children fell.)

Some psychologists argue that there are many more possible paths to success in adulthood than is often assumed, and that education must do more to foster attributes such as passion, determination and creativity. They emphasise the role of sheer persistence. Few researchers disagree with the idea that talent requires development, and that this should actually involve promoting hard work, as well as intelligence. (They might be talking about intensity, and ego strength; and the problem of environmentally fostered low expectations among bright but poor children must also be addressed.) *The Economist* piece concludes: 'so long as they are open to everyone, IQ tests still have a vital role to play. To find 'lost Einsteins', you have to look for them'

Israeli programmes for gifted children

With the exception of Haredi children the entire Israeli school population is tested at the age of 7 in arithmetic, reading and comprehension; the top 15 percent then go on to stage two, when the numbers are reduced to about one and a half thousand. The selected children then engage in various programmes – all in addition to the normal school day. A range of subjects is involved, subsumed under the heading 'enrichment'. The range of subjects is well beyond the normal school curriculum. Some of the schoolchildren even attend university classes. It is very likely, although comprehensive, longitudinal studies do not seem to have been carried out, that many of the schoolchildren concerned go on to such army units as 8200 and then on to high tech companies.

Nepotism: the son rises and does not fall

There's an old saying in England's north: 'clogs to clogs in three generations', meaning that while a family can escape clogs, (hard-wearing footwear worn in the past by manual workers and symbolising a hardscrabble life), it does so only relatively briefly, and clogs are later resumed. Considerable research, much of it in the US but also some in Israel, suggests that this is far from true in the 21st century; once success has been achieved, it is handed on to succeeding generations – often for many more than two.

According to *The Economist*,[238] 'In contrast to the past, for today's rich, it is increasingly possible to hand on to their children an asset which cannot be frittered away in a casino. It is far more useful than wealth, and invulnerable to inheritance tax. It is brains.'

'In the ever-burgeoning knowledge economy intellectual capital is crucial. Those who have lots of it get a large share of the pie, and it is increasingly heritable; far more than in previous generations clever, successful, men marry clever, successful, women. Thus, when like marries like, this increases inequality by 25 percent, since two-degree households typically enjoy two large incomes. They conceive bright children and bring them up in stables home – only 9 percent of college-educated mothers who give birth each year are unmarried, compared with 61 percent of high school drop-outs. And they stimulate them relentlessly: children of professionals hear 32 million more words by the age of four, than those whose parents are on welfare. They move to pricey neighbourhoods with good schools, and pull strings to get junior into a top-notch college'.

'The race begins early: competition for private kindergarten places among high status New Yorkers is farcically intense.... An educational consultant recommends that parents apply to 8 to 10 kindergartens, write "love letters" to their top three, and bone up on how to make the right impression when visiting. Some parents pay for sessions at which their children are coached on how to play in a way that pleases those in charge of admissions. The same influence of professional expertise on admissions is found also at entry-level to university: a firm with several ex-deans of admissions on its books provides advice on getting children into the best universities [...]

'The universities that mould the American elite seek out talented recruits from all backgrounds, and clever poor children who make it to the Ivy league may have their fees waived entirely, but middle-class students have to rack up huge debts to attend college, especially if they want a postgraduate degree, which many desirable jobs now require. The link between parental income and a child's academic success has grown stronger, clever people become richer... And education matters more than it used to, because the demand for brain power has soared. A young college graduate earns 63 percent more than a high school graduate if both work full-time – and the latter is much less likely to work at all. For those at the top of the pile, moving straight from the best universities into the best jobs, the potential rewards are greater than they have ever been'.

None of this is peculiar to America, but the trend is most visible there (together with Israel). Thanks to hyper-local funding, America is one of only three advanced countries where the government spends more on schools in rich areas than in poor ones. (Israel is one of the other two). 'Clearly, well-off people are not going to stop investing in their children, but the state should do a lot more to seek out and help clever children of poor parents'. This applies both to the US and to Israel: 'starting right from the beginning, when the brain is at its most malleable and the right kind of stimulation has the largest effect. There is no substitute for parents to talk and read to their babies, but good nurseries can help, especially for the most struggling families'. (Traditionally, Jewish mothers – and grandmothers – have both read to their children, and encouraged them to read and to talk).

According to *The Economist*[239] loosening the link between birth and success would make America richer – far too much talent is currently wasted. It might also make the nation more cohesive. (These injunctions apply equally to wealthy western nations in general.)

'The 1 percent solution – be born into it'
'For the first time the entire earnings distribution of (US) college graduates – and how that relates to parental income – is now

known, thanks to the Stanford University study of 30 million tax returns, headed by Raj Chetty. These data show that graduates of elite universities, with single-digit admissions rates and billion-dollar endowments, are still the most likely to join the top 1 percent of earners (although having wealthy parents further improves the odds). And despite recent efforts to change, their student bodies are still overwhelmingly wealthy... A rich student, hailing from a household in the top 5 percent, has about a 60 percent greater chance of reaching the income summit than a poor student whose parents were in the bottom 5 percent, even if they both attended one of America's most esteemed universities. Legacy admissions, which give preferential treatment to family members of alumni, exacerbate the imbalance. Of Harvard's then most recently admitted class, 27 percent of students had a relative who also attended. There is evidence that this system favours the already wealthy; MIT and the California Institute of Technology, two elite schools with no legacy preferences, have much fewer students who hail from the ranks of the super-rich'.[240]

According to *Dream Hoarders* by Richard Reeves,[241] 'although the top 1 percent have done best of all, the next 20 percent have also done well and are determined to protect their gains, (hence the 'hoarders' of the title), the upper middle-class fight to restrict housebuilding in their well-groomed neighbourhoods, thus making them unavailable for most Americans. They lobby for tax benefits for higher education, and home ownership, which disproportionately benefit the upper-middle-class. Figures from the Congressional Budget Office show that the top 20 percent of American households receive annual tax benefits worth nearly $450 billion (further enhanced by the tax cuts of 2018); benefits for the bottom 40 percent are roughly a third of that. Reeves goes on to argue that the 20 percent arm-twist elite universities into accepting their children, and draw on their network of successful friends and colleagues to place their offspring in the desirable internships and jobs that are the first rung on the ladder to success. The result is a chasm between the upper-middle-class and the bottom 80 percent of households. More than 40 percent of the children of the wealthiest 20 percent of households will themselves end up among the wealthiest 20 percent. Reeves goes on to argue that 'for American society to work as it should, your children, some of them anyway, must be downwardly mobile.[242] (Of course, this is simply not going to happen, at least not through parental intent.)

Gregory Clark drew upon research that uses surnames to track status over centuries. 'This has mined sources as varied as the Domesday Book, the Royal Society's records, and membership of the American Medical Association, in order to find surnames that are over- represented in elite positions. Researchers then tracked how long it takes those monied surnames to lose their wealth-predicting power.

'With surprising consistency across countries, and eras, social mobility is found to be painfully slow. Birth has predicted more than 50 percent of one's income or education status; erasing the legacy of past prosperity takes 10 to 15 generations rather than the three or four implied by sunnier estimates'. Mr Clark concludes that 'ability is strongly linked to underlying competence – an inescapable inherited trait. Only the intermarriage of people who are more prosperous and educated, with those less fortunate will dilute the genetic resources of well-off families, slowly pushing them back towards the average and preventing the rise of a permanent over class'.[243]

The most clear-cut case of nepotism is the probability of male baby boomers reaching the same level of success as their fathers. This was studied by Seth Stephens-Davidovitz and reported in an entertaining and persuasive piece in the *New York Times*.[244] He limited himself to fathers and sons because 'this was a highly sexist period in which women held few powerful political positions'. The results include the following:

1. Governors: He assumed that there were about 250 baby boomer males born to governors. Five of them became governors themselves, about one in 50, 6,000 times the rate of the average American.

2. The same methodology suggests that sons of senators had an 8,000 times higher chance of becoming a senator than an average American male boomer.

3. Generals: an American male is 4,582 times more likely to become an army general if his father was one.

4. A famous CEO: an American male is 1,895 times more likely to become a famous head of a major company.

5. Pulitzer prize: the son of a winner is 1,639 times more likely to win the award.

6. Academy award: the son of a winner is 1,361 times more likely to be awarded.

In all of these cases, the competitive playing field is hardly level; family example, opportunity and influence must always have played a part, in addition to genetic inheritance of relevant traits. In other words, nepotism is distinctly in evidence. The achievements to be particularly admired are of those of individuals with no family advantage.

The Lost Einsteins

In his poem "Elegy Written in a Country Churchyard", Thomas Gray (1716-1771), referring to the great English epic poet John Milton, muses on what might have been: "Some mute inglorious Milton here may rest".

Rather more prosaically, and also more indignantly, David Leondhart was 'left stewing over how many breakthrough innovations we may have missed because of inequality'.[245] He refers to another paper by the Harvard group, headed by Chetty, which looks at who becomes an inventor – and who doesn't. The key phrase in this paper is 'lost Einsteins, people who could have had highly impactful innovations' if they had been able to pursue the opportunities they deserved.... Nobody knows precisely who the lost Einsteins are, but there is little doubt that they exist'.

The researchers worked with the Treasury Department to link tax records with patent records. They were able to study the backgrounds of patent holders (the study focused on the most highly cited, significant patents) and were able to link these records to elementary school test scores for some patent holders. 'Not surprisingly, children who excelled in maths were far more likely to become inventors. But being a math stand out wasn't enough. Only the top students who also came from higher income families had a decent chance to become an inventor. Low-income students who are among the very best math students – those who score in the top 5 percent of all third graders – are no more likely to become inventors than below-average maths students from affluent families.... Children from the south-east are less likely to become inventors, so are African-Americans, Latinos and women.

'The gaps are enormous... Among upper-income students who excel at math, 6.5 out of every thousand are ultimately granted a patent. For low-income math stand outs, the number is 1.2.... Children who grow up exposed to a particular type of invention, or inventor, are more likely to follow that path'. Leondhart quotes a successful entrepreneur, Steve Case: "We do a pretty good job at identifying the kids who are good at throwing a football or playing the trumpet... But we don't do a particularly good job of identifying the kids who have the potential of creating a phenomenal new product or service or invention".

As far as Jews are concerned, lost potential is exemplified not only in the lack of opportunity for certain groups of able children in Israel, but – on a far greater scale – in the loss of 1.5 million children in the Holocaust. The next generation of potential Einsteins, who were born in continental Europe in the 1920s and 30s, and most of whom were murdered, had futures which can only be guessed at. But some information is provided by the long-term outcome of those who were able to escape – the data on the achievements, noted earlier, of the 10,000 Kindertransport children allowed into Britain in 1939.

In the field of music, an inkling of what might have been was provided by the successful result of a quest of nearly 30 years, by an Italian musician, Francesco Loreto, to track down music composed by Nazi concentration camp victims. His search yielded thousands of songs, symphonies and even operas, and involved scouring bookshops and archives, as well as interviewing Holocaust survivors. He accumulated about 8,000 pieces of music, including scores written on scraps of scavenged paper, toilet paper and newspaper. Several of the pieces were performed at a concert by the Ashdod Symphony Orchestra, in Jerusalem, to mark the 70th anniversary of the founding of Israel. Among them was a song written by a musician, author and poet, Ilse Weber. The song was never written down, but was memorised by Aviva Bar-On, a child in the same camp, Theresienstadt. She sang it at the concert for the first time since the war. Other pieces which were performed, included Tatata by Willy Rosen and Max Ehrlich, both prominent figures on the German cabaret scene in the 1930s, and both murdered in Auschwitz.[246]

(A final comment on the arresting title of Leonhardt's article: Einstein was neither an inventor, nor an American; his work was in theoretical physics and he spent his last decades in America only on account of Hitler's accession to power. A more apt title, referring to a prolific American inventor, might have been: 'The lost Edisons'.)

Nepotism and Israeli High Tech

Two articles in *Haaretz* tell the story of the close connection between parental status and their offspring's achievements in high tech. A high-tech career in Israel generally offers a path to a relatively high salary, and work in a competitive global environment. Large segments of the population are under-represented in high tech: Israeli Arabs, Jewish women, the less well-off, and Haredim. A study using data from the Israel's Central Bureau of Statistics focused on 102,000 people employed in the high-tech sector, which was then whittled down to a smaller group of people directly involved in technology. The profile obtained was that these high-tech employees came from families in which the parents had high incomes and levels of education. Moreover, a large number of successful high-tech employees grow up in relatively well-off Israeli communities. Seventy-five percent of them had taken and passed high-school maths matriculation at the highest level, five units, compared to 28 percent of the general sample studied. Moreover, people who had attended leading universities, where entrance requirements are high, had higher average salaries than those who studied at public colleges. The study also found that for men, the chances of entering higher education to study fields relevant to high tech was three times that of women from a similar background; for Israeli Jewish male students, the chances of studying the relevant subjects was four times that of Arab male Israelis with similar abilities.

For the latter group, matters are improving. The researchers found that between 1984 and 2014 only 1,600 Arab Israelis had graduated in relevant fields, such as software engineering and computer science. In 2016, however, a greater number of Arabs (2,200) were studying the relevant subjects than the combined total of Arab graduates in those fields during the previous 30 years. Nevertheless, the researchers also found that only 58 percent of Arab graduates[247] with the relevant degrees managed to find hi tech employment, compared to 75 percent of Jewish graduates.[248]

There is a continuing, and serious, shortage of well-qualified Israeli computer engineers. Nepotism clearly helps to explain this; as does the huge prestige attached to military service in units such as 8200. The part played by the highly selective programmes for gifted children also needs to be explored. There seems to be a conveyor belt process involving mostly secular Israeli Jewish males with well-off, well-educated parents. It begins early, proceeds via the school programs for gifted children and high-scoring achievements in maths and physics in the school matriculation examinations, continuing to army service in Unit 8200, followed by relevant degrees from the more prestigious universities and employment in high tech companies – alongside school and army buddies – headed by those who had come through the same route.

There is no doubt that the Israeli high-tech sector is extraordinarily successful, for the size of the country, and among the leaders in the world. But it could achieve even more if it were to become more accessible to currently disadvantaged groups: women, Arabs, students from poorer backgrounds. The same is true for Israeli universities. (This is without taking into account the rabbinical ban that generally prevents intellectually able yeshiva students leaving that world to study outside it, though this is slowly changing.)

Women

The Glass Ceiling Index
Compiled annually by *The Economist,* this ranks the best and worst countries to be a working woman. Each score is based on average performance in 10 indicators: educational attainment, labour market attachment, pay, childcare costs, maternity and paternity rights, business school applications and representation in senior jobs (in managerial positions, on company boards and in Parliament). In the latest report, the Scandinavian countries do well, while workplace parity for women in Japan, South Korea

and Turkey lags badly. America ranks only 19th out of the 29 OECD countries which comprise the index. Israel ranks 14th.

The universities: Israel

The general trend of educational performance between males and females over the past few decades in the Western world is clear: girls first performed better in their early teens, then in their late teens, and next at the undergraduate level, followed by superior postgraduate attainment. This has been the trend in Israel, too. However, throughout the West, including Israel, faculty appointments are still significantly in favour of men, increasingly so as the level of full professor is reached. Indeed, according to a report prepared by the Israeli Committee on the Advancement and Representation of Women in Institutes of Higher Education, women constituted only 29 percent of senior faculty at universities and 39 percent at (the less prestigious) public colleges. Israel ranked 30th among the 31 Western countries examined in the report. On average, women in those countries constituted 40 percent of senior faculty.

Moreover, the proportion of women is even lower at the highest levels of Israeli academia. Only 16 percent of full professors are women, again lower than the Western average. In the academic years 2010-2013, only 34 percent of new faculty hires at universities were women, and 45 percent at public colleges. This is of particular note since women now constitute a majority of the Israelis who receive doctorates every year. The proportion of women on the senior faculty is lowest in the exact sciences – only 11 percent in maths and computer science, and 13 percent in the physical sciences. (Even in the humanities, social sciences and education, women constitute a minority of the senior faculty.) The faculty gender gap is much larger than that among students. For instance, women comprise 25 to 31 percent of the student body in engineering, math and computer science departments, and 75 to 82 percent in departments of education and various paramedical professions.

This marked disparity between the sexes requires explanation, not only for evident reasons of gender equality, but also on account of the possible loss in quality at the highest level, which is likely to impinge on overall national achievement and on GDP.

What are the barriers to women's academic advancement? According to the report, one of the biggest is the lack of balance between personal and professional life

Women are still required to do the lion's share of housework and child care; many decide against doing overseas doctorates or post docs because, by that point in their careers, most are already mothers. Barriers also exist in the hiring process, which is neither transparent nor accessible to all, the report said. Openings for new academic staff are not widely publicised, and the advertisements generally don't encourage women to apply. Yet another barrier is the lack of awareness of gender issues.

The source of these barriers lies in social norms external to the academic system, the report concluded. For instance, one Education Ministry study found that 'girls are deterred from studying masculine fields by various open and hidden societal messages'.

A report by the Cyber Education Centre of the Rashi Foundation,[249] which surveyed 389 students in grades 11 and 12, about to take the 2017 matriculation exams in maths and computers, found that the girls were spending more time studying for the exams than the boys: 44 percent of them studied for over a week before the exams, compared to 31 percent of the boys, with only 15 percent of girls allocating just a day or two, compared to 24 percent of the boys. Moreover, the girls were twice as likely as the boys to use private tutors (30 percent and 15 percent, respectively). Another significant difference was in the level of drive: while the majority of both genders reported self-motivation as the main factor, the proportion among girls was a little higher – 65 percent compared to 59 percent; this was reversed with regard to those who said that parents were the main source of pressure, 32 percent of the boys, compared to 24 percent of the girls. A significant difference was also found between the genders in their perception of capability: 58 percent of boys believed that their chances of doing well in the exams were high, this was true of only 39 percent of the girls. A fairly large gap was also found in the students' future outlook: more boys than girls (71 percent versus 54 percent) thought there was a strong likelihood they would go on to a career in computers and maths, whether in academia or industry. Assuming that the sample studied by the

Rashi Foundation is representative, some important conclusions emerge. Whereas girls prepare themselves more assiduously than boys for these exams, they are less likely to be pressed by their parents, less likely to believe that they will do well, and to think that they will have a future career in the relevant fields.[250] Clearly, the negative expectations, held by both girls and their parents, will need to be addressed, if the – at least equal – level of female talent and effort in maths and computers is to be fully expressed over the 15 or so years between leaving school and pursuing academic appointments and successful grant applications. In short, female self-belief has to match their undoubted intellectual potential.

In the meantime, what can be done? The Higher Education Council report's main recommendation is that universities and colleges should institute affirmative action in the hiring process. Affirmative action is one of the main reasons other Western countries have higher proportions of women on the senior faculties; this has not led to any deterioration in the quality of the faculty. The report proposed drafting a multi-year plan to increase the proportion of women faculty members by offering financial rewards to institutions that meet the plan's goals. Prof Hagit Messer-Yaron, deputy chairwoman of the Council for Higher Education, said the council "had decided to include gender issues in all its rules and guidelines, when relevant. The council will also require all universities and colleges to report regularly on what they are doing to hire and promote more women," she added.

High Tech: Israel
Gender disparity is even more marked in high tech and particularly in those successful companies whose leading personnel are featured in newspaper articles and accompanying photographs – which tell a clear story: men outnumber women by at least 5 to 1. Even more than in university faculties and research teams, social and family life come second to achieving the coveted stock exchange quotation and an equity sale. Long and intensive hours of work are involved; even more than in university science and technology departments, married women are at a disadvantage – unless the company goes out of its way to subsidise high quality child care with long hours. Of course, the largely male 'buddy'

system of Unit 8200 also plays a part. Once again, both individual women and the overall economic performance of the country, lose out.

Elite institutions: closed and open

Every country has its elite universities, such as Harvard and MIT in the United States, Oxford and Cambridge in Britain. The key question is whether entry is strictly on merit, or whether there are other factors at play. Moreover, these institutions are supplied by similarly elite secondary schools. Here, too, the question arises: is entry on merit or not?

In Britain, easily the best-known example of an elite secondary school is Eton College, founded in the 15th century by Henry VI for 'poor boys'. Until fairly recently, poor boys, however clever, did not have much of a chance. Instead, for generations the school had a policy of allowing fathers, themselves the product of Eton, to register their sons (it has remained single sex to the present) at birth for the so-called 'Eton list'. In his essay on Eton, "1843", Christopher de Bellaigue,[251] himself an OE (Old Etonian), states that the List 'exemplified how the school had a built-in prejudice in favour of its own,' effectively allowing an OE 'to sew up a place for his son, while the boy was in nappies (diapers).' This continued, generation after generation. The next step was to attend one of the grander Oxford or Cambridge colleges, and then on to a successful career in a merchant bank or in politics. The immediate post-war period witnessed three Etonian prime ministers in succession (one of whom, Harold Macmillan, named no fewer than 35 OEs to serve in his governments of the late 1950s and early 1960s). The school also had links to the House of Lords, by the same hereditary principle. But it was a clear sign that the school could no longer count on its old connections with Parliament, when in 1999 almost 700 hereditary peers (many, if not most of them OEs) were expelled from the House of Lords; the vast majority of members of the House are now appointed only for life and (at least in intention) after a career of distinguished public service.

The governors of Eton read the message: the school needed to raise standards in order to maintain a market share in the process of feeding boys to Oxbridge. Entry to Eton was made strictly on merit, with a deliberate attempt to attract a number of poor, but clever, boys. However, the children of the nouveau riche were also admitted – the sons of Russian oligarchs and Chinese businessmen. Yet there is a continuing attempt to ensure that ability remains the pre-eminent factor. The result is clear: the percentage of pupils with an OE father went down from 60 percent in 1960 to 20 percent at present. About 20 percent of the student body now receive substantial, or complete, fee remission. The school recently took out a large loan to raise this number. Fortunately, it can also draw on a very large endowment (by British standards). In addition, wealthy parents are encouraged to make substantial donations to the school.

But the question remains: won't the new entrants, whether from poor parents, oligarchs, or 'traditional' OE, in their turn aim to send their own children to Eton, using all the means at their disposal, as do American elite parents?

The theme of 'poor but clever' certainly applied to City College of the City University of New York. According to *The Economist*,[252] City's 'golden era' came in the last century, when America's best-known colleges restricted the number of Jewish students they would admit, at exactly the same time that New York was teeming with the bright children of Jewish immigrants. In 1933-1954 City produced nine future Nobel laureates; Hunter, its affiliated, former women's college, produced another two. City-educated alumni included Felix Frankfurter, a pivotal figure of the Supreme Court (class of 1902), Ira Gershwin (1918), Jonas Salk, tinventor of the polio vaccine (1934) and Robert Kahn, an architect of the internet (1960).

But then it all went wrong: City 'dropped its standards– partly to do with demography (meaning that the Jews moved out of the catchment area), partly to do with earnest muddle headedness'. Only a small number of minority students were passing the strict test and that fact, critics decided, could not be squared with City's mission to "serve all the citizens of New York". In 1969, massive student protests shut down City's campus for two weeks. City subsequently scrapped its admissions standards altogether. By 1970, almost any student who graduated from New York's high schools could attend. The quality of education collapsed. In the

21st century attempts were made to remedy matters, and these continue. At the heart of the issue is the contention of one of the current key administrators: "Elitism is not a dirty word".

Chapter Sixteen

The Next Decade: Jewish Potential in the Diaspora and Israel

The big picture by 2030

Napoleon's well-known dictum from the early 19th century will become even truer than it is now: "China is a sleeping giant, which when it wakes will astonish the world." China's GDP will approach, perhaps surpass, that of the United States (which currently accounts for about a quarter of the world's total GDP). From being a large-scale manufacturer of consumer goods (like Britain in the 19th century, then said to be 'the workshop of the world'), China will increasingly dominate high tech, particularly the relatively new areas of artificial intelligence (AI), quantum computing and robotics. The centuries-old authoritarian nature of Chinese society will assist the goal of the communist leadership, which seems to be total surveillance of the entire population and of all aspects of daily life – governance by algorithm. China's increasing confidence and assertiveness on the geopolitical stage can only grow over the next decade. It now dominates the relatively close China Sea island chains, and encounters little or no response from the US Navy as it does so. By 2030, it is possible that much of the Pacific Ocean will no longer be 'the US pond', but 'China's lake'. It is quite simply the case that China's population is nearly five times that of the United States, and its government is firmly in control of national policy. The concomitant decline of the US (irrespective of which party controls the presidency and the Congress) and of Europe, as well as of Russia – economically dependent on the price of oil, and with a diminishing population and a kleptocratic leadership – will inevitably follow. And that is without mention of China's vast project, 'Belt and Road', to link China, via a series of roads and railways through the increasingly resource-rich and authoritarian central Asian 'stans', to the countries of the eastern Mediterranean and to Italy; a modern re-creation of the Silk Road of China's earlier heyday.

As far as Israel is concerned, it is largely a spectator in geopolitics outside the Middle East and this situation can only continue over the next decade, whatever the success of Israel's universities and high-tech companies. Its academic and technological leadership is well aware of this and has been assiduous in developing joint ventures with China, as well as with the US and Europe whenever possible. Russia will continue to be heavily involved in the Middle East, which it sees as a vital strategic interest, as it has done for the past 70 years. Throughout the world, the effects on work and employment of high-technology, particularly AI and robotization, will be increasingly felt. Governments will be hard put to either retrain displaced workers, whether blue or white collar, or to financially compensate them for lost jobs. Authoritarian governments, like China's, will find this top-down direction easier than liberal democracies, which will be increasingly challenged by populist movements. But the inability of the latter to solve practical problems may result in a swing away from populism before the end of the decade. Nevertheless, populist movements, whether in the US or Europe, will find it easy to blame traditional elites, as well as minorities and immigrants, for the inevitable economic difficulties arising from technological change in the short and medium term.

In another decade, the world in general will be a rather different place: the climate crisis will loom ever larger, and pandemics like Covid-19, caused by the coronavirus, are likely to recur. The pandemic erupted right at the beginning of the decade in the Chinese province of Wuhan and spread rapidly throughout the world causing millions of deaths, mainly among the elderly, people living in crowded housing, the obese and those with pre-existing medical conditions. The long-term political and economic effects are likely to be profound, but may well enhance the predicted and growing disparity between China and the United States. At the end of 2021, according to forecasts by the OECD, America's economy will be the same size as in 2019, but China's will be 10 percent larger. Whereas the latter, after initially denying the problem, then moved rapidly to respond, the former, under the flailing leadership of Donald Trump, did not, to say the least. Second and third pandemic waves have occurred in many parts of the world; the search for an effective vaccine has been the holy grail of international science and is achieving a high level of effectiveness and safety in the wealthier countries, though the economic effects will persist. World Jewry, particularly the most Orthodox segment, has been hard hit, with a death rate significantly larger than that of the general population. The same is true of Israel, which initially fared reasonably well, but relaxed too soon from an early "lockdown" and then joined the US and Britain in a rapidly rising rate of cases, before a successful vaccination campaign.

World Jewry by 2030

The demographic pattern will be as in 2020, only more so: two very large Jewish communities, in Israel and the United States, comprising between them more than 80 percent of the world's Jewish population. Towards 2030, an evident trend will become even clearer: the balance of numbers is constantly shifting towards Israel. In the US, as in the rest of the Diaspora, numbers are decreasing because the birth rate is exceeded by the death rate and, notably, because intermarriage typically results in the resulting offspring not being raised Jewish. Whereas American Jewry was considerably supplemented in the post-war period by a succession of Jewish immigrations, that was not the case for the earlier part of the 21st century, and the current pattern is set to continue. As 2030 approaches, severe demographic decline will be the norm in the many small Jewish communities that make up the remaining 20 percent of the world's Jewish population, which currently stands at around 14 and a half million.

European Jewry

There is every reason to expect the coming decade to be even bleaker, in demographic terms, for the European Diaspora: at least a third to a half of Jews will marry non-Jewish spouses; most of the children of such marriages will not identify themselves as Jews; even within all-Jewish marriages, fertility rates are significantly below replacement level – indeed the professional and business elites, to which European Jews increasingly belong, are failing to reproduce themselves. The success of Jewish social mobility in Europe over the past three generations has virtually eliminated the Jewish working class in the continent.

Whereas European societies in general have been considerably augmented by immigration from much poorer – mainly Moslem – countries, no such additions were available for the European Jewish Diaspora, except for the relatively small number from the dissolving Soviet Union, which moved to Germany. That reservoir is no longer available; Jews of the former Soviet Union will continue to emigrate, but mainly to Israel.

Jewish religious and cultural life in Europe will mirror the demographic decline. Apart from the entry and exit rituals of circumcision and burial, synagogue attendance is falling (though bar- and bat-mitzvahs will continue as lively social occasions). As for secular culture, there are leading playwrights and novelists who happen to be Jewish, but they write for general, not Jewish, audiences. There remains a thin patina of commercialised popular culture: *Fiddler on the Roof*, lokshen soup, 'Jewish' jokes.

A piece by Judy Maltz[253] sets out the numerical decline of European Jewry. In the last half-century Europe lost nearly 60 percent of its Jewish population; an estimated 1.3 million Jews currently live in Europe (barely one-tenth of one percent of the total population); almost two out of three European Jews live in France, Britain or Germany,

There is a single, striking exception to the likelihood of European Jewry's numerical decline continuing to 2030 and beyond: the UK's rapidly growing ultra-Orthodox community, which is characterized by early marriage (within the community) and large families. The result is rapid expansion and an increasing numerical share of Anglo-Jewry. Gateshead, a bleak town in the north-east of England, with an important yeshiva, is the smallest (8,000 in 2019) of the three main British ultra-Orthodox communities. However, the heterogeneous Leeds Jewish community is now even smaller (7,000) having shrunk from 20,000 sixty years ago. (The general population of Leeds is several times larger than that Gateshead.)

In another decade, the yeshiva in Gateshead may be rivalled by one that has been established in Canvey Island in 2017. The 'Island', about 40 miles east of central London, is a town of redbrick family houses inhabited by former Londoners, and one of the most pro-Brexit towns in the country. The move from heavily overcrowded Stamford Hill, a stronghold of London's Hassidic community, has been swift and is likely to accelerate further, assisted by local and Swiss Hassidic philanthropy. By early 2020, more than 75 families (about 500 people) had moved in and many others were keen to join them. But the response of the local community has been varied at best: some remember their own London origins; others point to the lack of 'mixing' with their new neighbours and wonder 'how many are on housing benefit'. A long-serving councillor stated "Canvey is a close-knit community... eventually problems will arise". But for now, the dream of this Yiddish-speaking, anti-Zionist segment of the Hassidic world is to recreate the shtetl existence of pre-War Europe in the heavily 'white British 'milieu of Canvey Island.[254]

In contrast to the continued decline of European Jewry (perhaps slowed by the significant numbers which will continue to attend Jewish day schools in both the UK and France) their economic status will improve still further by comparison with their non-Jewish neighbours; middle-class Jewish parents will ensure that their own success is replicated by their talented children, a pattern that can only strengthen over the next decade. But economic security goes together with resentment of that success, from the extremes of the political spectrum and from the rapidly increasing Western and Central European Moslem populations, whose share in the UK, France and Germany is likely to be around 8 percent or more by 2030, due both to continued immigration from Moslem countries, and young populations with a high fertility rate. In addition, the current pattern of Moslems holding much higher levels of antisemitic attitudes than the general population, is likely to continue. The resulting sense of physical, as compared to economic, insecurity, will maintain levels of emigration to Israel at approaching 500 per year from Britain and 2,500 per year from France. The Moslem populations of Western and Central European countries are set to grow, according to a report by the Pew Research Centre: *Europe's Growing Muslim Population*[255]. For example, the Moslem share of Germany's population could grow from 6.1 percent in 2016 to 19.7 percent in 2050, if high immigration levels continue. But even in a zero-immigration scenario, the Moslem population in Europe is expected to rise from 4.9 percent to 7.4 percent through natural increase, that is, a higher average fertility rate for Moslems, compared to non-Moslems.

What are the implications of this projected increase? It seems likely that the current, relatively high level of European Moslem antisemitic attitudes will be at least maintained over the next decade and, given the constantly increasing Moslem numbers, may have even more potential to result in actual violence. Moreover, the defeat of IS and Al Queda on the battle grounds of the Middle East may simply result in their surviving adherents going underground, particularly in Western Europe, with enhanced potential for terrorist attacks on both the general and the Jewish populations. The sharp rise in right-wing Western European antisemitism (see Chapter 9) is set to continue as post-war inhibitions against its expression erode over time and populist parties profit electorally. Eastern European antisemitism, in the context of hostile right-wing governments (probably set to continue in power) acting against vulnerable minorities, even in the continued absence of significant Moslem populations, will remain at high levels – antisemitism without Jews, although 'Jewish' cultural events will be popular with tourists, bringing much-needed foreign currency. European Jewish achievements will continue to depend on Jewish talent, on the relative rankings of the main European research universities and access to them for young Jews, most of whom live in elite cities such as London and Paris. Provided that Brexit does not impinge on elite universities, Oxbridge and the main London universities will hold their current world status as research centres, attracting and retaining the exceptionally talented and (crucially) high levels of research funding. British Jews will continue to be well to the fore: about 5 percent of Oxbridge undergraduates at present are Jewish, and around 10 percent of Jewish young people of undergraduate age study at Oxbridge, an extraordinary figure compared to the general population – only about one percent of which does so. The current numbers of Jewish students at Oxbridge are likely to continue over the next decade. The French government has established Paris-Saclay as a world class university; talented young French Jews will now have the same opportunity for exceptional achievement as their British counterparts.

American Jewry

What will the general situation be in 2030? Several predictions seem safe: the total number of American Jews will decline because of a relatively low birth rate, compared with the death rate; more importantly, the rate of intermarriage will continue at least at the current 50 percent level and will more likely increase; the relative shares of Conservative, Reform, and 'Just Jews' will decrease as compared to the Orthodox and ultra-Orthodox, particularly the latter, whose numbers will rise due to their very high birth rate. The many thousands of American-domiciled Israelis (secular, not religious of any stripe) have another self-imposed problem: how to preserve the 'Israeliness' of their children. A growing number are doing so by setting up after-school classes in Hebrew and secular Israeli culture. But unless the children return to Israel for their IDF service – as many do – it seems inevitable that they will assimilate over the years into the generic American secular culture.

A lively piece in *The Economist*[256] described the relationship between an American Strictly Orthodox community, Kiryas Joel, and their non-Jewish neighbours in the town of Monroe, about 40 miles north of New York City. It was founded in the 1970s as a part of the Satmar Hassidic sect and has grown from 500 in 1977 to more than 22,000 today. Conversations are conducted in Yiddish; there is little interaction with their non-Hasidic neighbours; Kiryas Joel already has its own school district, where boys and girls receive a religious education in separate classrooms. The community has increasing political muscle; more than half of all voters will be Hasidic by 2021. Many of the families are struggling, with more than half below the official poverty line. Other Strictly Orthodox American communities are also expanding rapidly, albeit from a numerically low base; there is little or no sign of the shift discernible among their Israeli counterparts towards entry into secular studies, increased employment among men, and military service. The key factors in this difference are that, in America, there is no draft, and no government pressure (albeit intermittent in Israel) to impinge on the Strictly Orthodox male lifestyle. This preserves the power of the rabbinical leadership to eschew anything more than minimal secular education for Strictly Orthodox boys. In Israel, however, the pressure of poverty may bring about change.

Further predictions for 2030 can confidently be made concerning the average American Jewish economic and educational situations. The former is likely to be even better, on average, than at present, as the remaining poor section of the community departs – mainly the more elderly Russian Jews who arrived at the end of the 20th century and the beginning of the 21st. (As noted above, however, the Strictly Orthodox community will continue to struggle with poverty unless the rabbinical leadership allows entry into the general economy.) At the rarefied upper end of the income scale, perhaps a fifth of American billionaires are Jewish, typically self-made; this pattern will continue into the future. A similar expectation of further improved performance is likely to be realized in the educational sphere; successful Jewish parents, like their non-Jewish counterparts, will seek to secure for their children at the least their own level of success, and even beyond. This will also very likely mean the same, probably a larger, proportional Jewish attendance at elite universities, from the undergraduate to the professorial level. Successful Asian-Americans will also be increasingly found at all levels. However, Nobel prizes for science and economics are usually awarded on the basis of seminal work of decades earlier so that, at least for the next decade, the disproportionate Jewish share of American prizes will probably continue.

In 2030 the voting patterns of American Jews will be as at present: the majority Democratic, the minority Republican – the latter heavily associated with those who are Orthodox or Strictly Orthodox.

The Democratic Party majority, particularly the younger end, will be ever more involved with general liberal causes – 'repairing the world' – rather than with specifically Jewish aims, and they will have a diminishing sense of kinship with Israel. Of at least equal importance is the financial support to Israel of successive US administrations. Towards the end of the Obama presidency a 38-billion-dollar military grant was agreed, to run over a ten-year period – a substantial increase over the previous decade. (As always, the bulk to be spent on US-origin armaments.) The close security cooperation between the two countries is set to continue into the future, supported by both House and Senate. But the result of the 2020 election – a very experienced Democratic President, Joe Biden, in place of the self-serving Donald Trump – will produce at least a partial shift: several Democratic lawmakers had already begun to link continued US military funding with a reduction in Israel's settlement project in the West Bank. The relatively frequent pattern of the incumbent party winning a second term would mean a Democratic-held White House through 2028. According to a trenchant *New York Times* piece by David M. Halbfinger,[257] President Trump's defeat left Israel and its long-time Prime Minister, Benjamin Netanyahu, on the receiving end of an abrupt demotion. He quotes Anshel Pfeffer, a Netanyahu biographer: "He's gone from Trump's wingman to the guy who polishes the canopy of the F-16".

Over the past century and more, antisemitism has been a concern for American Jews. A significant percentage of the general population continues to espouse antisemitic attitudes, encouraged by the rise of the alt right. Following the October 2018 massacre in a Pittsburgh synagogue, the deadliest attack on Jews in American Jewish history, American Jews have responded with a much-enhanced physical protection of synagogues and other Jewish institutions, including armed guards. Will there be also some form of 'push-back', perhaps by active legal challenges to the alt right presence on all forms of media? Crucially, Pittsburgh was not a one-off; it was repeated at Poway, California, exactly 6 months later, but with only one dead and several wounded – the shooter's gun jammed with over 50 bullets still unused. Future assailants may be more competent. The trend for antisemitic physical assaults in the US is on the rise.

However, in contrast to Europe, most American Moslems seek good relations with American Jews, as expressed in various joint activities, a pattern that is set to continue. They were enormously supportive post-Pittsburgh, both emotionally and financially (It is of note that, according to a Pew Research Centre projection, Moslems will shortly replace Jews as the United States' second largest religious group, due to a higher fertility rate than the national average, and certainly higher than the Jewish rate.) Among Christian denominations, Evangelicals stand out for their steadfast support of Israel, particularly for the right of its political spectrum, a pattern set to continue for the older generation. But the younger elements of the denomination appear less enamoured. By 2030 Evangelical support may be less clear cut. The marked trend noted in Chapter 10 – a growing rift between Democrats and Republicans with regard to Israeli policy in the West Bank – can only widen, particularly if the right remains in power in Israel, in contrast to the result of the 2020 US Elections: a Democrat victory in the presidency and the Senate, while retaining control of the House. Demographic trends suggest that the Democratic ascendancy will continue well into the decade; Trump will likely seek the nomination again in 2024.

Israel by 2030

1. Internal matters

Demography

If Israel continues to increase at around 2 percent per year, a rate that is typical of developing, not developed, countries (at most 0.5 percent per year), by 2030 its population will be well in excess of 10 million – in the same population bracket as Sweden and Belgium. By 2065, if the current growth rate continues, the situation will be dire: Israel will be the most crowded nation on earth with the exception of Bangladesh. But there is time to institute rational policies. By 2030 the population share of the Haredim will be greater than in 2020, despite a slowly falling birth rate, and hence it will still be higher than the rest of the Jewish population, at well over 15 percent of the total Jewish population. Unless government policy shifts sharply – to *dis*courage, not *en*courage large families – the current trend of rapid growth and serious overcrowding will continue. Any Israeli government must encourage Haredi male, as well as female, participation in the work force, a factor usually associated with smaller families.

The Arab population share will remain at about 20 percent due to a continued modest excess of Diaspora Jewish immigration over Israeli Jewish emigration, and a reduction in the Israeli Arab birth rate to about the combined Jewish rate, already the case in 2020. However, short of a catastrophic turn of events in the American and Western European Jewish communities, they will not – although potentially major sources of aliyah – fill the gap left by reduced emigration to Israel from the dwindling Jewish communities of the former Soviet Union. Over the next decade these FSU communities will be continually depleted, by an annual rate of departure of about 10,000 to 15,000, from a 2020 population of about 200,000. The combined result of continued Western Jewish prosperity and reasonable physical security, and a declining FSU Jewish population base, will be the gradual diminution in the annual addition to Israel of Jewish immigrants. But these trends are at the demographic margin; the main thrust of long-term government policy must be to confront the rabbinical promotion of very large families.

Education

By the end of the decade, given even reasonably sensible government policies, several groups – women, Arabs, Haredim, impoverished Jews, all currently under-represented in the STEM subjects – will be making more of a numerical contribution to them, at both the school and the university level. This will continue to high-tech employment, the demand for which will continue to grow from start-ups and established companies; there will likewise be a rise in these groups' percentage share of undergraduate entry, for subjects from business and law to engineering, first recorded in 2018. Another serious shortfall in a vital area of employment is in medicine. Israel is perennially short of doctors, a problem which will only worsen as large numbers of Russian-origin doctors retire over the next decade. At the same time, some 15 percent of first-year medical students come from abroad, paying three times the tuition fee paid by Israeli citizens. This has the effect of forcing Israeli would-be medical students to study abroad, despite performing at a high level in the entrance examinations, though just below that required. The medical schools benefit in the short-term from the high fees paid by foreign students, but in the longer term, the country loses their lifelong services, as they usually return to their country of origin, mainly the United States, where medical earnings are much higher than in Israel. Even a minimal adjustment by the medical schools and the government would see a more sensible state of affairs, with an increased annual intake by Israeli medical schools and the development of the new medical school of Ariel University.[258]

The last aliyah

Putting together the shortage of doctors and engineers with the undoubted intellectual talent hitherto locked up in the Haredi community, the Haifa Technion set up, some years ago, a quiet programme to identify, prepare and train Haredi doctors. The first of these graduated recently at the Technion, having completed in 18 months the usual 12-year pre-university schooling in secular subjects. While still young, Yehuda S., from a prestigious Haredi family, had been considered likely to become a leading rabbi. Instead, he fulfilled a secret childhood dream to qualify as a doctor. Out of an initial group of 35, identified as having the all-round potential to cope with the preparatory course and the Technion degrees in medicine or engineering, half graduated in the summer of 2018. Instead of only the less intellectually able Haredi boys being allowed to leave the yeshiva world for work (often intellectually undemanding), it is the most able who are sought by the Technion. Thirty-five (of a total Haredi student body of 60) are currently in medical school; the intention is to grow to an overall total of 200 in five years, and 400 in ten. (Other universities will no doubt follow suit, particularly in medicine and the STEM fields, in which shortages are also perennial). Professor Boaz Golan of the Technion, pointed out that Haredi boys brought with them from the yeshivas the habit of exceptionally hard intellectual work, and the ability to focus and apply logic. Economic necessity, as well as routine exposure to the secular world, will increase the pace of the male Haredi shift from exclusive Torah study to at least a 'mixed model' of work by day and study in the evening. A reasonable guess is for the proportion of Haredi men in paid employment to rise from one half to three-quarters, making a significant contribution to total GDP and to the Treasury, while reducing Haredi dependence on state hand-outs and also limiting the power of the rabbinical establishment. In addition, there must be a consistent effort by all future Israeli governments to ensure that it becomes the norm for Haredi children to receive a general as well as a religious education, preparing girls as well as boys for the world of work, at all educational levels and in all areas of economic activity. While the Haredi birth rate is declining, it will still exceed the national average. It should be seen not only as a demographic threat, but also as an opportunity, a reservoir of talent for the future. A recently formed group, 'working Haredim', will no doubt grow rapidly, with implications for political loyalties.

From the Diaspora

Foreign students are welcome in most university departments worldwide. In Israel, university fees are generally about one-eighth of those obtaining in the United States, except for the poorly off (which excludes the overwhelming majority of American Jews). Once again, good sense is likely to prevail in the long run and Israeli universities will seek foreign, mainly American, Jewish undergraduates. Even university fees markedly higher than those paid by native Israelis would undercut American university fees, a difference obviously attractive to American Jewish parents. One Israeli institute of higher education, the Interdisciplinary Centre at Herzliya, has made it a central feature of its appeal to potential students to offer across-the-board undergraduate degree tuition in English. It is a safe prediction that others will follow. The increased income will enable universities to employ more academic staff for both teaching and research on long-term projects in Israel – an alternative to moving to the United States.

The PISA elephant in the room

There remains Israel's glaringly poor performance in the international PISA rankings of school pupils. Will it improve to at least an average international level over the next decade? This will require a sustained effort and consistently increased educational budgets. Primary and secondary education are not areas that attract electoral votes. Cross-party agreement will be needed. Without it, the vital underpinning of continued high-level university performance will be at risk, as will the productive ability of the workforce to compete in world markets.

Economic indices

If the present rate of growth of about 3.5 percent per year can be maintained – a reasonable assumption given the likely increased involvement of both Haredi men and Arab women in the workforce – the Israeli GDP per head will reach at least $50,000, well above the European average. Another key index, government debt, may decline further to below the European Union target of around 60 percent. But there are two caveats: economic predictions could be upended by a major war with Israel's neighbours and regional rivals, or by another pandemic outbreak. In either case it is likely that unemployment would rise sharply, particularly among the young.

High tech

Once again, if major regional conflicts can be avoided, the development of Israel's high-tech sector will continue apace and across-the-board, with particular strengths in the cyber sector – scheduled for major development, both military and civilian, in the south of the country, in the economically modest city of Beersheba and at Ben-Gurion University, based in that city.

From the plethora of Israeli high-tech projects, it is worth noting two developments, both still at an early stage but with enormous long-term potential: producing electricity from bacterial activity, and laboratory-grown meat. Researchers at the Haifa Technion, together with colleagues from the Weizmann Institute and from Germany, demonstrated a process for generating electricity from cyanobacteria. These are a vital and widely-present part of the environment, forming a source of atmospheric oxygen and an essential source of organic material (they are largely made up of sugar), and they are the first link in the food chain. The process produces hydrogen, which the research team simply divert to generate electricity –demonstrating that cyanobacteria can be used as a source of clean energy. It is a far cry from a laboratory demonstration to the production of a viable energy source in the future. But this research opens the possibility of undoubted long-term benefits.[259]

The production of meat for human consumption is both very expensive and very wasteful–from the very large acreage required to produce cattle fodder, to the transportation of the animals, to the slaughterhouses, the process of manufacturing marketable meat, and finally the refrigerated space required to display the meat to prospective customers. Not to speak of the distaste many people feel for the whole sequence. If an edible product could be made which both looked and tasted like the meat familiar to and enjoyed by carnivores the world over, the economic and social benefits would be enormous. It is in pursuit of this worthy objective that a number of Israeli companies are growing meat animal cells in laboratories. The possibility has led to a $300 million deal between China and the Israeli companies concerned, a development that potentially opens access to the huge Asian economy for the Israeli companies. China imported meat worth more than $10 billion in 2016; as the country has modernised and the standard of living has risen, meat consumption has rocketed. The move would also be applauded by environmentalists as a step towards reducing greenhouse gases. Livestock produces methane, which results in 21 times as much climate warming as carbon dioxide; moreover, carbon dioxide is released when large tracts of forest are cleared for pasture. Globally, livestock raising is responsible for 14.5 percent of all greenhouse gas pollution. China has already announced a plan to cut Chinese meat consumption by half – hence the large initial investment in Israel. Many animal rights groups have welcomed the development of lab meat as an alternative to massive animal slaughter by the meat industry. As with bacterially produced electricity, Israeli technology could be transformative over large sections of the global economy by the end of the next decade.[260]

2. Internal politics

The 2018 edition of the Global Innovation Index of 80 combined indices ranked Israel at 6 (up from 17 in 2017) out of 180 countries, behind Switzerland, Sweden, the Netherlands and the UK, but ahead of South Korea, Japan and France. However, there are problems less tractable than economic ones: Israel lacks a political consensus to draft a constitution that will safeguard its democracy, and there are unresolved contradictions of state and synagogue which allow the rabbinate to control marriage and divorce. Israel's political parties remain fractious and fractionated, and this will continue to hamper progress in these less tangible areas. Political wisdom to solve them remains in short supply; political parties tend to prefer short-term electoral gains over long-term considerations. This is more likely than not to continue over the next decade, whether or not the prime ministership reverts to the hands of Mr Netanyahu, the most skilled political operator and electoral campaigner of the past decade and more. Next to David Ben-Gurion, Benjamin Netanyahu, known by his nickname 'Bibi', is the most remarkable Israeli political personality since 1948. Gifted but deeply flawed, he was accorded a leading editorial and an extended 'Briefing' by *The Economist*.[261] *Bibi*, a fine biography by Anshel Pfeffer,[262] explores his family background. His professorial father had been close to Jabotinsky, but was distant from Begin and the Likud, spending much of his time in the United States, having been denied a position at the Hebrew University. Netanyahu junior has long shared his father's sense of frustrated entitlement; his career development is detailed by Pfeffer.

The parliamentary elections of April 2019 resulted in a tie between Likud and a new party, Kachol Lavan (Blue and White) headed by a trio of former chiefs of staff, one of whom, the patently decent but politically inexperienced Benny Gantz, was the party head. Both main winners achieved their success at the expense of parties respectively to their left and right. On their left, Labour was reduced to a shadow of its former self as the heart of the Zionist enterprise. On their right, a mixed secular-observant, but hardline nationalist party was cannibalized by Netanyahu's clever but allegedly underhand campaign (reminiscent of his 'best friend', Donald Trump). Netanyahu tried to set up a coalition of Likud with rabbinically-dominated ultra-Orthodox MKs and religious nationalists. But his government-in-formation was stymied by another party's refusal to join the budding coalition: Israel Beiteinu (Israel Our Home) is an unequivocally secular (albeit nationalist) party largely composed of immigrants from the FSU and their descendants, led by the hard-boiled Avigdor Liberman. When Lieberman's refusal denied him a majority in the Knesset, Netanyahu instead called another election: the first 'do-over' election in Israel's history was held on September 17th, 2019. The result was essentially no change. Netanyahu was again mandated to form a government, but again failed to secure a working majority. The President then gave the task to Benny Gantz, the first time in over a decade that anyone other than Netanyahu had been given the responsibility. Gantz also had to admit defeat. A third election was called for March 2[nd,] 2020 with a similar result. But this time a functioning government was formed: a coalition between Likud, Gantz's section of Kachol Lavan, and the two Haredi parties, with Netanyahu again as prime minister, and Gantz as deputy prime minister (to change places after 18 months) and (a new position) alternative prime minister, to take office in the event of Netanyahu being "unable to fulfil his duties as prime minister" (for example by serving a prison sentence).

The tortuous legal process involving Netanyahu was suspended for the many weeks of the April 2019 election but resumed in October 2019 with a 'pre-trial hearing'; it would take many months, more likely years, to reach a final conclusion. An important landmark was reached when the Attorney General, a Netanyahu appointee, announced on November 21st, 2019, that he had decided all three indictments would proceed to trial. Throughout, the process has been marked by increasingly frenetic attempts by Netanyahu, his Likud party and their coalition allies, to secure immunity from prosecution for a sitting prime minister. But the manoeuvres failed; the Attorney General sent the three indictments to the Jerusalem District Court where the trial began on May 24th, 2020, the first in Israel of a serving prime minister. The most serious of the three charges carries a maximum sentence of 10 years' imprisonment. Over the next year or more, Netanyahu would divide his time between his prime ministerial duties and his legal travails.

In the event, the seemingly improbable outcome of that election was a win for a coalition of eight small parties, sworn in to govern on June 13[th,] potentially for the next four years, headed by Naftali Bennet, leader of the most far right of the eight, and including an Arab party, for the first time in Israeli history. After 12 continuous years as prime minister Netanyahu became leader of the opposition, probably facing challenges to his leadership of Likud from the most senior figures of that party. Whereas Netanyahu-led governments had always included the two Haredi parties they were also now in opposition, threatening their easy access to financial resources for their religious institutions, without any form of national service, or of secular education, for their young people.

3. Israel's neighbours near and far

Regarding the West Bank and Gaza, the former under Israel's direct control, the latter under its control by extension, there is much cause for concern about long-term Israeli policy.

The West Bank

Excluding the Jerusalem suburbs across the Green Line (the 1949 armistice line between Jordan and Israel), there are around 400,000 Jewish Israelis living on the West Bank in 2021. Of these, at least three-quarters live close to the Green Line in a number of medium-sized towns known as the 'settlement blocs'. There is a Jewish majority in this area (about 3 to 1) and a broad national consensus that, in any future agreement with the Arab world, the 'blocs' will probably remain within Israel and may even be formally annexed to it. The remaining quarter of Jews live in a much larger number of smaller settlements, towns and villages that are scattered throughout the West Bank. The total Palestinian Arab population of the West Bank amounts to about 2.5 million and has a much higher birth rate than the Jewish population, so that the demographic disparity is increasing annually; the Arab sector is much more heavily weighted towards the younger end. In the earlier years of the Jewish settlement enterprise, the scattered villages were able to attract new settlers, drawn by ideological fervour and by subsidised housing and continuing economic support from Israel. The incentives remain. Today the political parties are generally against removing the settlements, and many, like Likud, favour annexation. This trend is likely to continue, with the result that as far as Palestinian aspirations for independence are concerned, the juggernaut of Israel's hold over the West Bank will roll on. This, despite the fact that at least half of the working population of both the large settlement blocs and the scattered settlements are employed inside Israel proper. The demographic picture of Jews and Arabs in the West Bank is set to continue over the next decade; the population disparity, already very large, can only grow more acute, so that a relatively small Jewish population will be heavily privileged over an expanding Palestinian entity. What is to be done? A pragmatic view of what is desirable is very different from the ideological view held by Israel's right-wing parties, in power over the last decade but now replaced by a spectrum of parties from right to left, as described above. Left and centrist pragmatists would like to see some sort of enhanced Palestinian autonomy, though possibly not amounting to a sovereign state, and a gradual reduction of economic support for the Jewish population living outside the large settlement blocs. (An enforced withdrawal of settlers, on the lines of that carried out in Gaza in 2005, is highly unlikely, to the point of impossibility.)

What will be the likely position in 2030? In order to placate their very pro-Palestinian populations, the Arab states will continue to pay lip service to the Palestinian cause but, apart from limited subsidies, support will go no further. The one exception to the general tenor of Middle East states is Iran, since 1979 unshakably hostile to Israel. The large settlement blocs will continue to develop; the scattered Jewish settlements will attract modest new additions of population and even more of land; the Palestinian Authority will continue to cooperate with the Israeli security agencies to maintain the current situation of relative calm. A third intifada is thought to be unlikely. A positive current development, which is set to continue, is relatively large-scale outside investment in Palestinian towns such as Ramallah, including the growth of Palestinian high tech.

In short, the status quo will continue over the next decade, unless Israeli policy shifts in a more pragmatic direction. Moreover, Palestinian non-violence may not mean overall acquiescence. The West Bank leadership may take the radically different tack of demanding equal rights with Jews in a single state, encompassing both Israel and the West Bank, but excluding Gaza, where Hamas, still very much in charge, clings to a violent overthrow of Israel, however much of a chimera this is. A single state would be a return, geographically, to Mandatory Palestine. However attractive this might be to the Arabs of Israel and the West Bank, it is a non-starter for the vast majority of Israeli Jews of both entities. The old Brit Shalom aspiration, espoused by Martin Buber and a small group of like-minded colleagues, pre-1948, would be supported only by the far left of Jewish Israelis, vocal, but few in number.

So, short of new thinking that is acceptable to all parties, the West Bank impasse is set to continue over the next decade. This is in the context of the reality on the ground, a reality which remains unspoken by all the main players – Israel, the Palestinian leadership, the Arab states and the international community. It is the glaring disparity in all relevant areas, except the demographic, between Israel and the Palestinians: economic, military and strategic. To take only the first, Israel's total annual GDP for 2021 is 318 billion dollars and is growing steadily at 3 percent to 4 percent per year; the comparable figures for Gaza and the West Bank are both about 6.4 billion. This underpins the 'contest'; essentially, there is no contest. It ended with the 1947-8 failures of the Arab side – first the Arabs of Palestine and then the combined Arab states – to ' throw the Jews into the sea'. It was followed by the 1967 War which cost Jordan the West Bank. And the economic disparity is growing year by year. Moreover, while the Arab states were united, in November 1947, in rejecting partition and went to war against Israel in 1948, two states, Jordan and Egypt, later signed peace treaties with Israel. The wealthy Gulf Arab states are moving towards full political and trade relations. Seventy years on, the Palestinians are essentially on their own in the international arena. But the demographic factor remains the elephant in the room, as does the steady damage to Israel's democracy. How to square the aspiration of most Israelis – to be both Jewish and a democracy – is entirely unresolved and may remain so over the next decade. It is tempting to welcome the massive and growing Arab-Israeli across-the-board disparity, but the temptation should be resisted. The choice is between a continuation of Israel's often brutal military occupation of the West Bank, and a steady withdrawal undertaken from a position of overwhelming strength. Until the election of President Donald Trump in 2016 American policy, managed by the professional diplomats of the State Department, had sought to be neutral between the two sides, encouraging them to reach an agreed solution by negotiation, and to support the various UN agencies engaged in relief work with the Palestinian population. But with the accession of Trump all that changed. The professionals were replaced by three rank amateurs: two of the President's long-standing, personal lawyers, and his son-in-law, a youthful property developer. Their brief was to close the "deal of the century", finally solving this seemingly intractable problem to the satisfaction of both sides. Four years on, their only achievements were to further impoverish the Palestinians by slashing US aid, and to begin the process of moving the US embassy to Jerusalem, a step not yet emulated by any of the other Tel Aviv-based embassies (except for Nicaragua and Honduras) – although Guatemala has nibbled at the idea. And the US has recognised Israeli sovereignty over the Golan Heights – a move not supported by the international community. The replacement of President Trump by President Biden early in 2021 has meant a return to a more traditional foreign policy, and to a foreign policy team of experienced professionals instead of Trump's ragbag of amateurs. There will be a much more "even-handed" approach as between Israel and the Palestinians.

Gaza

One of the most densely populated places on earth (nearly 5,000 persons per square kilometer, ten times the density of the West Bank), Gaza has the status of an international ward and – to change the analogy – is in the intensive care ward. To the misfortune of its nearly 2 million inhabitants, it is controlled by a militant/terrorist organisation, Hamas, with smaller, even more extreme offshoots such as Islamic Jihad, all united in unrelenting hostility to Israel (although with intermittent offers of a long-term truce) and with little interest in mundane civilian affairs. Without a heavy UN contribution and day-to-day involvement, the population would be in even more dire straits. Since Israel's withdrawal in 2005 and Hamas's seizure of power two years later from the less militant Fatah organization – which controls the West Bank, alongside Israel – there have been three small but costly wars with Israel, and a resumption of hostilities is never far away (the flare-up of June 2021 lasted only 11 days but was again costly in human lives and material damage, particularly on the Gazan side). Over the next decade it is clearly in Israel's interest, as well as that of the Gazans, for current ambitious rehabilitation plans to be implemented – for a seaport, possibly an airport, desalination plants and efficient sewage disposal and electricity supply. While bellicose voices on the Israeli right are heard from time to time, there is more agreement across the political spectrum than concerning the West Bank, and little talk of an Israeli return. Instead, there is an increasing Egyptian involvement. Whether this amounts to a return to full Egyptian control, as between1948 and 1967, is much more doubtful. On the positive side, there is plenty of well-trained local talent (but many of these able young people are leaving if they can). Egypt probably holds the key; international investment is available. An optimistic scenario for 2030 is that the militant organisations will be a little more amenable to long term quiet, that Egypt will be increasingly involved – and that Israel will assist international efforts to move Gaza out of intensive care.

The rest of the Middle East

Current and likely future relationships with Israel's sovereign-state immediate neighbours are in a state of flux and likely to remain so over the next decade. Does the outlook look even reasonably positive, both for the avoidance of war and the development of normal trading and diplomatic links with Israel's geographic hinterland? The present situation is as if the US were to be severed from Canada. The mutual benefits of normality would be potentially enormous, including reduced defence outlays and increases in GDP due to two-way trade and tourism. An additional benefit for Israel, and potentially for its neighbours, would be increased funding for education at all levels, as well for research-based achievements across the board. But a dispassionate overview does not inspire much optimism other than for the avoidance of outright conflict. Iran – with which a growing understanding broke down in 1979, after the overthrow of the increasingly megalomaniac Shah by the ayatollahs – is a particular cause for concern. A common feature of all of these countries, which is particularly difficult to redress, has been the portrayal of Israel (usually referred to as the 'Zionist entity') and Israelis as close to the devil incarnate, in both official media and school textbooks. Very recently, however, there have been tentative efforts to tempt Israeli former citizens of a number of Arab countries, including Egypt and Iraq, to return. But there is little chance of this happening: sentimental memories aside, they are by now very elderly, well established in Israel, and there is no suggestion of compensation for property or possessions seized by the authorities many years ago. The restoration of a few synagogues and cemeteries, though welcome and likely to encourage Western tourism – as in Poland - will not bring back those who left, often unwillingly, more than half a century ago; their children and grandchildren, who know little of their parents' lands of origin, are even less disposed to leave the relative comfort of Israel, Europe and the US.

1. Egypt

The most populous, and in its own eyes the most influential Arab country, was the first to sign an armistice agreement with Israel after the 1948 War and the first to sign a peace treaty, in 1978. Apart from a brief interregnum from military rule, with the election of a Muslim Brotherhood government in 2013, rapidly brought to an end by a military coup, relations with Israel have been cool but correct at the official level, though the Egyptian street remains hostile. Israeli intelligence has assisted the Egyptian Army in combatting an Islamist insurgency in the Sinai desert, and Egypt has had an increasing involvement in Gaza. This mutually beneficial arrangement is set to continue, with possible further incremental improvements over the next decade. But the Egyptian street will be a perennial problem.

2. Syria

The Assad family, father and son, has maintained a very cold peace with Israel since the Yom Kippur War in 1973. The rule of Bashir al-Assad was under severe threat for some years following an uprising in 2011, but in 2018, thanks to considerable support from Russia and Iran and near non-involvement by the West, he 'can be said to have won, by bombing, gassing and starving his enemies out of the biggest cities...half a million people have died. Six million are displaced within Syria; a similar number have fled abroad. Most of the refugees are Sunni Arabs who made up most of Syria's pre-war population of 23m... so that Syria is smaller, in ruins and more sectarian'.[263] Throughout the Syrian conflict, Israel, just across the border in the Israel-controlled Golan Heights, has been concerned not to be involved, except for ensuring that its territory was not encroached upon. But it has consistently provided medical and surgical assistance to several thousand civilian casualties, who were treated in a field hospital and in permanent hospitals in the north of Israel. Substantial Iranian and Russian forces remain in areas of Syria adjacent to Israel, which seeks their removal. Beyond that, Israel would be well placed to assist in the reconstruction of Syria which will take many years, and is not an immediate prospect.

3. Iraq

America's 2003 'shock and awe' destruction of Saddam Hussein's Sunni minority dictatorship shifted power to the previously weak and impoverished Shia majority population. An important result has been to enable Iran to pursue its aim of a 'Shia corridor', running from Iran's border through Iraq and Syria (Assad's Alawites are a sect of Shiism) to the Lebanese Shia Hezbollah organisation, jostling for power in that country and unchangingly hostile to Israel. There is little prospect, for the foreseeable future, of any sort of positive relationship between Israel and the current (and likely future) Iraqi government; the West has withdrawn; Iran is in the ascendant.

4. Jordan

A peace treaty with Israel was signed in 1994, Jordan being the second Arab country to do so, followed by the mutual establishment of embassies. Not much has changed since then (except that Jordan has struggled to cope with a million Syrian refugees). The Hashemite dynasty is still in place (currently in the person of Abdullah II, great-grandson of Abdullah I who colluded with Israel and was assassinated for doing so). The king retains his special place as 'guardian' of the Temple Mount mosques. British influence is still strong (Abdullah II trained at Sandhurst Military Academy). Peace with Israel has held; Israeli tourists visit historic sites in Jordan, as they do those of Egypt. However much it might be willing to be a market for Israeli high-tech exports, Jordan, small in population, without oil and hence poor, offers little such prospect as compared to the far wealthier Saudi Arabia and other Gulf states.

5. Lebanon and Hezbollah

The Lebanon is a complex mix of populations: Moslem, both Sunni and Shia; Christian and Druze. It is the rapidly-growing Shia community, dominated by the militant/terrorist organisation, Hezbollah – essentially a state within a state and looking to Iran for its central ethos – which is unshakably hostile to Israel. It fought a bitter war with Israel in 2006, which left much of southern Lebanon, the main Shia area, in ruins, but has been rapidly rebuilding its weapons armoury, particularly of missiles, said to number over 100,000. Hezbollah is the Mediterranean end of Iran's ambitious 'Shia corridor'. Since 2006 Israel has developed an effective roster of anti-missile missiles, although a massive launch of Hezbollah's stockpile might well be beyond its capacity to counter. But Hezbollah is mindful of 2006. The most likely scenario in the foreseeable future is a continued stand-off, short of renewed hostilities. Much will depend on Iran. (In any event, Lebanon's small population, although quite well-educated, particularly the Christian community, is not a very promising market for Israeli products.)

6. Saudi Arabia

After decades of an implicit agreement between the royal family, including several thousand princes, and the very conservative religious establishment, allowing the latter to impose strict rules on social life and the former to live in idle luxury on the country's vast oil wealth, the dynamic Crown Prince, Mohamed bin Sultan (MBS), has changed the country's long-term social and economic course. The latter involves a radical shift by 2030 from a sole dependence on oil production to a much more diversified economy. In parallel, social life is set to be more relaxed, from women being allowed to drive and enter the work force, to the content of public entertainment. What are the implications for Israel? They are twofold: a gradual improvement in political relations with the Saudis concerning the Palestinian issue; an opportunity for Israeli science and technology and security intelligence to share in the Saudi plans for its economic future. Moreover, the two countries have a common enemy in Iran. So far, all this is potential, a window of opportunity rather than firmly agreed joint projects; but a degree of optimism is permitted over the prospects for the next decade, based on a partnership between MBS (aged 34, and heir to King Salman, aged 84) and any middle-aged Israeli prime minister. But this possibility is compromised by the Crown Prince's markedly autocratic, not to say murderous behaviour, and his possible international isolation as a result. On the other hand, Saudi Arabia is vastly wealthy; as long as the oil gusher continues, Western leaders, including Israel's, will ignore the negatives.

7. Other Gulf States

The same is true of several other Gulf states, smaller in population but also very wealthy, and equally unsavoury in internal policies. In September 2020 a long-gestating diplomatic and trade relationship was announced between the United Arab Emirates (UAE) and Israel. Close behind came Bahrein, more complex because it has a majority Shiite population and is much nearer, geographically, to Iran. Another wealthy Gulf state, Oman, has followed. A complicating factor is the firm request of all of them to receive from the US the F35 stealth plane, the world's most advanced fighter plane, on which Israel has hitherto had a regional monopoly, thus maintaining a 'qualitative military edge' over its neighbours. Israeli and Gulf companies are eagerly pursuing deals. There is much mutual benefit to be had. Saudi Arabia may follow; MBS is keen, his father, the very elderly King, is more cautious. But the political and economic partnership between Israel and the Gulf states will persist and develop over the next decade, irrespective of the names of the main political players. The Palestinians can only watch from the sidelines.

Notes

[1] Gilbert, M. (1976). *Jewish History Atlas: 121 Maps from Biblical Times to the Present.* p. 10 Macmillian Publishing Company

[2] Lebzelter, G. (1978). *Political Antisemitism in England 1918–1939.* Springer

[3] Murray, C. (2003). *Human Accomplishment: The Pursuit of Excellence in the Arts and Sciences, 800 BC to 1950.* p. 275 HarperCollins

[4] Vital, D. (1999). *A People Apart: the Jews in Europe, 1789-1939.* Clarendon Press

[5] Patai, R. (1996). *The Jewish Mind.* p. 272. Charles Scribner's Sons.

[6] Riasanovsky N. (1993) *A History of Russia.* p.283. Oxford University Press

[7] Pease, S. L. (2009). *The Golden Age of Jewish Achievement.* Deucalion

[8] Eban, A. (1978). *My People: The Story of the Jews.* p. 271. Random House

[9] Vital, D. (1999). *A People Apart: the Jews in Europe, 1789-1939.* p. 130. Clarendon Press

[10] Ferguson, N. (1999). *The House of Rothschild: Volume 1: Money's Prophets: 1798-1848,* Penguin

[11] Riasanovsky N. (1993) *A History of Russia.* p.395. Oxford University Press

[12] Elon, A. (2003) *The Pity of It All: A Portrait of the German-Jewish Epoch,1743-1933.* p.81. New York: Picador

[13] Ferguson, N. (2007). *The War of the World: Twentieth-Century Conflict and the Descent of the West.* Penguin

[14] Gilbert, M. (1976)

[15] Churchill, W. (1931). *The Unknown War.* New York: Charles Scribner's Sons

[16] Kochan, L. (1979) *The Jewish World.* pp. 271-2. Thames and Hudson.

[17] Babel, I. (1929) *Red Cavalry.* London, Knopf

[18] Elon, A. (2003) pp. 117-122

[19] Elon, A (2003) pp. 315-317

[20] Wasserstein, B. (2012). *On the Eve: The Jews of Europe Before the Second World War.* p. 286. Simon and Schuster

[21] Elon, A. (2003).

[22] Elon, A. (2003) pp. 358-363.

[23] Elon, A. (2003) pp. 232-236.

[24] Kershaw, I. (1999) *Hitler, Hubris.* p.32. Penguin

[25] Wasserstein, B. (2012) p. 286

[26] Johnson, P. (1988). *A History of the Jews.* p. 381 Weidenfeld and Nicholson

[27] Johnson, P. (1988). p. 382

[28] Johnson, P. (1988). p. 383

[29] Johnson, P. (1988). p. 384
[30] Johnson, P. (1988). Condensed from pp. 380-390
[31] Gilbert, M. (1976). p. 79
[32] Johnson, P. (1988).pp. 467-8
[33] Eban, A. (1978). p. 305
[34] Gilbert, M. (1976). p. 81
[35] Johnson, P. (1988). p. 467
[36] Johnson, P. (1988). p. 467
[37] Johnson, P. (1988). p. 465
[38] Gilbert, M. (1976). p. 81
[39] Gilbert, M. (1978). Exile and Return. p. 69. *London: Weidenfeld & Nicolson*
[40] Frankopan, P. (2015). *The Silk Roads: A new history of the world*. p. 342. Bloomsbury Publishing
[41] Most of this chapter has been extracted and greatly compressed from: Shapira, A. (2014) *Israel: A History,* Weidenfeld and Nicholson
[42] Elon, A. (2003) p. 11
[43] Extracted and summarized from: Kershaw, I. (2008). *Fateful Choices: Ten Decisions that Changed the World, 1940-1941*. pp. 436-7. Penguin
[44] Kershaw, I. (1999) *Hitler, Hubris*. pp. 423-437. Penguin
[45] Kershaw, I. (1999) pp. 423-427
[46] Kershaw, I. (1999) p. 199
[47] Kershaw, I. (2008). p. 65
[48] Elon, A. (2003) pp. 8-9
[49] Elon, A. (2003) pp. 9-10
[50] Gilbert, M. (2006). *Kristallnacht: Prelude to Destruction*. pp. 15-17. Harper Books
[51] Kershaw, I. (2008). p. 38
[52] Kershaw, I. (2011) *The End: Hitler's Germany, 1944-45,* Penguin Books
[53] *The Economist,17.12.2016*
[54] Kershaw, I. (1999) p. 470
[55] Kershaw, I. (2008) p. 470
[56] *The Economist,* 25.1.2020
    Kershaw, I. (2008) p. 243
[58] Kershaw, I. (2008) p. 243
[59] Kershaw, I. (2001). *Hitler 1936-1945: Nemesis*. pp. *271-5*. Penguin UK
[60] Kershaw, I. (2001). p. 669
[61] Kershaw, I. (2001). p. 670
[62] Kershaw, I. (2001). p. 670-675
[63] Cited by: Wasserstein, B. (1979). *Britain and the Jews of Europe, 1939-1945*. Footnote to p. 353. Oxford University Press
[64] Mazower, M. (1999). *Dark Continent: Europe's Twentieth Century*. p. 176. Penguin Books
[65] *Haaretz*, 26.3.18, p. 8
[66] Ferguson, N. (2007). pp. 447-9. Penguin

[67] Browning, C. R., & Gallagher, K. (1993). *Ordinary Men*. New York: HarperCollins

[68] Ferguson, N. (2006). p. 449

[69] Milgram, S. (1974). *Obedience to Authority*. Tavistock

[70] Feldman, M. P. (1993). *The Psychology of Crime*. Cambridge University Press

[71] Elms, A., Milgram, S. (1967). Personality characteristics associated with obedience and defiance towards authoritative command. *Journal of Experimental Research in Personality, 1*, 282–289

[72] Haney, C., Banks, W. C., & Zimbardo, P. G. (1973). A study of prisoners and guards in a simulated prison. *Naval research reviews, 9* (1-17)

[73] Elon, A. (2003) p. 81.

[74] Gilbert, M. (1976). p. 87

[75] Medawar, J. S., & Pyke, D. (2001). *Hitler's Gift: The True Story of the Scientists Expelled by the Nazi Regime*. p. 11. Arcade Publishing

[76] Medawar, J. S., & Pyke, D. (2001). pp. 54-5

[77] Medawar, J. S., & Pyke, D. (2001). p.xviii

[78] Elon, A. (2003) pp. 400

[79] Medawar, J. S., & Pyke, D. (2001) p. 56

[80] Medawar, J. S., & Pyke, D. (2001). p. 57

[81] Snowman, D. (2003) *The Hitler Emigrés: The Cultural Impact on Britain of Refugees from Nazism*. p. 357

[82] Elon, A. (2003) p. 395

[83] Medawar, J. S., & Pyke, D. (2001). p. 91

[84] Medawar, J. S., & Pyke, D. (2001). pp. 107-8

[85] Snowman, D. (2003).

[86] Snowman, D. (2003). pp. 241-248

[87] Snowman, D. (2003). pp. 249-250

[88] Marino, A. (1999). *A Quiet American: The Secret War of Varian Fry*. St. Martin's Press

[89] Laqueur, W. (2004). *Generation Exodus: The Fate of Young Jewish Refugees from Nazi Germany*. Tauris

[90] Silver, E. (1992). *The Book of the Just: The Unsung Heroes Who Rescued Jews from Hitler*. Grove Press

[91] Smith, M. (2016). *Foley: The spy who saved 10,000 Jews*. Biteback Publishing

[92] *New York Times* (18.11.2017)

[93] *New York Times* (14.10.2017)

[94] Extracted and condensed from Judt, T. (2007). *Postwar. A History of Europe since 1945*. pp. 90-99. Pimlico

[95] Forsyth, F. (1979). *The Odessa File*. Random House

[96] Elkins, M. (1971). *Forged in Fury*. Ballantine Books

[97] Freedland, M. (2011). *The Final Reckoning*. HarperCollins

[98] *The Economist* (06.2017)

[99] *The Economist* (31.3.2018)

[100] Roger Cohen, *New York Times* (2.3.2019)

[101] *Times of Israel* (6.9.2018)

[102] *Guardian* (11.4.2016)

[103] *Telegraph* (12.9.2017)

[104] From a report by Harriet Sherwood, *Guardian* (16.10.2017)

[105] Extracted and condensed from Wasserstein, B. (1997). *Vanishing Diaspora.* Ch.7

[106] The *New York Times* (30. 3.2018)

[107] Pew Research Centre. *Survey on Global Antisemitism* (2015)

[108] Pew Research Centre. *Survey on Moslem Antisemitism* (2006)

[109] Jon Henley, *Guardian (*15.2.2019)

[110] Extracted and condensed from Ignatieff, M. (1998). *Isaiah Berlin: a Life.* Chatto and Windus

[111] Pew Research Centre, *Survey of American Jewry* (2015)

[112] Verbit, M.F. *Encyclopaedia Judaica (*1983-92), pp. 57-64

[113] *Times of Israel* (18.02.2018)

[114] *Times of Israel (*20.10.2019)

[115] *American Jewish Committee* (11.02.2017)

[116] From the 2014 US Religious Landscape Study, reported in *Times of Israel* (05.2015)

[117] Based on reviews in *The Economist* and *The Jerusalem Report* of Karabel, J. (2006), *The Chosen: The Hidden History of Admission and Exclusion at Harvard, Yale, and Princeton*. Houghton Mifflin Harcourt

[118] Handlin O., American Jewry, pp. 282-3 in Kedourie, E. (1979) *The Jewish World: Revelation, Prophecy and History.* Thames and Hudson

[119] *Encyclopaedia Judaica* (1975-6), pp. 415-16

[120] *Encyclopaedia Judaica* (1983 -1992), pp. 377-79

[121] *New York Times* (10.2017)

[122] *Time* (22.10.2017)

[123] Pew Research Centre, *US and Israeli Jewry* (06.2018)

[124] Pew Research Centre, *US and Israeli Jewry* (04.2019)

[125] *The Economist* (20.1.2018)

[126] *The Economist* (13.4.2005)

[127] Craig, P., & Clayton, T. (2002). *End of the Beginning.* pp. 183-184. Coronet Books

[128] Kennedy, P. (1987). *The Rise and Fall of the Great Powers: Economic Change and Military Conflict from 1500 to 2000.* p.367. Unwin Hyman

[129] Hennessy, P. (2006). *Never Again: Britain 1945-1951.* p. 94. Vintage

[130] O'Brien, C. C. (1986). *The Siege: The Saga of Israel and Zionism.* pp. 265-6. Simon & Schuster

[131] Bethell, N. (1979). *The Palestine Triangle: The Struggle for the Holy Land, 1935-48.* pp. 121-122. Andre Deutsch

[132] Quoted in Shlaim, A. (1988). *Collusion Across the Jordan.* p. 57. Clarendon Press

[133] Montefiore, S. S. (2011). *Jerusalem: The Biography.* p. 557

[134] O'Brien, C. C. (1986). *The Siege: The Saga of Israel and Zionism.* p. 86

[135] Montefiore, S. S. (2011). p. 552

[136] O'Brien, C. C. (1986). *The Siege: The Saga of Israel* p. 281

[137] This material on Begin has been drawn from Silver, E. (1984). *Begin: A Biography.* Weidenfeld & Nicolson

[138] Shlaim, A. (1988). *Collusion Across the Jordan.* p. 7. Clarendon Press

[139] Shlaim, A. (1988). p. 7

[140] Shlaim, A. (1988)

[141] Montefiore, S. S. (2011). *Jerusalem: the Biography.* pp. 545-6

[142] Montefiore, S. S. (2011). p. 582

[143] Montefiore, S. S. (2011). pp. 558-9

[144] Morris, B. (2008). *1948: A History of the First Arab-Israeli War.* pp. 43-44. Yale University Press

[145] O'Brien, C. C. (1986). pp. 271-2

[146] O'Brien, C. C. (1986). p. 278

[147] Rose, N. (1986) *Chaim Weizmann.* p.427. Viking

[148] Morris, B. (2008). *1948.* p. 399

[149] Montefiore, S. S. (2011). p. 562

[150] Extracted and condensed from Morris, B. (2008). pp. 399 – 400

[151] Morris, B. (2008) pp. 125-8

[152] Shapira, A. (2014). p. 163

[153] Shapira, A. (2014). p. 164

[154] O'Brien, C. C. (1986). p. 286

[155] O'Brien, C. C. (1986). pp. 290-2

[156] Montefiore, S. S. (2011). p. 562

[157] Extracted and summarized from Shapira, A. (2014). pp. 164-174

[158] Morris, B. (2008). pp. 271-2

[159] Shapira, A. (2014). p. 196

[160] Montefiore, S. S. (2011). pp. 589-590

[161] *Times of Israel* (17.3.2018)

[162] *Haaretz* (14.5.2017)

[163] Shapira, A. (2014). p. 461

[164] *Haaretz* (24.1.2018)

[165] *Times of Israel* (07.3.2018)

[166] *Times of Israel* (05.03.2018)

[167] Central Bureau of Statistics, Israel, reported in *Times of Israel* (4.9.2018)

[168] *Times of Israel* (13.12.2017)

[169] Extracted from *Haaretz* (13.6.2018)

[170] Murray, C. J., Barber, R. M., Foreman, K. J., Ozgoren, A. A., Abd-Allah, F., Abera, S. F., & Del Pozo-Cruz, B. (2015). Global, regional, and national disability-adjusted life years (DALYs) for 306 diseases and injuries and healthy life expectancy (HALE) for 188 countries, 1990–2013: quantifying the epidemiological transition. *The Lancet*

[171] Senor, D., & Singer, S. (2009). *Start-Up Nation: The Story of Israel's Economic Miracle.* p. 255. Hachette

[172] *The Economist* (19.5.2018)

[173] Senor, D., & Singer, S. (2009). p.266

[174] *Haaretz* (11.6.2006)

[175] *Haaretz* (7.2.2018)

[176] Shapira, A. (2014). p.449

[177] *Haaretz* (28.11.2017)

[178] *Globes (*7.3.2017)

[179] *Times of Israel* (30.1.2018)

[180] *Times of Israel* (6.3.2018)

[181] *Times of Israel* (11.3.2018)

[182] *Haaretz* (2.1.2015)

[183] *Times of Israel,* (28.1.2018)

[184] *Times of Israel* (08.03.2018)

[185] *Haaretz (*6.2.2018)

[186] *Times of Israel* (15.2.2018)

[187] *Times of Israel* (19.12.2017)

[188] *Times of Israel* (26.3.2018)

[189] *Times of Israel* (24.11.2019)

[190] Katz, Y., & Bohbot, A. (2017). *The Weapon Wizards: How Israel became a high-tech military superpower.* St. Martin's Press

[191] *Globes* (19.3.2018)

[192] John Reed in *Financial Times* (10.7.2015)

[193] *Haaretz* (22.3.2018)

[194] *Times of Israel* (6.12.2016)

[195] *Times of Israel* (16.12.2016)

[196] *Jerusalem Post* (18.1.2018)

[197] Jewish Telegraphic Agency (25.1.2016)

[198] Slezkine, Y. (2004). In *The Jewish Century.* Princeton University Press.

[199] Chua, A., & Rubenfeld, J. (2014). *The Triple Package: What Really Determines Success.* Penguin Press

[200] Eysenck, H. J. (1995). *Genius: The Natural History of Creativity.* p. 50. Cambridge University Press

[201] Eysenck, H. J. (1995). p. 50

[202] Asbury, K., & Plomin, R. (2014). *G is for Genes: The Impact of Genetics on Education and Achievement.* John Wiley & Sons

[203] Pimlott, B., & Hennessy, P. (1992). *Harold Wilson.* p. 512 HarperCollins

[204] Cochran, G., Hardy, J., & Harpending, H. (2006). Natural history of Ashkenazi intelligence. *Journal of Biosocial Science, 38*(5)

[205] Russell, C., & Lewis, H. S. (1900). *The Jew in London: A Study of Racial Character and Present-day Conditions: Being Two Essays Prepared for the Toynbee Trustees.* T. Fisher Unwin

[206] Hughes, A. G. (1928). "Jews and Gentiles: Their intellectual and temperamental differences". *The Eugenics Review, 20*(2), 89

[207] Eysenck, H. J. (1995)

[208] Cochran, G., Hardy, J., & Harpending, H. (2006). Natural history of Ashkenazi intelligence. *Journal of biosocial science, 38*(5)

[209] Storfer, M. D. (1990). *Intelligence and Giftedness: The Contributions of Heredity and Early Environment.* Jossey-Bass

[210] Ortar, D. G. R. (1967). "Educational Achievements of Primary School Graduates in Israel as Related to Their Socio-Cultural Background". *Comparative Education, 4*(1), 23-34.

[211] Smilansky, M. and Smilansky, S. (1968). "The intellectual development of kibbutz-born children of "oriental" origin". *Research Report, No. 120,* The Ruth Bressler Centre for Education Research, Jerusalem

[212] David, H., & Lynn, R. (2007). "Intelligence differences between European and Oriental Jews in Israel". *Journal of Biosocial Science, 39*(3), 465

[213] Dunkel, C. S., Reeve, C. L., of Menie, M. A. W., & van der Linden, D. (2015). A comparative study of the general factor of personality in Jewish and non-Jewish populations. *Personality and Individual Differences, 78,* 63-67

[214] Eysenck, H. J. (1995). p. 8

[215] Cox, C. M. (1926). *The Early Mental Traits of 300 Geniuses.* Stanford University Press

[216] Eysenck, H. J. (1995) p. 114

[217] Snow, C.P. (1967). *Varieties of Men,* Penguin

[218] Patai, R. (1996). *The Jewish Mind.* p. 392. Charles Scribner's Sons

[219] Roth, P. (2011). *Portnoy's Complaint.* Vintage

[220] Eysenck, H. J. (1995). p. 258

[221] Post, F. (1994). "Creativity and psychopathology a study of 291 world-famous men". *The British Journal of Psychiatry, 165*(1), 22-34

[222] Eysenck, H. J. (1995). p. 117

[223] Reviewed by Helen Thompson, *Guardian* (21.8.2015)

[224] *Haaretz* (30.4.2017)

[225] Arai, J. A., & Feig, L. A. (2011). "Long-lasting and transgenerational effects of an environmental enrichment on memory formation". *Brain Research Bulletin, 85*(1-2), 30-35

[226] Cochran, G., Hardy, J., & Harpending, H. (2006). "Natural history of Ashkenazi intelligence". *Journal of biosocial science, 38*(5)

[227] The Cochrane account is reproduced from Murray, C. (2007). "Jewish Genius". *Commentary,* 123 (10 April), 29-35

[228] Some of these Sephardim are detailed in Schama, S. (2014). *The Story of the Jews: Finding the Words 1000 BC-1492 AD* (Vol. 1). Random House

[229] Botticini, M., & Eckstein, Z. (2005). "Jewish occupational selection: education, restrictions, or minorities?". *Journal of Economic History,* 922-948

[230] Darlington, C. D. (1969). *The Evolution of Man and Society.* New York: Simon and Schuster

[231] Murray, C. (2007). 29-35

[232] The work of geneticist Ariel Darvasi and his colleagues was reported in *Reuters* (12.7.2001)

[233] Murray, C. (2003). *Human Accomplishment: The pursuit of excellence in the arts and sciences, 800 BC to 1950.* HarperCollins

[234] Zuckerman, H. (1977). *Scientific Elite: Nobel laureates in the United States.* Free Press

[235] Stanley, J. C. (1996). "In the Beginning: The Study of Mathematically Precocious Youth". In C. P. Benbow & D. Lubinski (Eds.), *Intellectual Talent.* Baltimore: Johns Hopkins University Press.

[236] Chetty, R., Grusky, D., Hell, M., Hendren, N., Manduca, R., & Narang, J. (2017). "The fading American dream: Trends in absolute income mobility since 1940". *Science, 356*(6336), 398-406

[237] *The Economist* (24.3.2018)

[238] *The Economist* (24.10.2015)

[239] *The Economist* (24.1.2015)

[240] *The Economist* (28.1.2017)

[241] Reeves, R. V. (2018). *Dream Hoarders: How the American upper middle class is leaving everyone else in the dust, why that is a problem, and what to do about it.* Brookings Institution Press

[242] *The Economist* (1.7.2017)

[243] *The Economist* (1.2.2014)

[244] *New York Times* (23.3.2015)

[245] *New York Times* (3.12.2017)

[246] Based on an article by Peter Beaumont, *Guardian* (27.6.2018)

[247] Extracted and summarized from *Haaretz* (13.9.2017)

[248] Extracted and summarized from *Haaretz* (27.9.2017)

[249] From the report in *Haaretz* (22.10.2016)

[250] *Times of Israel* (9.5.2017)

[251] *1843* (16.8.2016)

[252] *The Economist* (23.1.2008)

[253] *Haaretz* (22.10.2020)

[254] Jacob Judah in *Haaretz* (10.2.2020)

[255] *Pew Research Centre: Europe's Growing Muslim Population* (29.11.2017)

[256] *The Economist* (4.11.2017)

[257] *New York Times* (11.11.2020)

[258] Based on an article in *Haaretz* (10.5.2018)

[259] *Times of Israel* (27.6.2018)

[260] *Times of Israel* (11.9.2020)

[261] *The Economist* (30.3.2019)

[262] Pfeffer, A. (2017). *Bibi: The Turbulent Life and Times of Benjamin Netanyahu.* Hurst & Co

[263] *The Economist* (30.6.2018)

Made in United States
North Haven, CT
24 May 2022

19478884R00192